The RETURN of COLLECTIVE INTELLIGENCE

Ancient Wisdom for a World out of Balance

DERY DYER

Bear & Company
Rochester, Vermont

Bear & Company
One Park Street
Rochester, Vermont 05767
www.BearandCompanyBooks.com

Text stock is SFI certified

Bear & Company is a division of Inner Traditions International

Cataloging-in-Publication Data for this title is available from the Library of Congress

ISBN 978-1-59143-352-1 (print)
ISBN 978-1-59143-353-8 (ebook)

Printed and bound in the United States by Lake Book Manufacturing, Inc. The text stock is SFI certified. The Sustainable Forestry Initiative® program promotes sustainable forest management.

10   9   8   7   6   5   4   3   2   1

Text design and layout by Debbie Glogover
This book was typeset in Garamond Premier Pro with Aries, Gill Sans MT Pro, and ITC Legacy Sans Std used as display fonts

To send correspondence to the author of this book, mail a first-class letter to the author c/o Inner Traditions • Bear & Company, One Park Street, Rochester, VT 05767, and we will forward the communication.

The RETURN of COLLECTIVE INTELLIGENCE

"At this critical, uncertain time in history, building interdependence and community resilience is crucial. To do this effectively, we need to bust out of our mental straitjackets and breathe in the freedom of collective intelligence. Dery Dyer's exciting book is at the leading edge of how to do just that!"

BILL PFEIFFER, FOUNDER OF SACRED EARTH NETWORK
AND AUTHOR OF *WILD EARTH, WILD SOUL:*
A MANUAL FOR AN ECSTATIC CULTURE

"We need to draw on our collective intelligence, and we need to realize that the best way of doing so is to 're-cognize' the intelligence that resides in each of us. Dery Dyer's book tells us why and how. A must-read in our critical times."

ERVIN LASZLO, PH.D., PHILOSOPHER AND AUTHOR OF
SCIENCE AND THE AKASHIC FIELD

"A compelling weaving of story, science, and mysticism that will help you remember who you are and the potential within and all around you. Dyer shows us how to release conditioning and misperception to see from the eyes of the heart and to root into primordial rhythms. She guides us into the mystery—to live in harmony with the Earth and the sacred circle of all life."

LLYN CEDAR ROBERTS, AWARD-WINNING AUTHOR
OF *SHAPESHIFTING INTO HIGHER CONSCIOUSNESS*
AND COAUTHOR OF *SPEAKING WITH NATURE*

"*The Return of Collective Intelligence* is much more than a book—it is a Michelin-star mind meal at what could arguably be humanity's last supper. Dery Dyer has dished out a veritable smorgasbord.

This beautifully crafted, highly readable ride through the latest literature and research on collective intelligence brings clarity while delivering a challenge to our hearts that (she rightly tells us) our intellects alone cannot answer—how do we cultivate wisdom in this information age? Dyer skillfully offers a clearer lens through which to evaluate the usefulness and limitations of our social networks and digital media platforms. By directing us to indigenous wisdom and Great Nature as the sanctuary and source of collective intelligence, her words ring the golden truth bell in our hearts. Our collective intelligence contains the resources required to right our world through love, empathy, and connection, if we act together. This is the promise and hope provided by the title of this work. May our collective intelligence indeed return, and quickly! Dery Dyer has certainly done her part to make it so."

ELIZABETH B. JENKINS, AUTHOR OF THREE BOOKS ON
INKA NATURE WISDOM, *THE RETURN OF THE INKA*,
JOURNEY TO Q'EROS, AND *THE FOURTH LEVEL*

"A richly textured tapestry, artfully woven from widely disparate threads of human experience—from ancient civilizations to modern medicine, education, and quantum science. If you harbor any doubt about the essential intra-connectedness of life across space-time, and that we are designed for the sole purpose of co-creating the magical TOGETHER, Dery Dyer's engaging narrative will relieve you of it!"

CHRISTINA STRUTT, PRINCIPAL THINKING PARTNER AT
COCREATING CLARITY

"I breezed through this book during the 24 hours when I was in the midst of tech-savvy people conferring about the internet's future. My neural excitation surpassed my ability to stay grounded in wisdom about who to be and what to do! I'm endorsing *The Return of Collective Intelligence* as a prompt for our fieldwork—to utilize Dery Dyer's great integration that stretches across times and cultures. The words on these pages are a robust pod for passing, the best collection I've seen—but how do we choose to live, applying what we learn? Please, let's not go back to sleep."

JOAN LEDERMAN,
STEWARD OF THE COLLECTIVE WISDOM INITIATIVE

To Pachamama
in ayni
and with greatest love

Contents

In Gratitude

As might be expected, this book is a collective effort.

It grew out of an innovative two-and-a-half-year doctoral program in New Paradigm thought created in 2002 by the late visionary educator Francisco Gutiérrez. Headquartered at Costa Rica's Universidad de La Salle, the Doctorado de la Tercera Cultura is also offered in Argentina, Brazil, Colombia, Guatemala, Honduras, Italy, Panama, and Spain.*

The program is unique in many respects. Instead of being taught by professors, you learn from the authors of books on a vast reading list—a bursting treasure trove of world wisdom most of us would never encounter otherwise.

Upon entering the program, you must declare your *chifladura* (madness, passion, obsession)—whatever it is you're hungering to know more about. (Three guesses as to what mine was!) Your reading and writing are done through the lens of your chifladura. You must also find a group of people with similar or related chifladuras and produce group work.

It was one of the most enjoyable, life-changing experiences I've ever had.

Like the rivers of wisdom that flow from so many different sources into this book, the wisdom from our work in the *doctorado* program

---

*For more information, contact asistentedoctorado@ulasalle.ac.cr or go to www .chifladuradoctorado.ac.cr.

flowed into what I'd learned over the years from native wisdom keepers and other friends and teachers, many of whom are quoted here. For these priceless gifts, which have enriched my life beyond measure, I'm deeply grateful.

The book has had good friends helping it every step of the way. My soul teacher Janine Fafard planted the seeds years ago during many late-night conversations; laughter-filled talks with soul sister Katya de Luisa made new insights bloom; Linda Moller, the soul sister who first set my feet on the Andean Path, bravely slogged through an embarrassingly boring and overwritten early draft and gave me excellent criticism. Ehud Sperling and Jon Graham generously offered incredibly valuable advice that inspired me to vanquish my timidity and write from my heart.

Along the way, I was delighted and humbled to discover that the editorial job requirements at Inner Traditions include infinite kindness and patience with clueless, fretful newbie authors. Special thanks to Patricia Rydle and Mindy Branstetter for gently shepherding this one through the bewildering publishing process.

And the book would never have happened without the consistent kindness of my husband (and fellow *chiflado*) Jim Molloy, who listened to me patiently; clarified my thinking with brilliant insights; contributed books, photos, technical and artistic skills, and countless hours of his valuable time; and repeatedly restored the peace—and my sanity—with timely interventions whenever he'd find me locked in mortal combat with my nemesis, modern technology.

May he and my other co-chiflados—Victoria Fontan, Jacqueline Gillet, Jan Hurwitch, and Steven Kogel—continue exploring, learning and helping the world. May the spirits of my parents, Elisabeth and Richard Dyer, see their work in this work. And may my many *waikis* (spiritual brothers and sisters), on Earth and in spirit, whose light illuminates this book and my life, recognize their contributions and know that I honor and thank them, even though I can't possibly list them all.

I am truly blessed by so many beings—including the unseen helpers who unfailingly placed the right books in my hands at precisely the perfect moments. *Mil gracias*!

What Is This Force Called Collective Intelligence?

It was magic!

Fifteen of us, representing various nationalities and ranging in age from our early twenties to our mid-sixties, were about to celebrate the final ceremony in our ten-day initiation journey through the Peruvian highlands. Our work had connected us with the energies in the land and ancient structures that marked places of power in the Inkas' spiritual tradition.

Our guide was Elizabeth Jenkins, fourth-level teacher of the Andean Path and author of three books on Inka spirituality. With great good humor, energy, and dedication, she had shepherded us flawlessly through the powerful energetic exchanges, rituals, and cleansings at each site—many of them quite challenging, some downright scary.

Now we were gathered at the massive stone ruins of the Wiraqocha Temple, and she was presenting us with what appeared to be the most difficult task of all. She asked us to separate into two circles—men in one, women in another—and immediately choose a High Priest and a High Priestess to conduct our closing ceremony.

We gaped at her in disbelief. Choose immediately? She had to be kidding! Our group contained an overabundance of likely candidates— even a kahuna from Hawaii!

Everybody agreed that Elizabeth simply wasn't being realistic.

What she was asking us to do would take hours of discussion and many rounds of voting.

She listened, grinning, as we voiced our doubts.

"You can do it!" she insisted. "Just consult your *qosqos*." (In the Andean tradition, the *qosqo* is the "spiritual stomach"—the energetic center of one's being.)

We finally agreed to humor her. Shaking our heads dubiously, we formed our circles, closed our eyes, and zeroed in on our qosqos.

Within seconds, my left hand shot out involuntarily and grabbed the arm of Juliet, the woman to my left. At that exact instant, three or four voices blurted, "Juliet!"

Everyone's eyes snapped open. Those who hadn't spoken were nodding vigorously, gazing at Juliet, who was even more astonished than the rest of us. A humble, soft-spoken woman in her sixties, she was not an obvious candidate.

But here she was—our instantaneous, unanimous choice. Our rational minds hadn't participated at all—they'd been bypassed by an immediate knowing that seemed to spring from somewhere in our bodies.

As we tied a *pareo* around her shoulders to honor her new status, Juliet seemed to grow taller, serene and proud, her gentle eyes radiating a power we had not noticed before . . . every bit the High Priestess.

The men took a little longer to choose the High Priest—about a minute. The youngest in the group, he was another unlikely (and unanimous) choice.

Priest and Priestess proceeded to lead the ceremony with an impressive intuitive certainty, as if they'd done it hundreds of times. All of us (except for Elizabeth, who was beaming proudly) were in awe.

It was magic!

It was the magic of collective intelligence.

* * *

What is this magic?

What is the mysterious force that enables flocks of birds, swarms of bees, parades of ants, and schools of fish to function together in perfect synchrony, obviously communicating and cooperating at some undetectable level, for the good of all?

What is the process that has always guided indigenous people to acquire the information they need to make important decisions, with no need for lengthy discussion or debate?

WHAT REALLY HAPPENED
IN OUR CIRCLES IN PERU?

As we will see in the chapters to come, the endlessly fascinating search for answers takes us deep into the discoveries of New Paradigm science—as well as into territory formerly reserved for shamans and mystics: sacred geometry, geomancy, multidimensionality, expanded states of consciousness, deep ecology, Black Madonnas, White Lions...? And we find that all the paths ultimately converge.

Modern humans, accustomed as we are to perceiving the world through our individualized lenses, find it hard to believe that it's possible to think, or act, as a single entity. But collective intelligence was a normal part of life for our ancestors and still is used by indigenous cultures throughout the world.

It lives on in native spiritual traditions and in universal symbols, which hints that it's encoded in us, as it is in all beings. Swarming and flocking behavior is its most obvious expression. At its most subtle, it's an instantaneous knowing, shared by members of a group, of the wisest course of action that will benefit all.

It may be Gaia's greatest gift to her children. And now, with all life on Earth critically endangered, I believe it has become her most urgent imperative.

If humans in the "developed" world can reconnect with this ancient gift, we may be able to repair our fragmented perception and reverse the devastation it has wreaked on our planet before it's too late.

PART ONE

ALL THAT IS

Fig. 1.1. Looking back: stairway in Machu Picchu, Peru.
Photo by Dery Dyer.

1

An Ancient Gift
The Interdependence of All Life

Perhaps, despite great destruction of human experience, ancient insight and wisdom are not lost. Somehow they are still part of us, inside us. These insights can and will come back to us when we need them.

ROBERT WOLFF[1]

We—you and I—are part of a collective.

Not just the collective formed by our family, our social circle, our nation, or even the human race. We're part of a collective that includes everything on Earth and beyond. Animals, plants, trees, bugs, bacteria, viruses, molds, cells, stones (stones? Yes!), wind and water, fire and earth, stars, sun, moon, cosmos.

All That Is.

Ancient spiritual traditions and now science tell us that each of us is a member of an intricately interconnected, infinitely complex whole that works cooperatively for the greatest good of all; each of us is a cell in a single immense organism that is constantly evolving . . . and intelligent.

It should be so obvious. You and I, the lone cells, couldn't survive for a second—much less thrive—by ourselves. From the instant of our conception we are utterly, inextricably dependent on All That Is— on sunlight, rain, bacteria, one another. At the same time, we are responsible for contributing to the success of everything we're part of.

We are not only participants in the awesome power of collective intelligence—we're proof of it.

But along the way, we humans forgot that we're part of this miraculous process. Our amnesia was so total that we deluded ourselves into believing we were autonomous, powerful, and immune. Our ability to manipulate the material world convinced us that our technology would guarantee our impunity, allowing us to act recklessly, selfishly, and destructively.

Fortunately, we're waking up. We're reconnecting with the ancient gift. Collective intelligence—aka collective wisdom, swarm intelligence, collective consciousness—has become a hot topic. Biologists, social scientists, computer researchers, robotics engineers, transport companies, and students of metaphysics, working through such organizations as the Co-Intelligence Institute, the World Café, the Collective Wisdom Initiative, and the Center for Collective Intelligence at the Massachusetts Institute of Technology, are all hard at work studying its implications for everything from traffic control to world peace.

Some researchers are concentrating on the behavior of animal groups; others are focusing on cities; still others are looking at circles of spiritual seekers. Most agree that collective intelligence occurs spontaneously when individuals who share a need and a purpose instinctively self-organize into a group and function with no leader or central authority. Whether they are flocks of birds, schools of fish, ant colonies, or gatherings of humans, such groups are somehow able to exhibit abilities much greater than what any—or all—of their members would normally possess.

"Where this intelligence comes from raises a fundamental question in nature," writes Peter Miller in his *National Geographic* article "Swarm Theory." "How do the simple actions of individuals add up to the complex behavior of a group? How do hundreds of honeybees make a critical decision about their hive if many of them disagree? What enables a school of herring to coordinate its movements so precisely it can change direction in a flash, like a single, silvery organism? The collective abilities of such animals—none of which grasps the big picture, but each of which contributes to the group's success—seem miraculous even to the biologists who know them best."[2]

I'm convinced that a group's extraordinary abilities are actually evidence of highly developed intelligence in its individual members. Each must be able to comprehend not only the big picture, but the *really* big picture—one that extends far beyond the success of the group. Each member of the group is smart enough to know that he or she has something of vital importance to contribute to the whole—and that the group does too.

As we'll see, our very use of collective intelligence implies an understanding of the importance of working together to ensure not only our individual survival and the success of our group, but the survival of our world.

And there's more. We'll be looking at how collective intelligence

- expands the definition of *intelligence* beyond standard accepted forms (logical, emotional, linguistic, spatial, musical, corporeal, intrapersonal, interpersonal, etc.). It includes but is not limited to brain function.
- appears to be hard-wired in all life forms. But most of humanity—with the exception of traditional cultures—has suffered such psychic fragmentation that we've lost much of our ability to use it.
- is based on wholeness—the interdependence of all life. As such, it always works for the collective good and benefits the entire web of life.
- was an important part of prehistoric spiritual beliefs and practices, conserved in esoteric traditions as well as by indigenous people, and is being remembered by many contemporary scientific theories.
- is the opposite of mob mind or groupthink. That's collective stupidity, which we'll be visiting in part 2.
- is much greater than what can be replicated by artificial intelligence. As experienced by ancient and contemporary humans, collective consciousness invariably includes the numinous.
- is available to all of us, all the time.

To comprehend the subtle and profound reaches of collective intelligence and how we can relearn to use it, we'll be looking closely at ancient and indigenous spirituality, the distortions in modern perception, the power of archetypal forces, and the many ways in which our ancestors worked—and native people continue to work—with energy. What we'll find is awe-inspiring, especially when seen through the lens of recent scientific thought.

THE VOLCANOES ARE TALKING

My experience in the circle in Peru was my first conscious brush with collective intelligence. But it wasn't my first taste of magic—or of the Andes (for me, the two are pretty much synonymous.)

Born in Brazil to two adventurous journalists from the United States, I spent my childhood in Costa Rica and Chile, punctuated by forays throughout the Americas, the Caribbean, and Europe, before going to high school and college in the United States.

As a child I found the dizzying power of the Andes intoxicating; as a grown-up, I was called to them again and again—ostensibly to learn about Andean spirituality, but also to bathe myself in the delicious energy emitted by the beautiful peaks and their people.

Everywhere I lived or traveled, magic was afoot somewhere in the natural landscape. In Latin America it blossoms with a continuous crop of inexplicable happenings that intrigue, baffle, and often terrify—such as when my U.S.-trained Costa Rican pediatrician, a close friend of my parents, confessed that he was haunted by the X-ray of a young TB patient whose lungs displayed a pattern of lesions that corresponded identically to pins stuck in the chest of a crudely made rag doll the child's parents had found in their yard.

In Costa Rica I spent my childhood in the Central Valley canton of Escazú, known as "Land of the Witches" because of its profusion of *brujos* who, since pre-Columbian times, healed with herbs or practiced sorcery in the hills beneath Mount Pico Blanco. This enchanted mountain is the home of the legendary witch Zárate, still said to work her powerful but benevolent magic in forest and fog.

I grew up savoring the rich soup of cultures with their fantastic tales of magic, miracles, spooks, and spirits. From the country folk who worked for us, I learned to hurry inside after dark if a certain owl hooted; it was announcing that its sidekick, the puma, was coming down the mountain. I learned that if it didn't rain on Good Friday, there would surely be an earthquake. I learned that one had to prune trees and cut hair only during the waning moon, and that the sheet lightning illuminating the mountain ridges was the volcanoes talking to each other.

And so much more. For children lucky enough to live immersed in wildness—untamed mountains, jungles, coastlines—the energies of the Earth are palpable and whisper of a mysterious world where anything is possible.

As I grew older, the enigmatic power and beauty of traditional cultures kept tugging at my soul. I felt that the ancients who had left traces of their vanished world on our land, and their descendants on every continent, had access to some kind of essential truth missing from the lives of "civilized" people.

All of this, of course, collided head-on with my rigidly rationalistic education, and certainly had no place in my subsequent journalism career, in which anything but the verifiable facts—especially anything woo-woo—was a no-no. But Costa Ricans live by the maxim *No hay que creer ni dejar de creer* (one must neither believe nor cease to believe)—in other words, be skeptical, but keep an open mind.

So, neither believing nor ceasing to believe, I lurched back and forth between "the facts" and the magical world I had often experienced, always wondering if there was a way to reconcile these paths that were so different.

After years of seeking, I finally found it—first in the spiritual wisdom of native cultures, then in the new science that has come to validate it for those of us still arrogant enough to need convincing.

THE PARADIGM SHIFT

For many new-science pioneers, the idea of collective intelligence easily follows the great discovery that everything is interconnected and interdependent. If, at the quantum level, we are all one, how extraordinary is it, really, that we are able to think and act together?

Numerous aspects of the New Paradigm, such as systems theory, chaos theory, and field theory, as well as exciting discoveries in many different branches of science—biology, cosmology, genetics, neurobiology—all shed light on collective intelligence. At the same time, they provide dramatic evidence that the spiritual beliefs and practices of traditional people, which mechanistic science couldn't and wouldn't touch, had it right all along.

Native people and modern people see things so differently that sometimes it seems as though they're not looking at the same world. The indigenous person sees the living links between Earth and her children and knows that there is no action any of us can take that won't have some effect, for good or ill, somewhere.

This means that each of us bears an immense responsibility for what happens to the world, each other, and all beings. It's an ethical burden most people in "developed" societies, mindlessly "getting and spending," consuming and polluting, have never even contemplated, much less carried.

But it's not our fault. Over millennia, we of the dominant culture gradually lost our connection with nature. And the more technology took over writing our life scripts, the harder it became to perceive the subtle energies that weave the web of life. All we could see were isolated fragments of reality—bits and pieces of the whole. The big picture eluded us; it was just too vast to grasp.

Yet more and more modern people sense, at a deep level, that something vital has gone missing. We may no longer be able to perceive the cosmic web, but we are still part of it.

"The key insight coming from the new paradigm in the sciences is not technological, it is the confirmation of something people have always felt but could not give a rational explanation for: our close connection to each other and to the cosmos," writes philosopher and systems theorist Ervin Laszlo. "Traditional people have known it and have lived it, but modern civilization has first neglected and then denied it. Yet genuine spiritual experience offers direct evidence of our links to each other and to all of creation, and now science confirms the validity of such intuitions."[3]

THE BIG PICTURE

For me, many studies of collective intelligence, while valuable and interesting, don't go far enough. I believe the story isn't just about the amazing self-organizing behavior of ant colonies, slime-mold cells, flocks of birds, or cars in traffic; the big story is about the even more exciting big picture: the ways in which those ants, birds, slime molds (sorry, the cars don't count), and increasing numbers of humans are contributing—wisely, intelligently, altruistically—to the maintenance of life. Laszlo notes:

> A fresh look at our connections in the framework of the new sciences—quantum physics above all—began to indicate that the "oneness" people sometimes experience is not delusory and that the explanation is not beyond the ken of the sciences. As quanta, and entire atoms and molecules, can be instantly connected across space and time, so living organisms, especially the complex and supersensitive brain and nervous system of evolved organisms, can be instantly connected with other organisms, with nature, and with the cosmos as a whole.
>
> This is vitally important, for admitting the intuition of connections to our everyday consciousness can inspire the solidarity we so urgently need to live on this planet—to live in harmony with each other and with nature.[4]

ONE WITH ALL THAT IS

I am one with All That Is,
All That Is is One:
Rocks and trees and
Hawks and bees,
All beneath the sun.

OWL WOMAN[5]

Nature is the source of all indigenous wisdom because it shows the way—the *only* way—to live in harmony with All That Is.

According to Tom Cowan, author of *Fire in the Head: Shamanism and the Celtic Spirit,* what the Eskimos call *sila* "is similar to the divine power the Polynesians call *mana,* the Algonquin *manitou,* the Lakota *wakanda,* the Iroquois *orenda,* the Pawnee *tirawa,* and the !Kung *ntum.* It is very much the same idea expressed as *brahman* in India and the *tao* in China and Japan. In the European esoteric tradition, it is often called *magick.* It is the God-Without-Form, the Great Spirit or wondrous mystery behind all that is and, in fact, it *is* All-That-Is." Cowan says the ancient Celts believed that this power resides in everything, so "the vital essence of the universe interconnects all living things."[6]

Native people throughout the world hold this same view, venerating Mother Earth and honoring "All My Relations," the myriad beings who share their world, as brothers and sisters.

While learning the Andean spiritual path from native shamans, Elizabeth Jenkins frequently found her eyes opened to a startling reality in which what was metaphorical to us was literally true. "Again and again my exposure to this tradition has revealed to me as obvious the fact that on levels often too subtle to notice, human beings, plants, animals, nature, and mother earth all constantly communicated, affected, and exchanged energy with one another, and that should these incalculable inter-species exchanges cease, life itself as we know it would also cease," she writes. "Together, we formed an immense living system in which each part performed some necessary service essential to the survival of the whole."[7]

The elements show us the awesome power of the collective. A single drop of water, a soft breeze, a pebble, or a spark might go unnoticed, but when each contributes its energy to the whole, rivers, hurricanes, avalanches, and flames resculpt our world in a continuous process of creation.

The new science is confirming what native people have been insisting for thousands of years: Mother Earth is not just a colorful metaphor. Now that we've finally begun to wake up, we're amazed to learn that she really is the one running what we thought was our show. Moreover, unlike the ham-fisted, destructive humans who think they're in charge, she maintains harmony with astounding delicacy, precision, and care. As "new thinker" Ken Dychtwald points out:

> Since all aspects of the universe can be seen to exist as energetic systems, then the rigid line between living and nonliving systems immediately disappears and we see that everything is quite alive in some very fundamental way. Not only are the tiniest atomic particles to be considered whole, intelligent and alive systems, but we must also view the planet earth, the solar system and the galaxy as being alive, whole and self-intelligent at a fundamental energetic level.[8]

Physicist, systems theorist, and deep ecologist Fritjof Capra writes:

> The earth . . . functions not just *like* an organism but actually seems to *be* an organism—Gaia, a living planetary being. Her properties and activities cannot be predicted from the sum of her parts; every one of her tissues is linked to every other tissue and all of them are mutually interdependent; her many pathways of communication are highly complex and nonlinear; her form has evolved over billions of years and continues to evolve.[9]

"Only now are we realizing that the Earth is a self as well," adds cosmologist Brian Swimme, author of *The Universe Is a Green Dragon*. "The Earth is a self-organizing process of astounding complexity and achievement."[10]

AWARENESS OF ONENESS

The universe is a multiform event. There is no such thing as a disconnected thing.

BRIAN SWIMME[11]

The universe came into being with us together; with us, all things are one.

CHUANG TZU[12]

The heart of indigenous spirituality is the heart of the new science.

"Traditional people look at the world and everything in it as 'wholes,' as universals: each a universe in itself, a microcosm of the macrocosm, each a part of an infinity of other wholes, and itself comprising an infinity of other smaller wholes," writes James David Audlin in his compilation of teachings of Native American elders.[13]

He could be talking about systems theory, which introduced the idea that "systems are integrated wholes whose properties cannot be reduced to those of smaller units." Every organism, says Fritjof Capra, "from the smallest bacterium through the wide range of plants and animals to humans—is an integrated whole and thus a living system."[14]

Our indigenous ancestors were clearly more observant of what was actually going on in the natural world than were the mechanistic scientists who sought to separate, label, and categorize.

"The mechanistic view of reality separated substance from process, self from other, thought from feeling," say systems theory scholar and deep ecologist Joanna Macy and writer Molly Young Brown. "In the systems perspective, these dichotomies no longer hold. What appeared to be separate and self-existent entities are now seen to be interdependent. What had appeared to be 'other' can be equally construed as a concomitant of 'self,' like a fellow cell in a larger body."[15]

Wholeness is also the basis for chaos theory. In a chaotic system, say holistic theorist John Briggs and holistic physicist F. David Peat, "everything is connected, through negative and positive feedback, to everything else. . . . Chaos theory, like the image of our incredible planet in space, offers us a perception . . . of an interconnected world—a world organic, seamless, fluid, whole."[16]

According to Ervin Laszlo, field theory proposes that "human beings and all living things are a coalescence of energy connected to every other thing in the world." The discovery that energy fields link everything has led to the realization that "the reality we call universe is a seamless whole."[17]

THE ILLUSION OF ISOLATION

A human being is part of the whole, called by us the "Universe," a part limited in time and space. He experiences himself, his thoughts and feelings as something separated from the rest, a kind of optical delusion of his consciousness. This delusion is a kind of prison for us, restricting us to our personal desires and to affection for a few persons nearest to us.

Our task must be to free ourselves from this prison by widening our circle of compassion to embrace all living creatures and the whole of nature in its beauty.

ALBERT EINSTEIN[18]

The tendency of individuals to self-organize into groups is an essential quality of living systems, and it's where collective intelligence reveals itself.

"The social insects—bees, wasps, ants, termites and others—form colonies whose members are so interdependent and in such close contact that the whole system resembles a large, multicreatured organism," Fritjof Capra explains. "Bees and ants are unable to survive in isolation, but in great numbers they act almost like the cells of a complex organism with a collective intelligence and capabilities far superior to those of its individual members."[19]

Of course, *nothing* can survive in isolation. We humans may live under the illusion that once we become adults, each of us is independent and can easily live on our own. But just try it. We wouldn't last very long without our support group of countless beings and systems inside and outside of us.

"Many of us think that our mind is separate from the world around us," writes Joan Halifax, author of several books on Buddhism. "Gregory Bateson said that this divided notion of the self was the great epistemological error of Western civilization. There is a larger mind of which the individual mind is only a subsystem. This mind is immanent in the totally interconnected social system of our planetary ecology."[20]

Halifax offers the example of corn to show how "we interpene-trate one another and are coextensive with all creation. We inter-are. . . . [Corn] cannot grow to maturity outside the body of the Earth, so therefore she is part of the Earth. Nor can she grow without sun, moisture, and human care. . . . She cannot 'be' in isolation. Rather, she is part of the continuum of life whose unique expression of maize-ness is part of an interactive web of identities and events that give rise to her beingness."[21]

The New Paradigm weighs in to agree. Lecturer and journal-ist Lynne McTaggart says that the discoveries of quantum scientists "blurred the boundary lines of our individuality—our very sense of separateness. If living things boil down to charged particles interacting with a field and sending out and receiving quantum information, where did we end and the rest of the world begin?"[22]

There's just no getting around it (or away from each other): we are all entangled.

"The visible body just happens to be where the wave function of the organism is most dense," biologist Mae Wan Ho explains. "Invisible quantum waves are spreading out from each of us and permeating into all other organisms. At the same time, each of us has the waves of every other organism entangled within our own make-up."[23]

This entanglement is quite visible to indigenous masters, who can perceive a universe that modern people not only can't see but can't even imagine. Well-known author Deepak Chopra says that the Sanskrit word *maya* describes the modern person's handicap: it's "the illusion of boundaries, the creation of a mind that has lost its cosmic perspective."[24]

But we can learn to see our connections again. As part of a "large, multicreatured organism," humans too are capable of collective intel-ligence working for the greater good.

WHOLENESS AND HOLINESS

It is enough for me to contemplate the mystery of conscious life perpetuating itself through all eternity; to reflect upon

*the marvelous structure of the universe, which we can
dimly perceive, and to try humbly to comprehend even an
infinitesimal part of the intelligence manifested in nature.
This is as good a definition of God as I need.*

ALBERT EINSTEIN[25]

*Attempting to understand a phenomenon as mysterious as
collective wisdom . . . is a bit like trying to understand God.*

CRAIG HAMILTON[26]

Awareness of wholeness is awareness of holiness, and pioneering theoretical physicist David Bohm was fond of pointing out the common
root of both words. (They come from the Indo-European root *kailo-*,
meaning "whole, uninjured, of good omen," according to *The American
Heritage Dictionary of the English Language.*)

Our ancestors perceived no difference among what Western minds
later divided into the material, the energetic, and the sacred. They
understood that the same energy animates a blade of grass, a hurricane,
a mosquito, and us. The sacred was not remote, exclusive, or difficult to
touch; it was an intimate part of every being's life.

Specific points on the Earth and places in nature—mountains,
forests, bodies of water—as well as cyclical celestial events such as sol-
stices, equinoxes, and the appearance of certain stars, were acknowl-
edged as openings to divine energy. Working with air, water, fire, and
earth in sacred places at certain times, ancient people used tools such as
the circle to exchange energy with the cosmos, thereby fulfilling their
responsibility to the forces of creation and receiving infusions of grace.
Sacred reciprocity—the energetic give-and-take the Andeans call *ayni*—
became the cornerstone of indigenous spiritual life.

Tom Cowan stresses that in the mystical literature of all peoples,
regardless of religion or century, "we find vestiges of the belief that the
natural landscape is spiritually alive and that an indwelling spirit animates each living or created thing."[27]

"When we speak of the human animal's spontaneous interchange with the animate landscape, we acknowledge a felt relation to the mysterious that was active long before any formal or priestly religions," adds philosopher, cultural ecologist, and performance artist David Abram. "The instinctive rapport with an enigmatic cosmos at once both nourishing and dangerous lies at the ancient heart of all that we have come to call 'the sacred.'"[28]

We see this rapport in children, which implies that spirituality may be something every human is born with. Ramón Gallegos Nava, sociologist and author, maintains that "children are spiritual beings by nature. Their recognition of the mystery and wonder of life places them in contact with an immense non-material world ready to be discovered."[29]

Interestingly, the syncretism that followed every effort by dominant religions to eradicate traditional beliefs epitomizes the wholeness-holiness link. Instead of disappearing, ancient and indigenous Earth spirituality simply incorporated elements of the new religions being imposed on them. From prehistoric Goddess-worshipping cultures to Afro-Caribbean religions to Mayan and Andean spirituality, native peoples' insistence on blending ancient and recent shows that they don't admit the doctrinaire divisions created by modern minds.

Our ancestors were also well aware that collective activities facilitate communication with divine energies. Not surprisingly, the sacred pops up often in contemporary discussions of collective consciousness.

"Miraculous"—a word frequently used by scientists examining the behavior of animal groups—is voiced repeatedly by awed humans who have experienced collective intelligence. Reports contain such phrases as "You feel the presence of the sacred," "It was as if something larger than me was speaking through me," "It was totally magical," and "We're absolutely convinced that we're experiencing the beginnings of an evolutionary shift that's greater than anything we've ever experienced."[30]

If mechanistic science falls short when trying to explain the apparently miraculous behavior of animal groups, it's at a loss to deal with such dramatic experiences among humans.

According to Fritjof Capra, science and the sacred can no longer be on separate pages. He explains, "In the stratified order of nature, individual human minds are embedded in the larger minds of social and ecological systems, and these are integrated into the planetary mental system—the mind of Gaia—which in turn must participate in some kind of universal or cosmic mind. . . . In this view, the deity . . . represents nothing less than the self-organizing dynamics of the entire cosmos." Therefore, he says, "the systems view of mind seems perfectly consistent with both the scientific and the mystical views of consciousness, and thus to provide the ideal framework for unifying the two."[31]

For biologist Rupert Sheldrake, "God is not remote and separate from nature, but immanent in it. Yet at the same time, God is the unity that transcends it." He quotes fifteenth-century mystic Nicholas of Cusa, who said that "divinity is the enfolding and unfolding of all things in such a way that all things are in divinity"—presaging Bohm's theory, centuries later, of the implicate order unfolding into the explicate.[32]

"Far from destroying God, science for the first time was proving His existence—by demonstrating that a higher, collective consciousness was out there," writes Lynne McTaggart. "There need no longer be two truths, the truth of science and the truth of religion. There could be one unified vision of the world."[33]

Fig. 1.2. Leaf-cutter ants at work. Photo by Jim Molloy.

ANTS, INTELLIGENCE, AND ALTRUISM

"Ants aren't smart. Ant colonies are," says biologist Deborah Gordon.[34]

Author Steven Johnson looks at the collective intelligence of ants from the standpoint of emergence theory, describing Gordon's studies of "the connection between the microbehavior of individual ants and the overall behavior of the colonies themselves." He calls this "a particular kind of emergent, self-organizing system."[35]

Gordon says the queen ant, housed in a safe chamber deep at the bottom of the colony, is not an authority figure; she lays eggs and is cared for by the workers.[36] It would be impossible for her to direct every worker's decision about which task to perform and when. According to Johnson, this makes ants perfect models of "bottom-up" or "emergent" collective intelligence.

Gordon points out that individual ants have no way to "assess the global situation" but still manage to "work together in a coordinated way . . . using only local information. *"Local* turns out to be the key term in understanding the power of swarm logic," Johnson writes. "We see emergent behavior in systems like ant colonies when the individual agents in the system pay attention to their immediate neighbors rather than wait for orders from above. They think locally *and* act locally, but their collective action produces global behavior."

Johnson maintains that ants, which Gordon says communicate with each other by means of pheromone trails, have no way to perceive the big picture. "There are no bird's-eye views of the colony, no ways to perceive the overall system—and indeed, no cognitive apparatus that could make sense of such a view," he points out. "'Seeing the whole' is both a perceptual and conceptual impossibility for any member of the ant species."

Therefore, he concludes, ants fulfill all the requirements for "emergent" behavior: a critical mass of numbers, ignorance of the big picture, random encounters, the ability to read patterns, and interaction with their neighbors. Together, he says, these mean that "local information can lead to global wisdom . . . the most important lesson the ants have to give us, and the one with the most far-reaching consequences."

So far, so good. But it may not be that simple.

Gordon has also been probing another mystery: the fifteen-year life spans of ant colonies, which are tied to the life span of the queen, and the fact that colonies grow stronger and more successful as they age— even though individual ants live for only a year.

This, along with Johnson's observation that "it's in the colony's best interest—and the colony's gene pool—to keep the queen safe," raises intriguing questions that he neglects to answer.[37] He uses emergence theory to explain persuasively *how* ants might achieve collective intelligence, but we're left wondering *why*. He suggests that collective intelligence aids in the ants' survival, but why did they develop this particular survival strategy? He misses the all-important link between the group and the greater whole—between the colony and Gaia.

German theoretician Marco Bischof stresses that "quantum mechanics has established the primacy of the inseparable whole. For this reason, the basis of the new biophysics must be the insight into the fundamental interconnectedness *within* the organism as well as *between* organisms, and that of the organism *with the environment*."[38]

One measure of collective intelligence is that it benefits the entire web of life. If individual ants can't live to see the success of their colony, yet they work toward it anyway, could they be driven by a greater awareness than we currently understand? Compare this behavior with the Native American ethic of making every decision based on its possible effect on one's descendants seven generations from now.[39]

This attitude suggests altruism. The ants' care of their queen also hints that altruistic intelligence may be at work. "Their genes instruct them to protect their mother," Johnson writes.[40]

At the deepest possible level, ants know that protecting their mother is essential for the good of the whole: each individual ant benefits, the colony benefits, future generations benefit, the ecosystem of which the colony is a part benefits. Ultimately, all beings on Earth benefit.

Now translate this into human scale. Native people know that protecting their mother—Mother Earth—is essential for their own and all beings' survival. How do they know this?

Perhaps the knowledge needed by both ants and humans lies in the infinite field of information to which all beings have access, and which can be tapped into when needed—especially when a group of individuals is functioning as one.

Maybe individual ants are a lot smarter than Gordon gives them credit for. Maybe, just maybe, each little ant, making its contribution for the good of all, comprehends far more about the big picture—the *really* big picture—than we do.

THE *REALLY* BIG PICTURE

The *really* big picture, according to New Paradigm scientists, is that "everything is intelligent"[41]—including bacteria, viruses, and plants—and not only intelligent, but altruistic.[42]

Bacteria, says Lynn Margulis, are part of "a single global superorganism . . . an incredibly large community of highly intelligent interactive subparts" that "have the ability to make choices; they possess free will."[43]

Viruses display altruistic behavior, sacrificing part of their swarm when they need to "stabilize and retain their self-organized state," says herbalist and author Stephen Harrod Buhner. And plants protect and support "not only their own health but the health of the ecorange in which they live."[44]

Forest expert Peter Wohlleben cites eye-opening recent studies that show how trees cooperate to benefit one another and the forest as a whole. He says trees communicate by means of olfactory, visual, and electrical signals, as well as by low-frequency sound waves, aided by fungal networks that transmit signals from one tree to the next "like fiber-optic internet cables . . . helping the trees exchange news about insects, drought, and other dangers."

Trees also share resources, "equalizing differences between the strong and the weak," Wohlleben adds. "Whoever has an abundance of sugar hands some over; whoever is running short gets help," he says. "It's a bit like the way social security systems operate to ensure individual members of society don't fall too far behind." The well-being of each tree, and the entire forest, "depends on their community."[45]

David Bohm, who laid the groundwork for much current research in human collective intelligence, believed that through dialogue, a self-organized group of people could produce intelligence far greater than what any single member—or all the members trying to find consensus—could come up with. "What I propose is that it is possible now for a number of individuals who are in close relation . . . to establish a one-mind. In other words, that the consciousness is one, acting as one." Such a group "would have a power immensely beyond one."[46]

VISA founder Dee Hock, another collective-intelligence pioneer, pointed to ballet as one example of "teams whose performance transcends the individual" and developed the term *chaordic* to describe the collective process. He defined this as "any self-organizing, self-governing, adaptive, nonlinear, complex organism, organization, community, or system, whether physical, biological, or social, the behavior of which harmoniously combines characteristics of both chaos and order."[47]

When Hock tried to explain his ideas to people throughout the world, he said women, people from Eastern cultures, and native people had no trouble understanding them. "Those who had the most difficulty with the concepts were often Caucasian men from Western societies in positions of power. People like me!"[48]

Buhner offers a possible explanation for this: "Deep examination of the brain and physiological sciences has found that populations in the West, most especially in the United States, are abnormal when compared to the majority of humans on the planet. Most people don't think like we do . . . and they never have." Members of WEIRD (Western, educated, industrialized, rich, and democratic) societies, he says, "are among the least representative populations one could find for generalizing about humans."[49]

To begin to grasp the *really* big picture, we may need to start thinking like an ant . . . or a tree . . . or a virus.

* * *

That said, I watch with alarm as parades of leaf-cutter ants) march grooves in the earth around our house, bobbing along, each with its prized piece of leaf from the tall tropical oak tree they're busy stripping bare. It's the third tree they've killed in as many years.

The leaf-cutters are becoming a plague in this secondary forest that has grown up during the last sixty-five years on what used to be typical rich farmland in Costa Rica's mountain-ringed Central Valley, a mixture of pastures, cornfields, and coffee plants interspersed with small stands of shade trees, some four thousand feet above sea level. Now dirt from the ants' vast network of underground tunnels and chambers is forming mounds on paths and hillsides.

I can't help but wonder: what's intelligent about this? Are the ants really working for the good of all? Aren't they simply destroying their environment, just as we humans are destroying ours?

I have to remind myself that we've been disrupting the ants' ecosystem for a long time. Humans, not ants, were the first to deforest this land. In the early fifties, when my family settled here and allowed the forest to start growing back, the use of highly toxic pesticides was rampant. Later came uncontrolled urban sprawl, gobbling up the few remaining patches of surrounding wilderness.

Finally, climate change started making itself felt. Wildlife that used to call this area home—coyotes, sloths, kinkajous, and many species of birds—disappeared. Species never seen at this altitude—toucans, boas, golden orb spiders, *Aedes aegypti* mosquitos—made their appearance. All of the inhabitants of our microclimate (including us) have had to adjust to the disturbances.

If I could perceive the *really* big picture, perhaps I would trust nature's processes and understand that what I'm witnessing right now as a plague of ants is really the wisdom of Gaia, slowly, patiently working to put things back into balance—over eons, if necessary—through collective intelligence.

2

We Can't See

The Crisis of Perception

Reality is the vision we have of what surrounds us, but there are other, much more subtle realities that are more important. As humans evolved, they lost this ability to perceive and are thus disconnected from the cosmos, in a state of neglect that they seek to fill with material goods.

RAMÓN CARBALA[1]

Living is easy with eyes closed, misunderstanding all you see.

THE BEATLES

Something there is that doesn't love a wall.

ROBERT FROST[2]

We can't see—even though we think we can.

Five hundred years of perceiving reality through the lens of mechanistic science has fragmented our thinking, creating boxes in our brains. More than brainwashed, modern people are brain-boxed: bolstered by scientific certainty, we have learned to sort everything into carefully walled-off categories and hierarchies, with names, rules, scripts, and maps. We have built walls not only between things, but between ourselves and the many dimensions of reality, each other, and all other beings. And we have built walls within ourselves, arbitrarily dividing mind, body, and spirit.

As apparently distinct individuals, we know who we are, what's real, what we believe, what we like, where we stand. We stuff everything that comes along into one box or another, and if something doesn't fit, we build another wall to keep it out. Without our boxes' comforting walls, we'd find ourselves in terrifying free fall. Like our well-developed ego boundaries, the walls help us feel safe. But such a sense of security has come at a terrible price.

Cut off from the finer perceptions of heart and body, we can no longer sense the Earth as our Mother, or all her beings as our brothers and sisters. We can't detect the spirit in a stone or a thunderstorm; we can't hear the voices of trees or recognize the intelligence in the tiniest insect.

When we lost contact with the layered deliciousness of divine mystery in nature, our vision rigidified, becoming mechanical, sterile, and soulless, finally splintering into what David Bohm calls "illusory perception . . . shaped by fragmentary thought"[3] and complexity theorist Edgar Morin calls "fractured thinking."[4]

Now, instead of a loving, abundant, responsive universe, all we can see is a lifeless world of human greed and need, fear, pain, and conflict. We feel alone, hopeless and helpless. It's as if we cast ourselves out of Paradise.

Bohm believes that "man's essential illness today is his feeling of fragmentation of existence, leading to a sense of being alien to a society that he himself created, but does not understand. Thus, he cannot assimilate his whole field of experience into a totality felt to be beautiful, harmonious, and meaningful."[5] This feeds our illusion of isolation, in which each of us sees ourselves as a distinct "self" different from, and in continuous competition with, anything and everything outside our defining, limiting skin. Of course, if I am so measurably different from you and him and them, then what happens to any or all of you is of no concern to me.

"It is our mistaken notion of the *other* that threatens to destroy us," notes author China Galland.[6] Joan Halifax believes that our alienation is expressed in "split atoms, schizoid psyches, and divided selves, human against human, nation against nation, and human against nature."[7]

Self-described "maverick ecologist" Bill Pfeiffer, founder of the

U.S. NGO Sacred Earth Network and author of *Wild Earth, Wild Soul,* calls this a "basic error in our perceptual lens—our operating system, if you will, from which our creations emanate."[8] Fritjof Capra says it's a "crisis of perception" and insists that we need to reorganize "the entire way in which we conceive of our world."[9]

"The way people see the world around them has a profound effect upon the manner in which their society functions," F. David Peat points out. "Western society, for example, is based upon the notion of the primacy of the individual. This is profoundly different from an Indigenous society where each person is first and foremost a part of the group, and the group itself is an aspect of the natural world."[10]

"The earth is one household," stresses Bohm. "We are the earth, because our substance comes from the earth and goes back to it. It is a mistake to say it is an environment just surrounding us, because that would be like the brain regarding the rest of the body as part of its environment. It is essential to see the world as one, because these households are not independent."[11]

DISTORTIONS AND DECEPTIONS

If we can't see, how can we know what's real?

John Briggs and F. David Peat believe that "habits of mind, the supposed certainties of our 'knowledge' about the world, produce distortions and deceptions about reality."[12] Mind-body medicine pioneer Larry Dossey calls this

a kind of collective hypnosis, a cultural trance, that prevents us from seeing things the way they really are. We are like flies crawling across the ceiling of the Sistine Chapel. We cannot see what angels and gods lie underneath the threshold of our perceptions. We do not live in reality; we live in our paradigms, our habituated perceptions, our illusions; the illusions we share through culture we call reality, but the true . . . reality of our condition is invisible to us." [Quoting William Irwin Thompson][13]

Says James David Audlin, "Persons who hold the modern literal understanding of reality become observing minds separated from reality," whereas the traditional person "does not feel divorced from reality, but closely interrelated with it."[14]

"Because what modern people see is constrained by what they believe they *can* see, everything that's not conveyed to the mind by the eye and ear is missing from the modern view of the world," says Ervin Laszlo.[15]

As a result, we have no clue about what reality might "really" look like. Safe within our walls, we've excluded the best parts of it. But as David Bohm reminds us, the new science has found that the walls and boxes we think we're seeing don't exist. "Because of its atomic structure no object can have a sharp boundary," he explains. "Rather, there is always an interpenetration of different kinds of atoms when two substances are in contact."[16]

Our indigenous ancestors knew this and participated with their whole selves in the whole of reality, not just pieces of it. Shamanism teacher Sandra Ingerman points out that in shamanic cultures, "'seeing' is a full-bodied experience."[17]

The perception of native people, which involves "the heart and the whole being," enables them to touch "the inner essences of things," says Peat. "While Western thought grasps at the surface, the Indigenous heart, mind, and being seek the 'inscape'; that inner voice and authenticity that lie within each experience and aspect of nature."[18]

Stephen Harrod Buhner believes that if we could perceive what he calls the "metaphysical background" of reality, "we would begin to experience, once again, the world as it really is: alive, aware, interactive, communicative, filled with soul, and very, very intelligent—and we, only one tiny part of that vast scenario."[19]

With such an expanded vision, we'd realize that we no longer need to act out of fear, greed, indifference, or hatred, perpetuating vicious circles of separation and destruction. As Bohm puts it, "What is at the origin of evil is just the fact that each man pursues his own fragmentary notion of the good."[20]

WHY WE CAN'T SEE

The individuals described as "wise" seem to be much fewer
in number than those described as "intelligent."
ROBERT KENNY[21]

We built boxes in our brains as information became more abundant and complex. Collecting and processing it to ensure individual well-being—organizing it and turning it into immediately usable knowledge—became more important than slowly developing wisdom, the understanding of the big picture that springs from the awareness of wholeness.

We acquire wisdom by participating deeply in life, which is why it is the gift of elders (although children, who are still connected to the unseen worlds, can also be very wise).

Robert Kenny of the Collective Wisdom Initiative says that intelligence is "the ability to learn or understand from experience . . . ; to acquire and retain knowledge . . . ; use of the faculty of reason in solving problems." Wisdom, on the other hand, is "the faculty of making the *best use* of knowledge, experience, understanding, etc. It involves not just reasoning, but also intuition, and therefore more direct and multiple modes of sensing and knowing." Arriving at wisdom, he says, "often requires inner change and deep reflection upon experience."[22]

Without wisdom, we're operating from what the authors of *Homeland Earth,* Edgar Morin and Anne Brigitte Kern, call "blind intelligence," which "breaks the complexity of the world into disjointed pieces, splits up problems, separates that which is linked together, and renders unidimensional the multidimensional. Incapable of seeing the planetary context in all its complexity, blind intelligence fosters unconsciousness and irresponsibility."[23]

In traditional societies, wisdom inspired a deep sense of responsibility for the well-being of all life. Yet "our instinctive empathy with the earthly surroundings remains stunted in most contemporary persons," says David Abram. "Hence, whenever we moderns hear of traditional peoples for whom all things are potentially alive . . . such notions seem to us the result of an absurdly wishful and immature style of thinking, at best a kind of childish naïveté. . . . Rocks alive? Yeah, right!" And yet, he argues, "it seems unlikely that our ancestral lineages could have survived if the animistic sensibility were purely an illusion."[24]

Dee Hock says that native societies,

> which endured for centuries with little increase in the capacity to receive, store, utilize, transform, and transmit information, had time to develop a very high ratio of understanding and wisdom to data and information.
>
> They may not have *known* a great deal by today's standards, but they *understood* a very great deal about what they knew. They were enormously wise to the extent to which they were informed, and their information was conditioned by an extremely high ratio of social, economic and spiritual value.[25]

It was with the rise of the first cities, says F. David Peat, "that individuals began to function with an increasing sense of their own independence . . . separate in a rigid sense from society and nature."[26]

Humans' loss of wisdom has been bad news for the planet. Our "blind intelligence" and diminished empathy now threaten the survival of all life with "vast technological power unleashed with inadequate understanding of its systemic propensity for destruction, or sufficient wisdom to guide its evolution in holistic, creative, constructive ways," according to Hock.[27]

THE FATAL SHIFT

> *While in the primordial condition humans possessed an instinctive knowledge of the sacred unity and profound interconnectedness of the world, a deep schism arose between humankind and the rest of reality with the ascendance of the rational mind. The nadir of this development is reflected in the current ecological disaster, moral disorientation, and spiritual emptiness.*
>
> Ervin Laszlo[28]

We lost our most vital source of wisdom when we lost our connection with the feminine. This marked the fatal shift from collective to individual, when we broke our bond with Mother Earth and each other.

According to theologian and professor Leonardo Boff and sociologist Rose Marie Muraro, authors of *Femenino y masculino* (Feminine and Masculine), the feminine in both man and woman is "that moment of mystery, of integrality, of vast profundity, the capacity to think with one's body, of deciphering messages hidden beneath signs and symbols, of interiority, of the feeling of belonging to a greater all, of receptivity, of treasuring in the heart, of the power to generate and nurture, of vitality and spirituality." Without these qualities, we are left with only the masculine—"reason, objectivity, ordering, power, materiality and even aggression"[29]—which has brought us unimaginable technological prowess, but also a spiritual Dark Age and a devastated planet ruled by collective stupidity.

Author John Perkins says his Mayan teacher Viejo Itza told him that "the most significant—the most disastrous—shapeshift in human history" was the shift away from the feminine.

"'This world is basically feminine, you know,'" Viejo Itza said. "'It's what allows survival. Not 'survival of the fittest'—that's just a male concept. Survival is all about nurturing, loving, sustaining—the feminine aspects. Without them, where would we be?'

"'My culture here worshiped the goddess, as did people all over the world—all over *Mother* Earth—until recent history, a few thousand years before Christ,'" he added.[30]

According to Riane Eisler, author of *The Chalice & the Blade,* early Goddess-worshipping societies were peaceful, creative, equalitarian, and technologically advanced and lived in harmony with nature.

"It was not the fight for survival of the strongest that guaranteed the perseverance of life and of individuals," Boff observes. "It was rather the cooperation and the co-existence between them."[31]

And then everything changed.

* * *

In Viejo Itza's words, "a great and terrible shapeshift took place. The ego got in the way of wisdom. What has always amazed me is how it seemed to happen simultaneously in so many places."[32]

For some reason, much (but fortunately not all) of humanity lost the ability to fully use both hemispheres of the brain, which cut off much of our access to the feminine.

"Modern man, in spite of all of our accomplishments, is brain imbalanced," says physician Melvin Morse, coauthor of *Where God Lives*. He explains that "the bicameral mind is the mind humans had for the first 195,000 years of their existence. It has been in the past 5,000 years that we have suffered from a lack of communication between the two sides of the brain, leaving an unhealthy dominance of the left temporal lobe and a relative atrophy of the right temporal lobe."[33]

Biologist Humberto Maturana's breakthrough confirmation of neuroplasticity proved that brains change in response to environmental influences, establishing new neural pathways.

So what happened to change our brains? A few theories:

Catastrophe

Joseph Chilton Pearce in *The Biology of Transcendence* speculates that the fatal shift may have been sparked by some deeply traumatic catastrophe "that left survivors with good reason never to trust the Great Mother as in the past."[34] He suggests a possible culprit: the gigantic volcanic eruption that blew out the center of the Mediterranean island of Thera in 1628 BCE.

According to archaeologist Charles Pellegrino, this single horrendous cataclysm, which has not been repeated anywhere on Earth since, caused disastrous tsunamis and climate change throughout the world and wiped out the peaceful, Goddess-worshipping Minoan civilization that had flourished in the eastern Mediterranean for fifteen hundred years.[35] Pellegrino argues persuasively that the Thera explosion gave rise not only to the legend of Atlantis, but to countless other accounts of catastrophe, including the biblical Flood.

"Perhaps through trauma our species suffered a setback, breeding an intellect based on distrust, fear, and the attempt to predict and control a hostile natural world in the interest of protecting against it, which ultimately produced culture as we know it today," Pearce suggests. "Our biology influences our culture and our culture influences our biology. A sufficient number of children born predisposed to defensiveness and quick reflexive survival reactions will tend to change the nature of the society in which they grow up."[36]

Soul Loss
Shamanic cultures claim that traumatic events can cause soul parts to break away, flee, and hide, leaving the victim disabled in mind, body, and spirit. Sandra Ingerman notes that soul-retrieval ceremonies are practiced in Siberia, Central Asia, Indonesia, northwest Africa, New Guinea, Melanesia, and Australia.[37] If the victims of some ancient catastrophe were unable to heal their soul loss with shamanic help and restore their trust in Mother Earth, could those fragmented souls have carried the wounds from one generation to the next?

Language
When humans began to communicate through speech, their brains may no longer have needed to rely so heavily on intuition, causing the left brain to become dominant.

"The convenient tools of language enable us to decide before-hand what we think things mean, and tempt us all too easily to see things only in a way that fits our logical preconceptions and our verbal formulas," says theologian Thomas Merton.[38]

David Abram suggests that the development of alphabets that permitted silent reading damaged our ability to interact with the world around us.

As our eyes, moving across the lines of text, learned to provoke an internal flow of words, a tight neurological coupling between the visual focus and inner speech arose in the brain. Given the growing emphasis upon the practice of reading for the cultivation of the self, it inevitably began to influence—and interfere with—other forms of seeing.

Soon our visual focus, even as it roamed across the visible landscape, began to release a steady flood of verbal commentary that often had little, or nothing, to do with the terrain.[39]

Conquest

Riane Eisler traces the fatal shift back to the Neolithic, when Goddess societies were overrun by violent nomadic warrior cultures and "the original partnership direction of Western culture veered off into a bloody five-thousand-year dominator detour."

In what sounds eerily like our current situation, she describes a shift "toward more effective technologies of destruction. This is accompanied by a fundamental ideological shift. The power to dominate and destroy . . . gradually supplants the view of power as the capacity to support and nurture life."[40]

In this scenario, the demands of a warlike culture would have required masculine attributes to prevail, shaping our brains accordingly. This in turn would have produced the patriarchy, which Boff and Muraro describe as "a complex pyramidal structure of domination and hierarchization, a structure stratified by gender, race, class, religion, and other forms of domination by one party over the other."[41]

* * *

For whatever reason, the one-sided brain that most of us rely on today is not the whole brain our ancestors used. And because of the feedback loop between biology and culture, we continue to reward masculine, left-brain analysis over feminine, right-brain intuition, violence over peaceful coexistence, separation over oneness. Only those in whom right-brain activity prevailed—poets, artists, musicians—were able to resist the shift. Fortunately, perhaps because of their relative isolation despite increasing efforts by dominant cultures to destroy or absorb them, most native people have been able to escape the worst effects of the brain deformations, which unfortunately are still taking place in the "developed" world.

For example, in the late 1960s, professors at Germany's University of Tübingen noticed a serious drop in sensory perception and general awareness in their students, Pearce, quoting the study, reports. "The same drop was noted in 1966 in the United States," he says. "Students didn't appear to be as aware of information from their environment or schooling or didn't seem to register it as young people had previously."

Working with the German Psychological Association, the university tested some four thousand young people over a period of twenty years and concluded that "our sensitivity to stimuli is decreasing at a rate of about 1 percent per year. Delicate sensations are simply being filtered out of our consciousness."

Significantly, studies by child psychologist Marcia Mikulak in the 1980s revealed that children from primitive settings averaged levels of sensory sensitivity and conscious awareness 25 to 30 percent higher than those of children in industrial-technological countries.[42]

Stephen Harrod Buhner claims that modern humanity's "conceptual monoculture that can't see outside its limitations"[43] is the result of "sensory gating channels . . . tiny apertures or gates or doors in specific sections of the nervous system's neural network." These channels, he says, are similar to the lenses in our eyes "that can expand or contract as needed to increase or decrease the amount of data allowed in. They act to prevent sensory overload."[44]

There's no question that people in modern societies have been suffering more and more sensory overload for generations, which means that we're likely becoming less and less able to see. "What you are taught does in fact shape what you are able to perceive," Buhner stresses. "And it alters brain structure accordingly." Echoing the findings cited by Pearce, he adds: "It turns out that sensory gating is a lot more open" in less "developed" cultures. "The further away you get from industrialized reductionism, the more open they are. What those other cultures see is actually there. We in the West just can't perceive it."[45]

WHAT WE CAN'T SEE

If we are to believe New Paradigm researchers, traditional people have always perceived the world in the way it actually is: a fluid universe of self-organizing creativity, the enfolding and unfolding of realities— what F. David Peat calls the "living universe."[46] It's the universe of mystery, magic, and metaphor we forgot we belonged to.

In the indigenous world, everything is energy: alive, conscious, meaningful, and indivisibly linked; time is not linear; the universe is multidimensional; and the Earth, our mother, needs loving care. It's a world in which paradox flourishes because the limits we thought were demarcating time and space, matter and energy, you and me, don't exist.

All beings give and receive, participating in the continuous exchange of energy that keeps the world in balance. Taking the Hermetic dictum of "as above, so below" a step further, native people also understand that "as within, so without." Reality is permeable, in constant flux.

The power to shapeshift—to not only see but participate in myriad dimensions, life forms, and consciousness—is one of the living universe's gifts. Peat points out that "transformations of being and consciousness are totally natural to Indigenous cultures in which a bear can transform into a man, or in which a mask can be imbued with animating power. . . . Their existence is more fluid and their ability to enter into other worlds is more highly adapted."[47]

The Shuar shaman Chumpi asks us:

Was I not a tree? Will I not be one again? And the bat—I know that soon my human form will disappear when I shapeshift into a bat. Does this mean I have sunk lower, become something less than I am now? Of course not. . . . We see the reality in our oneness. . . .

The priests hallucinate and in their confused state declare that man is above all others. We are not separate from these things in nature; we are them, and they are us.[48]

According to Tom Cowan, shamans can shapeshift because they understand that

on the Web of Life all created things share in the same power, and can *exchange* power, life, and consciousness.

Recognizing that creation is more loosely knotted than it may seem, shamans enter the experiential state of other entities and allow other entities to share in the shamans' own conscious experiences. It is like trading heads for a time, or emptying your own head so that it can be filled with new perceptions and new life.[49]

The ability to shapeshift is not limited to shamans; it's inherent in all beings. The fact that our ancestors knew this reveals that they were also aware of the basic truth of our interchangeability, as expressed in the Mayan phrase *in lak'esh* (You are me and I am you),[50] and confirmed by the discovery of quantum entanglement.

"The implicate order would help us to see that everything enfolds everything," David Bohm points out. "To see that everybody not only *depends* on everybody, but actually everybody *is* everybody in a deeper sense."[51]

THE OWL AND THE PINE CONE

For double the vision my eyes do see,
And a double vision is always with me.
With my inward eye, 'tis an Old Man grey;
With my outward, a Thistle across my way.

WILLIAM BLAKE[52]

With no brain-boxes to circumscribe their reality, traditional people see the world with Blake's "double vision."

According to James David Audlin, "When a traditional person and a modern person look at the same thing, it is *not* the 'same thing' because they perceive it in such fundamentally different ways." He tells a story about a modern person and a native person walking through a forest:

They both see something in a distant tree. "It looks like an owl," they both say. As they get closer they look again. Now they agree, "It looks like a pine cone."

"At first I thought it was an owl," says the member of the dominant culture, "but, as I got closer, I realized it was a pine cone."

The Native American says, "When I was farther away it appeared to me as an owl, but, as I got closer, it changed its appearance into that of a pine cone. It was an owl at first, but it became a pine cone."

The Native American is happy to have had a vision that affirms for him the presence of the Creator and the spirits all around him. The member of the dominant culture may feel foolish . . . and wonder if he should make an appointment with an optometrist.[53]

WHAT WE EXPECT IS WHAT WE GET

Traditional people expect to inhabit a world in which owls can turn into pine cones and humans can become trees and bats; modern people expect the world to fit into their rigid-walled brain-boxes, which admit no such possibilities. Reality helpfully obliges all of us, meeting both groups' expectations.

A possible explanation for this might be found in brain scientist Karl Pribram's groundbreaking work with holograms and the brain. Pribram theorized that when we observe the world, "we do so on a much deeper level than the sticks-and-stones world 'out there,'" writes Lynne McTaggart. She adds:

Our brain primarily talks to itself and to the rest of the body not with words or images, or even bits or chemical impulses, but in the language of wave interference: the language of phase, amplitude, and frequency—the "spectral domain." We perceive an object by "resonating" with it, getting "in synch" with it. To know the world is literally to be on its wavelength. . . .

The art of seeing is one of transforming. . . . In the act of observation, we are transforming the timeless, spaceless world of inter-ference patterns into the concrete and discrete world of space and time—the world of the very apple you see in front of you.[54]

Physicists probing the mysteries of the zero-point field built on Pribram's theories. McTaggart notes, "What they all discovered was something that Pribram's work had always hinted at: perception occurred at a much more fundamental level of matter—the nether-world of the quantum particle. We didn't see objects *per se,* but only their quantum information and out of that constructed our image of the world. Perceiving the world was a matter of tuning into the Zero Point Field."[55]

It's therefore up to us whether we expect to see an owl, a pine cone, or both—or something else entirely. Indigenous people and quan-tum scientists agree that the universe offers us an unlimited array of options—including the possibility that an image can be both a univer-sal archetype and a tangible, functioning part of our everyday reality.

Keeping this in mind, we can understand how a given popula-tion's perception can end up fashioning its reality. What we expect—individually and together—is exactly what we get.

A WORLD OF MEANING

Being able to see and interpret the messages offered by the living universe opens the door to other dimensions, readily accessible to traditional peo-ple but off-limits most of the time to handicapped modern brains. The ability to move in multiple levels of reality permits people to experience synchronicities—the "meaningful coincidences" that point to the exis-tence of what quantum theorists call a "participatory universe."[56]

In the indigenous view, says James David Audlin, "every event has meaning, every creature its message and teaching," and native people see meaning as "a fundamental characteristic of all things, not something that originates in our mind but in nature itself."[57]

According to F. David Peat, a synchronicity "begins with the very fact of meaning in life and in nature." During a synchronicity, he says, "a person experiences a strong sense of meaning which unites inner thoughts, dreams, and feelings with patterns of events in the outer world."

Whenever synchronicities happen to modern people, we tend to feel that something rare and uncomfortably paranormal is taking place. But synchronicities are a natural part of native consciousness, occurring all the time.

"If such epiphanies of meaning were to be sustained throughout the whole of life then clearly the human mind would operate on a different level," Peat points out. "Rigid structures of thought would be dissolved and creativity would operate through the whole field of consciousness."[58]

In his book *Original Wisdom,* Robert Wolff says that he couldn't figure out why, every time he decided to visit the Sng'oi people of Malaysia, someone was always sitting by the side of the road, waiting to accompany him to the village. "When I was with them I was moved by the strange synchronicities that so often occurred," he writes. "How was it possible that people without a telephone knew that I was coming to visit, when I did not know myself until a few hours before I left home? How could one person know what another was thinking and feeling and dreaming?"[59]

Later, he realized that

> they were not waiting for *me.* They were just sitting there as I happened along. Only then did it become clear to the people who were sitting by the path that *to escort a visitor* was why they were waiting. . . .
>
> When I understood this much about the [Sng'oi] People, I realized how truly different their reality was. My reality is made in my head; I create roles for myself, I create a structure that requires certain activities and prohibits others. I live in time; I have an agenda.
>
> Their existence had no reality until they lived it . . . each day a blank page, to be written as one lives it.[60]

3
Subtle Energy
The Flow of Life

From Wakan-Tanka, the Great Spirit, there came a great unifying life force that flowed in and through all things—the flowers of the plains, blowing winds, rocks, trees, birds, animals—and was the same force that had been breathed into the first man. Thus all things were kindred, and were brought together by the same Great Mystery.

GRANDFATHER LUTHER STANDING BEAR[1]

God is energy, and we are a reflection of that intelligent cosmic energy, that cosmic consciousness.

HUNBATZ MEN[2]

Ancient cultures throughout the world were aware of a "vital, animating energy of existence"[3] known in Eastern traditions as *prana, chi,* or *qi.* This is the "sacred energy . . . constantly flowing through everything" in native societies;[4] it's what Deepak Chopra calls the "unseen energy waiting to coalesce into atoms";[5] it's David Bohm's implicate order;[6] it's the zero-point field;[7] and it's Ervin Laszlo's Akashic Field.[8]

Mayan scholar Hunbatz Men says that Mayan sages "reached the scientific understanding that everything is born of energy, which gives life as well as form."[9]

"Andeans are born into a world that they believe is as conscious of them as they are of it," says Joan Parisi Wilcox. For them, all beings inhabit a "vibrating field of pure energy."[10]

Author Johanna Lambert tells us that for the Australian Aborigines, all of manifest reality is an expression of the Dreamtime, "a period when great mythical powers and beings pervaded infinite space. . . . In Aboriginal cosmology the Dreamtime epoch concluded," she writes. "However, the energy and vibrational patterns from the exploits of the great Ancestors congealed the initially limitless space into the topography and forms that we now experience as the material aspect of the universe."[11]

"Hindu and Chinese cosmologists have always maintained that the things and beings that exist in the world are a concretization or distillation of the basic energy of the cosmos, descending from its original source," says Laszlo. "The physical world is a reflection of energy vibrations from more subtle worlds that, in turn, are reflections of still more subtle energy fields. Creation, and all subsequent existence, is a progression downward and outward from the primordial source."[12]

Concurring with such beliefs, the new science has determined that "on our most fundamental level, living beings, including human beings, [are] packets of quantum energy constantly exchanging information with this inexhaustible energy sea," writes Lynne McTaggart, and that "there may be such a thing as a life force flowing through the universe—what has variously been called collective consciousness or, as theologians have termed it, the Holy Spirit."[13]

BUBBLES AND EGGS

What I can't explain is the fact that I'm seeing energy. It only happens when I sit next to Don Eduardo. When I go more than a few feet away from him I sense nothing. It's like he is surrounded by an electric space, where the air actually tingles. When I'm inside his space I see everything he sees.

ALBERTO VILLOLDO[14]

The vast flow of cosmic energy includes the energy fields emitted by everything, including supposedly "inanimate" objects such as stones and mountains. The Andeans call these fields *poq'pos,* or "bubbles." Carlos Castaneda's teacher, Yaqui sorcerer don Juan Matus, told him that people are surrounded by "eggs" of energy, perceptible when one's ability to "see" the deeper layers of reality is developed.[15]

According to author and shamanism teacher Alberto Villoldo:

> We all possess a Luminous Energy Field that surrounds our physical body and informs our body in the same way that the energy fields of a magnet organize iron filings on a piece of glass. Indian and Tibetan mystics who documented the existence of the Luminous Energy Field thousands of years ago described it as an aura or halo around the physical body.
>
> At first it seemed odd to find the same concept of a human energy field among the jungle and mountain shamans in the Americas. Once I grasped the universality of the human energy field, however, I understood that every culture must have discovered it.[16]

In the Andes, the world of living energy, known as the *kawsay pacha*, contains two kinds of energy: *sami,* which is ordered, light, and refined, and *hucha* (pronounced and sometimes spelled *hoocha*), which is heavy, disordered, and dense.

"Hucha is created only by human beings, and it manifests because we do not live in perfect ayni—reciprocity—with the kawsay pacha and with each other," explains Joan Parisi Wilcox. "At our current level of consciousness, we cannot seem to exist on Pachamama [Mother Earth] without creating disorder—without hurting others or undermining ourselves, without upsetting the harmony of the environment or threatening other species—and so hucha cannot be avoided."

Significantly, the principal way to cleanse *hucha* from one's bubble is to consciously release it to Pachamama, for whom heavy energy is delicious food, not waste. Wilcox quotes Peruvian shaman and anthropologist Juan Núñez del Prado: "She needs living energy, and if you release hucha to her you are empowering her. Also you are empowering yourself." Working with both heavy and refined energies is a continuous activity in the Andes, where, as in other native cultures, people strive to "maintain at all times the ecology of our energy environment."[17]

"We in Western culture were so programmed to categorize everything in terms of 'good' and 'bad,'" notes Elizabeth Jenkins. "But the Andeans followed Nature and in Nature there were no 'bad' plants, no 'evil' animals—everything, even humans, had a purpose in the great, interdependent ecosystem of planetary life. So with living energy, some of it was heavier, some more refined, but it all served a purpose."[18]

VOICES OF THE EARTH

Everything that exists is energy, and everything has a frequency or vibration.

CARLOS BARRIOS[19]

Earth has many, many voices. Those who understand that Earth is a living being know that Earth is a community that is constantly talking to itself, a communicating universe.

JOAN HALIFAX[20]

The energies of the cosmos express themselves in vibrations, which traditional cultures have used to navigate, recognize sacred power spots and objects, and even—some indigenous traditions hold—build gigantic structures.

Sound plays a vital role in native healing and spiritual practices. Medicine people sing, chant, play drums, and shake rattles to enter altered states of consciousness and journey to other worlds.[21] Shamans in Siberia believe their drums contain spirits that aid them in healing and journeying. For Native Americans, drumming aligns them with the heartbeat of Mother Earth.

"There is an innate tendency in the universe, within Gaia, for self-organized systems to vibrate in harmony, to share rhythms," says Stephen Harrod Buhner.[22]

According to F. David Peat, many traditions believe that sound, vibration, and song are the creative, generative forces of the cosmos.[23] Deepak Chopra notes the similarity between superstring theory, which holds that "billions upon billions of unseen strings pervade the universe, and their different frequencies give rise to all the matter in creation," and the teachings of the Vedic sages (*rishis*) that "the fundamental level of the whole world . . . is made of sounds."[24]

There is also the low-frequency "silent sound" inaudible to us, known as infrasound, emitted (and heard) by animals such as rhinoceroses, elephants, and whales, as well as by trees and forests, thunderstorms and hurricanes, and tectonic plates and volcanoes. (Maybe the volcanoes of my childhood really *were* talking to each other!) The Earth itself "rings a bell" in infrasound that travels out into the galaxy, says botanist and forest medicine expert Diana Beresford-Kroeger, adding that some humans can hear silent sound.[25]

Martín Prechtel was raised on a Pueblo Indian reservation in New Mexico and as a young man was initiated as a shaman and village chief by the Tzutujil Maya in Santiago Atitlán, Guatemala, where he lived until his village was torn apart by the violence of the 1980s. In his magnificent trilogy describing his experiences, he mentions the importance of sound in the creation of the Tzutujil cosmos:

> To the shaman, all the places, animals, weather, plants, and things outside in the world are also inside of you . . . the layers then stretch outside and inside simultaneously to create the House of the World, or World Body. This structure is made by the Builders, certain Owners or Gods with their original sounds and words.
>
> These sounds and words become tangible meaning, made to live as they are spoken. Each God word builds the House of the World by echoing off other words. These spirit world soundings, when made all at once, form the spiritual song of the world.

> This combined sound . . . grows the world in the form that we see and are. The song is the nervous system of the Universe.[26]

Shamans in many native traditions seek a "song of power" that enables them to fulfill their healing mission. According to author Holger Kalweit, "it is holy, because it comes from the very core of that which pervades everything."[27]

Peat says African pygmies played a sacred instrument and sang to the forest, "for the forest looked after everything, the insects, the birds, and the people. . . . If the forest slept, maybe it would forget about them, but if they sang to it and made music, then the forest would be happy, and the people would also be happy and not get sick."[28]

For the Dineh (Navajo) people, *nílch'i,* or "Holy Wind," carries the messages of all beings to one another. "It is through this Holy Wind that the world came into being," says Joan Halifax. "For from the Wind came the Word. The vibrations of words solidified into phenomena. Thus all things are related through the Holy Wind and the Word."[29]

Australian Aborigines "listened through all their senses to the various languages that permeate the natural world—for example, languages emitted by trees, celestial bodies, rocks, wind, water, fire, shadows, and seeds," Johanna Lambert reports. "The Dreamtime stories arose from listening to the innate intelligence within all things. . . . In many Aboriginal languages, the word for *listen* and the word for *understand* are the same."[30]

Exploring the link between the sounds of language and symbols encoded in ancient Mayan art, Hunbatz Men reveals how the sounds of words find expression in stone carvings, which convey spiritual messages. The carvings include the circle and the spiral, which, as we'll see, are important transmitters of energy and sacred information. We'll also be looking at the remarkable connection between sound and stones.

Now let's listen to the sound of those whose role in collective wisdom is legendary.

BLESSINGS FROM THE BEES

The awesome ability of bees to work together for the good of their communities and ecosystems has made them stars in collective-intelligence research. It's probably no coincidence that since humanity's beginnings, bees also have been revered in spiritual traditions throughout the world.

"Working in the hive, a home buzzing with the airiness of the artist's studio rather than with the gloom of the factory," bees are "a universal quickening power between Heaven and Earth," symbolizing the vital principle and incarnating the soul, write Jean Chevalier and Alain Gheerbrant. "It is this dual dimension—collective and individual, material and spiritual—which enriches their symbolism as a whole."[31]

Bees' vital role as pollinators is well known. Taking nectar and leaving pollen, they act in perfect *ayni*—reciprocity. Their honey sweetens, nourishes, and heals the lives of many beings. Significantly, each individual bee is important to the life of the hive.

And there's more. Could the sound created by bees' collective buzzing create a frequency that opens a door to the information-filled field? Diana Beresford-Kroeger notes that bees can communicate with infrasound: when they hear the silent sound generated by hurricanes, thunderstorms, or tornadoes, they change the frequency of their own sounds to a higher pitch.[32]

Bees' humming is echoed in the sacred syllable OM, which, according to Deepak Chopra, is the "primordial sound . . . that breaks the cosmic silence [and then] subdivides into different frequencies that compose the matter and energy of our universe." Chopra claims that the rishis heard this sound as a "cosmic hum."[33]

"If intoned correctly, [OM] vibrates the cranium and the central cortex of the brain, causing a sound similar to the humming of bees," notes Layne Redmond in her book *When the Drummers Were Women*. In addition, she says, the yogic practice called *bhramari,* in which the practitioner vibrates the central nervous system, brain, and body by buzzing the vocal chords, "refers to the sound of the absolute, of undifferentiated reality . . . which is reminiscent of the sound of bees buzzing."[34]

BEES AND THE GODDESS

Since Paleolithic times, bees have been considered emissaries of the Goddess.* According to author Barbara G. Walker, they were associated with healing, resurrection, and the power of female sexuality.

> Bees are still called *hymenoptera,* "veil-winged," after the *hymen* or veil that covered the inner sanctum of the Goddess's temples, the veil having its physical counterpart in women's bodies. Defloration was a ritual penetration of the veil under the "hymeneal" rules of the Goddess, herself entitled Hymen in the character of patroness of the wedding night and "honey-moon."

The hexagons that form the cells in a honeycomb are sacred geometric shapes with mystical significance. According to Walker, the number six (*hex* in Greek, *sex* in Latin) was known as the number of sex, as well as the perfect number. In Tantric Hinduism, the hexagram represented the union of the sexes.[35]

The "hex" cast by witches arose from the dangerous aspects of the Goddess; the honeycomb was the symbol of Aphrodite, Greek goddess of love. When the Goddess was demonized, Aphrodite's mystical number—666—became the biblical "number of the Beast." Layne Redmond tells us that bee goddesses—including the Paleolithic Queen Bee; Demeter, Rhea, and Cybele (Sibyl) of ancient Greece; Deborah, the biblical Queen Bee; and Bhramari Devi of Hindu cosmology—embodied the importance of sound in contacting the divine. Bee-goddess priestesses, known as *melissae,* invoked the Goddess by drumming.[36]

Andrew Gough, author of *The Bee,* says bees were associated with the Egyptian goddess Neith, whose "House of the Bee" contained an

---

*Riane Eisler is apparently unaware of the Goddess-bee connection, or of bees' mastery of collective intelligence. Despite her eloquent criticism of hierarchy, she falls into anthropocentric as well as hierarchical thinking when she dismisses bees and ants as species of "very limited capacity" when compared to the "vastly superior minds" of humans (Eisler, *The Chalice & the Blade,* 173).

inscription that said, "I am All That Has Been, That Is, and That Will Be. No mortal has yet been able to lift the veil that covers Me." Bees also played a role in the veneration of lion deities in Egypt and were linked to the Greco-Roman goddess Artemis/Diana at Ephesus, whose name is believed to derive from the pre-Greek word *apasus,* meaning "bee."[37]

Author Simon Buxton recounts his initiation into an ancient European shamanic tradition known as the "Path of Pollen." He tells how his Welsh beekeeper teacher, the "Bee Master," began chanting and beating a metal drum known as a *quoit,* a technique he called *"tanging:* hitting a piece of metal in such a way that the bees respond to the sound and may be easily subdued. . . . The strange sound filled the room until it became something akin to the hum of the entire hive." Buxton writes, "The thought occurred that this was not just humming. Rather, it was the wisdom of the ages that the bee shamans had whispered into the hive over centuries, and it was being spoken aloud now by this man chanting the language of the bees. Some form of information was being conducted directly to my brain. I had become a conduit for this knowledge, yet I knew not what electricity compelled it to me in such a way."[38] This was the first of many shamanic journeys Buxton claims he took with the aid of bees.

Hunbatz Men found numerous examples of the sound "G" in ancient Mayan hieroglyphs, which he maintains stands for the energy of the Milky Way, "the seed from which all life—human or otherwise— springs." Depicted as a spiral in drawings of hieroglyphs from the Madrid Codex reproduced in Men's book *Secrets of Mayan Science/ Religion,* it appears with the Bee Lord.

According to Men, the drawing on the left shows a bee flying over an altar "where the 'G' is fully active—moving the energy of the Milky Way." In the drawing on the right, the Bee Lord, also known as Lord of the World, suctions what it holds in its hand, "making contact with the energy of the Milky Way."[39]

Bees universally seem to have extraordinary connections with other dimensions. And it's worth noting that in many indigenous cultures, the Milky Way is believed to play a vital role in the flow of energy on Earth.

BEES AND BALANCE

Significantly and tragically, bees now are threatened with extinction. Domestic honeybee populations in many "developed" countries have been declining at an alarming rate since the 1990s, with ominous implications for Earth's other inhabitants. Scientists fear that wild bee populations may follow suit.

Bees' disappearance in the industrialized world is blamed on a deadly combination of devastating changes in their environment, the result of ecological destruction and mismanagement by clueless humans. These include extreme temperatures due to climate change; inadequate nutrition, as greedy producers began feeding bees high-fructose corn syrup instead of the bees' own honey; monocultures—many genetically modified to repel insects—replacing the wildflowers that supply the

Fig. 3.1. The Bee Lord. Illustrations from
Secrets of Mayan Science/Religion *by Hunbatz Men.*

variety of pollens bees need to maintain their resistance to parasites and viruses; and the widespread use of neonicotinoid pesticides.[40]

Energetically, what we have here is a dramatic breakdown of *ayni:* humans are no longer living in reciprocity with the Earth and her beings. Instead of giving gratitude and care in exchange for nature's gifts, we have disrupted their fragile balance by seeking to dominate, exploit, and destroy.

Interestingly, highly defensive Africanized "killer" bees—which have caused more than a thousand human deaths throughout the Americas since 1957, when twenty-six queen bees brought from Africa escaped from a laboratory in Brazil and migrated north, "Africanizing" existing populations of docile European bees—seem more resistant to environmental stresses.[41] Along with greater numbers and productivity, Africanized bees received their African ancestors' instinct to prevail against threats of all kinds.

Could this be Gaia and her sacred bees writing new rules in an effort to repair the imbalances?

4
The Magic of the Circle
A Symbol of Unity

Everything an Indian does is in a circle, and that is because the power of the world always works in circles, and everything tries to be round.

BLACK ELK[1]

God is an infinite circle, whose circumference is nowhere, and whose center is everywhere.

NICHOLAS OF CUSA[2]

The path to collective intelligence goes in a circle. In fact, we can't begin to comprehend the ancient gift until we look closely at circle magic.

Energy unfolds in circles; nature expresses itself in circles.

Primordial symbol of unity, the circle is a powerful archetypal force, alive and active in the movements of wind, water, and planets and in the instincts of the tiniest insect.

"We cannot exist without the presence and support of the interconnecting circles of creation—the geosphere, the biosphere, the hydrosphere, the atmosphere, and the sphere of our sun," notes Joan Halifax. "All are related to us; we depend on each of these spheres for our very existence."[3]

Gaia's message regarding the circle couldn't be louder or clearer: we are inseparable from Earth, from each other, from the whole.

In their plea for a "planetary consciousness or global mind,"[4] Edgar Morin and Anne Brigitte Kern make a wonderful declaration of circularity: "We belong to the Earth which belongs to us."[5]

For people who revere the Earth as Mother, the circle is a constant reminder of our oneness with All That Is, binding us together in a form that comforts us in the deepest reaches of our souls. At the same time, it's a dynamic dimensional portal through which mystical and magical transformation can occur.

The circle—and its extensions, the spiral and the sphere—are among the most ancient and frequently seen forms in prehistoric art throughout the world, and they're basic to indigenous spirituality. Our ancestors worked with the circle on many levels—physical, psychic, magical, and spiritual (which we mustn't forget are arbitrary Old Paradigm distinctions used to describe what is essentially the same thing).

"The power of the circle as an access point to a field of higher wisdom was first recognized by Earth's indigenous people," write Bruce Lipton and Steve Bhaerman. They quote Native American elder Manitonquat, who told them, "Our people noticed long ago that the circle is the basic form of Creation. In the circle, all are equal; there is no top or bottom, first or last, better or worse."[6]

In his book *The Wind Is My Mother,* Creek medicine man Bear Heart puts it this way:

Both the sweat lodge and the tipi are round—in fact, most Native dwellings are round. We even have a dance we call the Round Dance. A circle is without end—there's no time element to any part of it. When people come together in a circle, there's a spirit of oneness, a sense of sacredness that comes from inside us. The circle contains an appreciation, an acknowledgment, of all the created forces at our command if we so desire.[7]

Forming circles seems to help human groups generate collective wisdom. People automatically tend to gather in circles when they congregate spontaneously, or "self-organize." When native elders meet to solve problems, they almost always sit in circles. (And I can't forget that our magical election of Priest and Priestess in the Andes happened in circles.) As author Michael S. Schneider notes, "We draw circles and they draw us."

To ancient mathematical philosophers, Schneider continues, the circle symbolized the number one,

> the source of all subsequent shapes, the womb in which all geo-metric patterns develop . . . the Monad. The message of the shape bypasses our conscious mental circuitry and speaks directly to the quiet intelligence of our deepest being. The circle is a reflection of the world's—and our own—deep perfection, unity, design excel-lence, wholeness and divine nature.[8]

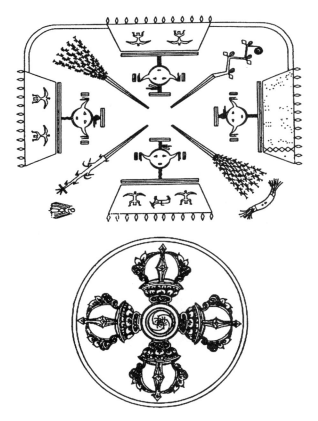

Fig. 4.1. Mandalas: at top, Navajo; at bottom, Tibetan.
Illustration from Navajo & Tibetan Sacred Wisdom *by Peter Gold.*

When much of humanity moved away from the circle as a defining power, we became alienated from one another, the Earth, and other beings, and vulnerable to domination by hierarchical structures.

SEEKING THE CENTER

In nature, in the psyche, and in sacred art, the circle unfurls into mandalas. *Mandala,* the ancient Sanskrit word for "circle," is defined by Tibetan Buddhists as "an integrated structure organized around a unifying center."[9]

Tibetans and Navajos create complex, beautiful mandalas to express their spiritual world. For both peoples, says author Peter Gold, "the mandala is almost always a visual expression of the perfect pattern in all things and a prime metaphor of the quest of the spiritual hero toward the central still point in a changing world."[10]

In moving toward the center, the seeker becomes transformed—like the seeker who enters a sacred labyrinth, moving into the center in search of answers—and then carries the answers back out to the world. Interestingly, according to James N. Powell's book *The Tao of Symbols,* the Cretan labyrinth (below) is one of the symbols used by the Hopi to represent the structure of the *kiva* (their underground ceremonial chamber), the Earth, and the human form. The vertical line in the center of the labyrinth is the *kiva's* ladder.[11]

"A mandala from the Buddhist perspective is a complete system emerging from the field of emptiness," says Joan Halifax. "It is a map as

Fig. 4.2. The Cretan labyrinth.

well as a protector. . . . It can be a symbol of the individual as the world or the universe."[12]

Pioneering shamanism researcher Michael Harner notes that "the concentric circles of a mandala often resemble the ribbed aspect that the Tunnel [experienced in shamanic journeys] frequently presents, and meditation with a mandala can lead to an experience resembling the entrance into the Tunnel."[13]

Psychologist Carl Jung spent months drawing and painting mandalas, "unconscious of what they might mean."[14] Finally he concluded that the mandala "is an archetypal image whose occurrence is attested throughout the ages. It signifies *wholeness of self*."[15]

SACRED SPACE

Peace enters the human soul when it recognizes the oneness with the universe and that the Creator dwells in the Seventh Direction, at the center of the universe, which is everywhere and within each person.

BLACK ELK[16]

When one perceives reality as circular instead of linear, the sacred is everywhere around us. "Wherever we are, we are at the center of the universe," says James David Audlin. "The horizon around us reminds us of that fact. No matter how far we go, we will still see the edge of the visible Earth equidistant around us in all directions. No matter how far we go, the Sky still stretches itself over us."[17]

Acknowledging one's placement at the center of the universe is basic to shamanic practice and Earth-honoring rituals throughout the world. To open sacred space for ritual, one creates a circle around a center point—a mandala—by invoking the spirits of the four cardinal directions, plus the Creator (above) and Mother Earth (below).

Each direction has special powers associated with the elements, stages of life, and guardian animal spirits. One can also invoke the seventh direction, the universe within. This acknowledges the circle's center, which Audlin calls "the direction we travel . . . in dream, in vision or at the end of this physical life."[18]

Says Bear Heart:

> Our old teaching is that the universe is in harmony as long as we keep the Sacred Hoop intact. The Sacred Hoop is the circle of all life—the Four Directions, the Earth, and everything that lives on the Earth. It includes not only the two-leggeds, but also the four-leggeds, the wingeds, those that live in the waters, those that crawl on the earth, even the plant life. Everything is part of the Sacred Hoop and everything is related. Our existence is so intertwined that our survival depends upon maintaining a balanced relationship with everything within the Sacred Hoop.[19]

Tom Cowan points out that "shamanically speaking, invoking the directions creates a timeless-spaceless realm that transcends physical reality, even as it uses the elements and directions of physical reality. By creating a circle that is both present and not present, both here and not here, we put our consciousness in a framework that is both temporal and eternal, similar to the shaman's trance consciousness."[20]

Interestingly, the symbol for Earth in astrology—which astrologer and Jungian scholar Alice O. Howell says dates back at least six thousand years[21]—is a circle surrounding a cross with equidistant arms, depicting the four directions. This image is repeated in the Native American medicine wheel and appears in ancient and native art throughout the world.

The circle's center point is ever-present in indigenous consciousness, as it was in the psyches of our ancestors. Howell points out that "the symbol for God Manifest in us is that of a circle with a dot in the center. This is also the symbol for the Sun and the metal gold."[22] The latter connection is especially interesting, as we'll see later.

Layne Redmond says that the *omphalos*—navel of the Earth and seat of the Great Mother in ancient times—is often depicted as a dot within a circle. As shown in figures 4.4 and 4.5, the *omphalos* symbol depicted

Fig. 4.3. Native American medicine wheel.
Photo by Jim Molloy.

on a coin from Delphi from around 480 BCE bears an uncanny resemblance to the concentric circles into which water self-organizes when subject to sound vibrations, as shown in experiments conducted by wave-form researcher Hans Jenny.[23]

Fig. 4.4. The omphalos coin, 480 BCE.
(www.coinproject.com)

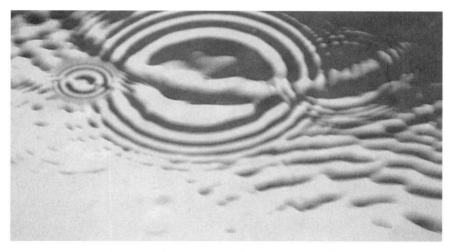

Fig. 4.5. Concentric circles in water ripples.

The field of cymatics, developed by Jenny, showed how sound applied to sand, metal filings, or water on a metal plate causes the materials to organize into mandala-like shapes, illustrating the unfolding of universal energies into sound and then sacred geometry.

According to Hunbatz Men, circles and mandalas in ancient Mayan hieroglyphs were representations of the sacred vowel O, which symbolized "awakened consciousness."[24]

Fig. 4.6. Mayan hieroglyph. Illustration from Secrets of Mayan Science/Religion *by Hunbatz Men.*

LINKING THE WORLDS

Buryat shaman Sarangerel tells us that the center of the Mongols' traditional round dwelling "is the focal point of an axis that runs up to the sky and down to the earth. At that very point heaven and earth meet." Through this center point—the *axis mundi*—the shaman can journey to parallel realities in the lower and upper worlds, by way of a tunnel or a tree.[25] According to historian of religions Mircea Eliade, some native cultures depict the *axis mundi* as a pillar, a ladder, a mountain, or a vine, which "connects and supports heaven and earth and whose base is fixed in the world below. . . . Such a cosmic pillar can be only at the very center of the universe, for the whole of the habitable world extends around it."[26]

Author and shamanism teacher Ross Heaven notes that the World Tree, a sacred motif that occurs in many traditional societies and early religious writings, "connects all of the human and spiritual worlds. It is generally viewed as the very center of the universe, and is connected to the attainment of knowledge through interactions with the gods. [The World Tree of Vodou, known as the *porteau mitan,*] stands at the center of the *peristyle* [Vodou church], at the very heart of sacred ceremony."[27]

During his time with the Shuar people of the Amazon, John Perkins learned about the Cosmic Tree:

> Our hammocks were tied at one end to the central pole and at the other to separate support poles in the outer wall, like spokes radiating out from the hub of a wheel. To the Shuar the central pole is far more than a structural support that holds up the roof, for it represents the Cosmic Tree, the Tree of Life, connecting the upper world with the middle and lower worlds. It is a sacred place that provides both an entryway for spirits to visit the world and a ladder for us to travel to parallel worlds.[28]

The conical dwellings of the Bribri people in Talamanca, in southeastern Costa Rica, likewise echo their vision of the Cosmic House—layered circular worlds united, and accessible, by a central axis, as shown

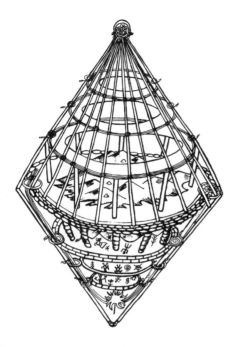

Fig. 4.7. Talamanca cosmos. Illustration from La casa cósmica Talamanqueña.

in the illustration (above) from *La casa cósmica Talamanqueña* (The cosmic house of Talamanca).[29]

Followers of the Andean spiritual path learn to explore the *ukhu pacha* (Lower World), *kay pacha* (Middle World, where we live), and *hanaq pacha* (Upper World) in a variety of ways, including through the *mesa,* the bundle of sacred objects carried by every *paqo* or *curandero* (shaman/healer). The three worlds also correspond to the three levels of consciousness.

In the Pachakúti Mesa tradition, the shaman creates an altar by opening his *mesa* and arranging its contents to correspond to the four directions and center point. This creates sacred space from which he can "commune with Spirit, mediate change, provide healing, and access information from a greater totality of existence."[30]

"People who conceive of the universe as holographically structured, as archaic cultures seem to have done, can locate the Center of the World in any tree or spot so designated," Tom Cowan points out. "In a holographic universe, the part incorporates the whole; every detail contains the totality; within the microcosm we find the entire macrocosm."[31]

Our ancestors already knew what we're just rediscovering: as we've seen with Pribram's work and as we'll see in more detail later, contemporary researchers are focusing on holography to help them decipher a number of mysteries—including the mystery of collective intelligence.

SPIRALS OF ENERGY

Energy coils and uncoils into and out of the circle's center and can operate in three dimensions. Galaxies and hurricanes swirl in spirals, "the purest expression of moving energy," in Michael S. Schneider's words. "Wherever energy is left to move on its own it resolves into spirals. The spiral's role in nature is transformation."[32]

"The self-replicative trait of spirals can be observed in the stunning imagery of fractals, where the whole is in the parts and the parts are in the whole," writes Lori Bailey Cunningham, artist and author of *The Mandala Book*. "Fractals are created by a recursive equation that folds back into itself, resulting in images that offer a taste of the cosmos as well as a window into the patterns of natural forms."[33]

Mayan elder Carlos Barrios says that the source of universal energy is "a giant macrospiral that arises right next to the Pleiades. This sole spiral contains everything that has a material form, what we call *teos,* or the universe."[34]

When Andean master Américo Yabar works with a group in a circle, the circle forms the bottom or top of a spiral that enables him to direct the group's energy upward or downward.[35] Sarangerel notes that "in some rituals the participants may dance around the shaman in a sunwise [clockwise] direction, creating a spiral of energy. In much the same way, the merging of time and space . . . can be visualized as a spiraling of all things toward the center."[36]

According to Wiccan priestess Phyllis Curott, "All energy moves in a circular manner, that is, in a spiral. . . . When you work with energy within a circle you are working in harmony with the organic flow of all energies. . . . Our circle is actually a nexus joining the worlds of spirit and matter, divine and human." She says that witches working in a group often direct energy raised in a circle for healing or attainment of a goal. The energy is shaped into a cone, the point of which is high above the circle. Then it's "directed to spiral upwards, [clockwise], into the cone's apex, where it is then directed either downward into a person or object, or up and out."[37]

This process, she says, may have been the origin of the classic conical witch's hat.

WE'RE NOT IN KANSAS ANYMORE

The spiral can form a vortex, which has long been associated with travel to other realms. (Remember the tornado that carried Dorothy to Oz?)

"Anchor and transmission points, or natural vortexes, are also understood as places on Earth that inherently possess sacred space," writes Matthew Magee in *Peruvian Shamanism*. "Shamans the world over have utilized these vortex points as sacred ceremonial ground. Many believed the veil between this world and the spirit world was more easily breached in these places, and a blending of the two worlds was more evident."[38]

Ervin Laszlo tells us that vortices are conveyors of information from the quantum vacuum and could carry information about the state of the whole universe.[39]

The vortex also represents the continual movement between the individual and the collective, with the paradoxical conclusion that there is no difference between them. "A vortex [in a river] is a distinct and individual entity, and yet it is indivisible from the river that created it," John Briggs and F. David Peat point out. "In a vortex, a constantly flowing cell wall separates inside from outside. However, the wall itself is both inside and outside. The vortex suggests the paradox that the individual is also the universal."[40]

WHIRLING WHEELS

In ancient times the Goddess was often represented as a "whirling wheel of life" that generated spiritual transformation.[41] In the human energy

*Fig. 4.8. Swastikas on
ancient Siberian fabric.
Photo by Jim Molloy.*

body, the centers along the spine described in the Hindu system of the chakras are depicted as whirling wheels.

The swastika appears in ancient sacred iconography worldwide and describes this whirling process: "a rotary movement around a fixed centre . . . a cyclical symbol of activity, manifestation and perpetual regeneration," according to authors Jean Chavalier and Alain Gheerbrant.[42]

Olga Kharitidi's spiritual teacher in Uzbekistan told her that the swastika's four arms (which correspond to the Four Directions) "connect the right and left sides of our brain, and by doing so, they connect past with present. They also connect action and perception in a way that is different from our usual experience, so a sense of unity is created in the center of the symbol. . . . The center of this image serves as a gate that opens to the dream space."[43]

Unfortunately, Adolf Hitler was well aware of the swastika's age-old archetypal power when he chose it for the Nazi symbol, forever contaminating it.

CIRCLE OF RECIPROCITY

*Whatever befalls the earth befalls the sons of earth. Man
does not weave the web of life, he is merely a strand in it.*

Whatever he does to the web, he does to himself.
CHIEF SEALTH (SEATTLE)[44]

Elizabeth Jenkins calls *ayni*—sacred reciprocity—"the one law of the Andean mystical tradition."[45] The giving and receiving of *ayni* form an unbroken circle—a unifying force that binds together All That Is.

Reciprocity is a crucial concept that appears again and again when we look closely at collective intelligence. Defined as "to give and take mutually," it's at the heart of traditional spiritual beliefs, based on the understanding that because we are all part of a greater whole, we cannot take—from Mother Earth or from one another—without giving back.

Significantly, *ayni* is itself an energetic force: the indigenous worldview makes no distinctions between individual spiritual awareness, ethical action, and simply living in harmony with the sacred in nature.

Ayni is also "a relationship of 'today for you, tomorrow for me,' a concept that weaves the people and the Earth together into the same luminous tapestry," says Matthew Magee.[46] As Peruvian *paqo* Fredy "Puma" Quispe Singona explains to Joan Parisi Wilcox, "*Ayni* is a whole way of being. . . . *Ayni* is responsibility and respect. *Ayni* is love and compassion. *Ayni* is everything. We are in so much *ayni* with each other!" Quispe stresses, "For billions of years now, and maybe even beyond that, we have been connected. . . . We are in *ayni* with *Pachamama,* between each other, with our creator. We are in *ayni* with everybody."[47]

Among the Australian Aborigines, "the process of giving, receiving, and belonging to a group is cultivated . . . rather than personal or individual achieving, acquiring, and possessing," writes Johanna Lambert. "This habituation toward sharing and reciprocal exchange is as fundamental to Aboriginal life as buying and selling are in the contemporary world."[48]

"We are biologically, psychologically, and spiritually designed to collaborate with Mother Nature," Jenkins points out, "and these sacred reciprocal exchanges are the basis of life, i.e., BREATHING!"[49]

THE GIFT OF GIVING

Indigenous people everywhere perform *ayni* in their ceremonies, which maintain balance by giving to Mother Earth to thank her for her gifts and keep her strong. In the Andes, these take the form of elaborate *despacho* offerings, in which participants infuse carefully selected coca leaves, flower petals, sweets, seeds, seashells, spices, incense, drops of pisco, and other treats for Pachamama with their finest energy and arrange them artistically in a sacred package, which they burn ceremonially or give to a body of water.

In North America, native people make offerings to the Earth and nature spirits and perform sacred giveaways in which they share their wealth with the community. Siberians leave offerings of colorful cloth prayer ties, tobacco, coins, stones, and personal objects at shrines constructed of piles of stones and poles known as *ovaas,* and in sacred groves of trees.

"In all of these we are giving to all living things and to the Creator," James David Audlin explains. "This kind of giving is not contractual, in which one gives only if one is sure to be given something of equal value, but covenantal, in which one gives and *trusts* that balances will be maintained."[50]

* * *

Ayni may, in fact, be humans' ultimate raison d'être in the cosmic scheme.

"What if nature needed us just as much as we needed nature, to achieve a collective supreme evolutionary purpose?" Jenkins wonders.[51] Says Hunbatz Men: "The gods need human beings and human beings need the gods."[52]

Our conscious exchanges of energy with All That Is help empower everything around us as well as ourselves. When we fail to participate in the sacred give-and-take, we end up disempowering and destroying.

"In the Inka view, humans are not *un*important, but neither are we *all*-important," Jenkins points out. "*We exist as part of a larger system. We are part of the family of Nature.*"[53]

WOMB, CHALICE, CAULDRON

Circle magic is feminine magic. The circle is the womb where life is created—the holy chalice, magical cauldron, Mother Earth.

Riane Eisler describes power in early Goddess-worshipping cultures as "linking, not ranking," which "from time immemorial has been symbolized by the circle. . . . The secret of transformation expressed by the Chalice was in earlier times seen as the consciousness of our unity or linking with one another and all else in the universe."[54]

"When one sits in a circle with others, everyone is equal and linked," says Maureen Murdock, author of *The Heroine's Journey.* "No one person is in power, the power is shared, and there is no place for egocentrism. Because everyone is interrelated and derives meaning only through the relationship of the circle, each person's vision is transformed as the circle takes form. Magic occurs in circles. A circle is a hug of giving and receiving: it teaches us about unconditional love."[55]

Ceremonies celebrating the Goddess took place in caves, circles of trees, or circles of stones. Participants gathered and danced in circles, whose mystical power enabled them to experience direct, ecstatic communion with the divine.

BIRTHING THE WORLD

The vesica piscis ("vessel of the fish"), which, Murdock notes, is "a symbol of the feminine as vessel," is formed when two circles intersect.

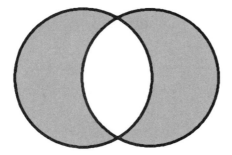

Fig. 4.9. Vesica piscis. Artwork by Jim Molloy.

The vessel "was transformational," she says. "The vessel was used to heal and it was always made by women. Perhaps that is because women understand what it is to allow transformation to occur within their womb."[56]

According to Michael S. Schneider, the almond-shaped space of the vesica piscis "is the crucible of the creating process. . . . The *vesica piscis* is a *yoni* (Sanskrit term for the female generative organs) through which the geometric shapes and patterns of our universe emerge."[57]

Teacher of shamanism José Luis Stevens says that the vesica piscis is known to shamans worldwide as "a portal to the Tao or, as shamans refer to it, the Spirit World. . . . The Christian association of Christ with the fish is for good reason," he writes. "Jesus was well aware of this portal."[58]

The intersecting circles can also be viewed as the two brain hemispheres working together—the *yoni* becoming the brain's corpus callosum, the bridge between the hemispheres. The world birthed by the Goddess requires, and expresses, wholeness. Wholeness, in turn, demands interaction between the circle and other sacred geometric forms. Interestingly, invoking the Four Directions creates not only a circle but also a square.

Hunbatz Men notes that "the Maya classify the Supreme as Hunab K'u, the Only Giver of Movement and Measure, and proudly represent the concept with a square superimposed on a circle, a synthesis of universal geometry based on the human body."[59] And Phyllis Curott in her book *Witch Crafting* points out that when the square and the circle are joined in the process of casting the circle, they represent a joining of "intuition and intellect, spirit and matter, divinity and humanity."[60]

DIVINE FEMININE, DIVINE PARADOX

The Goddess is a loving mother. But she can also kill. The sacred feminine is the essence of paradox.

Anthropologist Gregory Bateson reminds us that the word *sacred* comes from the Latin *sacer,* which means both "holy" and "cursed."[61] The sacred contains within it both light and darkness: the circular potential for becoming its own opposite.

This is nowhere more evident than in the two faces of the Goddess—the benevolent, nurturing Great Mother with her gentle touch and welcoming, comforting lap, and her terrifying opposite, the ferocious, raging Kali, draped in her necklace of severed heads, blood dripping from her sword. Often represented by the snake, the Goddess is at once beautiful and dangerous, a symbol of birth, death, and rebirth.[62] One interpretation of the ancient image of the *ouroboros,* the serpent consuming its own tail, is "the marriage of the chthonian world, represented by the serpent, and the celestial world, represented by the circle . . . the marriage of opposing principles, Heaven and Earth, night and day, the Chinese *yang* and *yin.*"[63]

The Goddess's ever-changing dual nature reflects nature's cycles: day changes into night and back again, winter turns into summer, birth becomes death. Every element—air, fire, water, earth—has its life-giving and life-taking aspect.

In yoga, the sacrum ("holy bone"), the triangular bone at the base of the spine that ends in the tailbone, is the human being's connection with the Earth—as well as with the two faces of the Great Mother.[64] This is where kundalini—the divine power inside each person, represented by a coiled serpent—lies dormant. When awakened, depending upon how it is channeled, kundalini can either enlighten or kill.

Jungian psychologist M. Esther Harding notes that for early people, the supreme deity

> was like the moon, not like the sun. She was dual in her very nature. She lived her life in phases, manifesting the qualities of each phase in turn. In the upperworld phase, corresponding to the bright moon, she is good, kind, and beneficent. In the other phase, corresponding to the time when the moon is dark, she is cruel, destructive, and evil.[65]

"It's clear that Mother Nature gives life with gusto and takes it back with gusto," writes Robert Bly, author and pioneer of the mythopoetic movement. "She hints at immortality, then kills you; she produces children and then eats the children with no more emotional distress than a boa constrictor. This is uncomfortable to contemplate."[66]

Comfortable or not, it's important to remember that even when taking back life, the Great Mother is always seeking balance. When she needs to destroy, she's not being vengeful or punishing. Her destructiveness is generalized and impersonal: some cells in every organism must die so that the whole can thrive.

Paradox is at home in the human psyche: what we fear we also need. Yet fear of the divine feminine in her terrifying aspect became fear of nature itself. This was why, for many humans, nature had to be subdued and the sacred ended up behind the "safe" man-made walls of patriarchal religious institutions.

Leonardo Boff distinguishes between *dualism,* which he considers an expression of the masculine, and *duality:* "Dualism considers things to be apart, while duality sees things together, as dimensions of the same unique reality."[67] Before the split in our psyches placed modern humans firmly in dualism, people were able to live comfortably in duality, accepting paradox as simply part of life.

In dualism, we could no longer live in harmony with the Earth—or with differentness in any form. Fundamentalism became the most extreme expression of our psychic split.

"There has been and always will be a primal struggle with all of nature for human survival," writes Jungian scholar Fred Gustafson. "The earth can very quickly take back into itself what it has given. But the struggle with nature is different from its exploitation. Struggling to survive with nature can result in a harmonious cooperative relationship with it; while the result of our exploitation of the earth is epidemic despair (often mislabeled depression) and a sense of disconnectedness from our most elemental selves."[68]

Interestingly, natural disasters always bring people together: those at odds with each other during good times suddenly find that their differences vanish when collective solidarity is needed. Could such events be one of Gaia's strategies to remind us of our oneness?

Tom Cowan describes the legendary quest for the Holy Grail as a journey into a world of feminine circularity that "contains shapeshifting powers, where friendly foes become foelike friends. It is the true world of the unconscious, where the conscious mind's binary categories fail to explain reality. Black and white, good and bad, ally and enemy, sacred and profane, are not easily distinguished. The Grail is a cup, not a box. There are no separate corners for saints and sinners. On the contrary, the Grail, like its pagan antecedent, the Cauldron of Mystery, contains a heavy, hallucinatory brew of seekers, fools, risk-takers, failures, and fighters. . . . If we dare to look into the round, spherical vessel of the Grail, we become, like its contents, stirred, mixed, and intermingled, losing our sense of separateness. For ultimately, that is the lesson of self-discovery; we are not separate, but part of the whole.[69]

"INDIAN TIME" GOES IN CIRCLES

Past, present and future are only an illusion, albeit a stubborn one.

ALBERT EINSTEIN[70]

Paiute medicine man Hidden Wolf used to drive his nonnative students crazy with what he called "Indian Time." (He never used the politically correct term "indigenous"—which he jokingly pronounced "indidjoous.") Asked what time a sweat lodge ceremony would be starting, he'd reply, "When it's supposed to." Asked how long the sweat lodge would last, he'd hold his hands out in front of him, palms facing each other.

"About this long," he'd say.

Like the cycles of Nature, Indian Time can't be regimented by clocks or calendars. It simply unfolds, expanding and contracting in sync with many different, often mysterious (to us) variables.

"The very nature of time, within Indigenous science, is different from what we in the West normally experience," notes F. David Peat. "Indigenous people have access to dimensions within the spirit of time that we have forgotten."

Indian Time has prevailed in every traditional ceremony I've been lucky enough to take part in. Whether celebrated in North, Central, or South America or Siberia, the rituals begin and end "when they're supposed to" and seem to take place outside of time as we perceive it.

"A ceremony begins: *that* is the time of the ceremony," says Peat. "People come together, through the action of a general consensus, or a group mind, or in response to the movements of the winds and heavens—and the ceremony commences. *It is at that moment that a time is created for the ceremony.* From that numinous instant time is broadcast backward into the past and forward into the future."[71]

With no time pressure, indigenous ceremonies are deeply peaceful and characterized by infinite patience. Slow, deliberate preparations—building a fire, carefully donning regalia, or painstakingly selecting coca leaves—are part of the rituals themselves. Although a ceremony may have a specific purpose, there is no sense of moving toward a goal or outcome: native elders obviously relish the delicious significance of each moment for its own sake.

Each ceremony takes on a life of its own, moving to its own rhythms and carrying its participants with it. I've never felt time (our time) passing during a ceremony and have always been surprised afterward at how much—or little—has gone by.

"Sacred events, being sacred, happen outside of time altogether," James David Audlin points out. "Not really in the past, present, or future, but in one transcendent infinite moment that cannot be located on the time line of linear events." He adds, "The Native American does not conceive of time as a line extending from a fixed past to an indefinite future, but as an intermingling of circles. Place too is an intermingling of circles."[72]

For Mongols, "past, present, and future wind tightly around themselves, and therefore, past, present, and future all touch each other. . . . All times that have been or will be are the present," says Sarangerel. "In the same way, all places in the universe touch at this point."[73]

Martín Prechtel offers a remarkably similar description of time as experienced by the Maya: "All existences—the unfolding Present as well as that which has already been and visibly disappeared known as the Past, along with the Future continually coming to us like a good friend not yet arrived—are all organically tethered to a central umbilical point, which in Tzutujil Maya is called Camic, meaning Now."[74]

Indian Time hints at the field-theory world described by Lynne McTaggart—"a subatomic world of pure potential, [where] life exists as one enormous present."[75] It also suggests the chaos-theory notion of "fractal time"—time that curves and curls in upon itself, moving sometimes quickly, sometimes slowly, in sync with the rhythms of nature.

"Chaos theory argues that there are no simple lines in nature," John Briggs and F. David Peat point out. "So what about time, that line we assume to run from past to future? Why should it be the only one-dimensional line remaining in nature? What if the linear time of our technological world is no more than a convenient delusion of our mechanistic world, concealing a living vibrant time within the vibrant curling details of a fractal?"[76]

The change in humans' perception of time, Peat says, contributed to the fragmentation of the modern psyche. "As the consciousness of society broke away from the direct contact with the harmonies of nature, and planning, control, and the first technologies began to develop, a new time order began to evolve in which the notion of 'becoming' dominated over that of 'being,'" he explains. "Society did not remain with itself in an eternal 'now' but constantly moved away from itself in an attempt to become 'better.'"[77]

* * *

As we can see, the circle is much more than a handy metaphor.

David Bohm established it as the form for group dialogue because "such a geometric arrangement doesn't favor anybody."[78] When there is no obvious leader, each person is uniquely valuable, and everyone has something to contribute.

Hal Zina Bennett, author of *Spirit Animals and the Wheel of Life*, describes contemporary "council circles" modeled after native gatherings, in which friends, business associates, or community members come together to seek answers to difficult questions.

> When the powers of the council circle are working, their magic carries us into and beyond the finite truths of our individual lives, bringing us face to face with the infinite truths of our oneness. [Eventually] a stillpoint emerges . . . as we reach a quiet place in our minds . . . undisturbed by our individualized perceptions and interpretations. When two or more in the circle touch this place, the experience swiftly spreads around the circle . . . our illusions dissolve and we open to a greater Truth—a Truth with a capital "T." We see, among other things, that this greater truth is a collective effort.[79]

The dynamics of the circle coincide perfectly with Bohm's notion of wholeness as "undivided flowing movement, unbroken, all-encompassing. Every individual is in total contact with the implicate order, with all that is around us," he explains.[80] He recalls the native understanding that the center of the universe is within each person when he notes that "each individual manifests the consciousness of mankind."[81]

Collective intelligence is not only a product of the circle; it's a way back to the circle—a way to mend our splintered world, and yet another circular dynamic.

5
Collective Intelligence
"Amazing and Insane"

How do indigenous people experience and use collective intelligence?

The phenomenon seems to spring naturally from a shared sense of purpose, and in some cases, a shared need—as well as from mutual trust and comfort. Collective intelligence is active, alert, and participatory: everybody involved understands that he or she is working for the well-being of the whole.

Danil Mamyev, director of a 60,000-hectare specially protected indigenous area in the Altai Mountains of south-central Siberia and

Fig. 5.1.
Danil Mamyev:
modern science and
traditional wisdom.
Photo by Jim Molloy.

founder of a school specializing in "spiritual ecology," is using modern science to try to validate the traditional wisdom of his people, who have inhabited the area since the Stone Age. As both a native elder and a modern scientist, he's very familiar with collective intelligence.

During the Soviet era, when native culture was brutally repressed, Mamyev left his village to study in Kyrgyzstan, where he became a geologist and geographer. Ancestral ties pulled him back to the Altai, where he has been working to protect the land and preserve its rich traditions, now threatened by globalization.

He was our guide during a 2008 visit organized by the U.S.-based nonprofit Sacred Earth Network. In addition to connecting us with ancient sacred sites, he encouraged us to interact with many different people, including a traditional healer, teachers and students, the owner of a village museum, an expert on ancient petroglyphs, an elder writing a book about Altai spirituality, and two sisters who prepared feasts of traditional delicacies.

All of the villagers we met were eager to explain how they had chosen to contribute to their communities, and Mamyev pointed out that this was collective intelligence in action. "Every single person can change what happens [in a native village], because they have no dogmas," he told us. "The most important thing is who they are as a person. These cultures are closer to truth, because every single person carries knowledge. In the Altai, there are no rules—no one keeps to a plan. Everyone is doing his or her own little bit, creating an assemblage point. . . . It looks unstructured, but suddenly it becomes clear what the rules are."

In native societies everywhere, collective intelligence takes a similar form, with no planning, rules, or leaders. David Bohm mentions a North American tribe of some fifty people, who gathered in a circle and "just talked and talked, apparently to no purpose. They made no decisions. There was no leader. And everybody could participate. . . . The meeting went on, until finally it seemed to stop for no reason at all and the group dispersed. Yet after that, everybody seemed to know what to do, because they understood each other so well. They could get together in smaller groups and do something or decide things."[1]

Oren Lyons of the Onandaga Iroquois describes tribal council sessions during which everyone sits in a circle: "We meet and just keep talking until there's nothing left but the obvious truth."[2]

Ojibway native Wilfred Pelletier told John Briggs and F. David Peat how his community put a new roof on its council hall with no apparent prior planning or leadership: "People start coming together, helping out, lending a hand, throwing in their two cents. Nobody's leading particularly, but things get done."[3]

John Perkins quotes Shuar shaman Tuntuam as saying that "when we face a crisis, we sit in a circle, drink *chicha,* and work it out. Someone steps forward as the leader to help us move through that crisis. He forms his own circle, they take action, then it's over."[4]

Martín Prechtel offers a priceless description of the way the elders in his Tzutijil Maya village solved problems:

All the council would leap to their feet, blankets flapping, eyeballs rolling, eyes bulging and squinting, faces wrinkling, some cocked to one side, jaws moving and tongues clucking. Everyone had an opinion, and they all talked at once to everybody they could see to the front, side, back, or far away.

Miraculously, everyone listened to everybody else simultaneously, pointing and gesticulating, pouncing forward, pacing, jumping up and down, yelling, laughing, or preaching in a low oratory.

Amazing and insane, the roar of such a meeting was like a plane taking off. Just as quickly as it began, it stopped, everyone having understood and been heard simultaneously. And in the second of silence it took everybody to sit back down, and calmly go back to smoking and waiting for the next issue, the headman would state matter-of-factly, "That's decided then," and the royal crowd would grunt in affirmation. Then the next issue would be presented.

At first I couldn't understand how anything got heard or what plan had been adopted. Sometimes I wasn't even aware of what was being argued about, and I never comprehended the outcome. Gradually, however, I too became a participant in the word orgy of the decision making and learned to hear as I was being heard.

It was a most gratifying experience to merge into the oneness of diversity of the village mind, where all opinions and ideas mattered and all went into a distillation process run by chaos, humor, and God, from which a strong policy emerged that was understood by most.[5]

WHAT'S GOING ON HERE?

Audlin would explain such experiences as the workings of Spirit.

Among traditional peoples, communication is in essence a living being, a spirit being, in its own right. It does what it wishes and exists on its own terms. It's not that some person decides to communicate, but that Spirit decides to speak through that person to the people listening. Spirit can choose to be evoked anywhere, at any time, and not necessarily in linear terms . . . the "speaking" may come after the "hearing," or there may be hearing without any apparent "speaker."[6]

Briggs and Peat see chaos theory at work in native societies using collective intelligence, because indigenous communities are "open, creative, nonlinear systems that self-organize."

Chaos theory would answer that the "organization" in Pelletier's roofing project was self-organization. It began with chaos—all that disorganized talk beforehand about the leak. The first guy on the roof was a bifurcation point that became amplified. The feedback between the first fellow and the next one who came along started a cascade that coupled the community together around the project, and then the system got the job done.

They stress that the diversity of interacting systems—the individual members of a group—is what gives the group its creative power.

As individuals—each with their own self-organized creativity—couple together, some degrees of freedom are given up but other degrees are discovered. A new collective intelligence emerges, an open system, unpredictable from anything one could have expected by observing the individuals acting in isolation.[7]

Rupert Sheldrake proposes that morphic fields are formed by a process of morphic resonance, "the influence of like upon like through space and time. . . . The fields of a given species . . . contain a kind of collective memory on which each member of the species draws and to which it in turn contributes," he explains. "The fields are the means by which the habits of the species are built up, maintained, and inherited." When native people exhibit collective intelligence, he says, it's because the group "is included within the social field of the tribe and the fields of its cultural patterns."[8]

According to Melvin Morse, early humans did not have an individual sense of consciousness: "They were so linked to each other that they thought of themselves as sharing consciousness, not only with other humans but with everything in the universe." Echoing almost exactly Danil Mamyev's description of collective intelligence in contemporary Siberian villages, Morse notes that people such as the Vikings "adhered to the early human concept of a shared community and 'group thinking.' Yet each individual had a particular skill that he or she used to contribute to society as a whole."[9]

What happens in a group "is creative in unpredictable ways," say Joanna Macy and Molly Young Brown. "From the interactions, connections are woven that are unique to each particular mix of people. The synergy of a group reveals the profoundly collaborative nature of life itself."[10]

Contemporary collective-intelligence researchers are learning that having a shared purpose seems to open a group's access to the magical flow of information. Robert Kenny and his colleagues at the Fetzer Institute and the Institute for Noetic Sciences say that "through coordinated intention, synergistic groups can metaphorically form a chalice, a container, a structure of unified, transpersonal consciousness that draws in and expresses

Spirit and from which emerges group wisdom, a level of insight and realization that is greater than the sum of individual understanding."[11]

"We begin to experience, first hand, the ecosystem of the soul," adds researcher David La Chapelle. "The differing modes of perception and being that any group exhibits are all in service of the revelation of an underlying unity."[12] Religious studies professor Christopher Bache calls this "Sacred Mind"—"the unbounded awareness within which all individualized experience occurs, the living matrix within which minds meet and engage."[13]

Groups of humans "can amplify and make explicit wisdom itself," La Chapelle stresses. And Kenny maintains that group wisdom, "by synthesizing diverse perspectives and types of experience," can lead to "holistic and comprehensive" solutions to complex problems. Collective-intelligence groups employ a variety of techniques, including resonance, or "empathetic vibration and rapport"; attunement, which brings members into harmony with each other; alignment, the "development of a common orientation"; and entrainment, "guiding into a common state."[14]

This may seem like a lot of work to achieve what native people have always done automatically—but remember that fragmented modern humans have millennia of separation to overcome.

ALL THAT IS, IS ONE

Quantum mechanics has forced us to move to deeper levels of perception of the world.

F. DAVID PEAT[15]

Anything that is holographic is just that, a graph of the whole—and each of us is that.

JOSEPH CHILTON PEARCE[16]

The deeper we delve into the workings of the universe as experienced by our ancestors and contemporary native people, the more often we run into holography.

For the ancient Celts, says Tom Cowan, there was "an unspoken sense that the nature of the universe is fluid, and that our personal identity is not bounded by skin and ego, but is holographically present through all time and space and can manifest in physical forms other than the one in which we currently dwell. We can be a hawk circling overhead, the sharp point of a sword, or the lure beyond the ends of the earth."[17]

According to James N. Powell, "The Hopi say that events are prepared and emerge from deep within the heart of all things, which is the heart of nature, of human beings, of plants and animals."[18]

Fast-forward to the present, where the new science proclaims the recently explored unified field as "a space-filled medium that underlies the manifest things and processes of the universe. . . . It carries the universal fields: the electromagnetic, the gravitational, and the strong and the weak nuclear fields. It carries the ZPF, the field of zero-point energies." Perhaps most importantly when we consider the way indigenous people have always perceived the world, the unified field is also "the element of the cosmos that records, conserves, and conveys *information*."[19] Ervin Laszlo calls this the Akashic Field, "the rediscovered ancient concept of Akasha," known to ancient Indian philosophers as "an all-encompassing medium that *underlies* all things and *becomes* all things." The new physics describes this as "the original field out of which emerged particles and atoms, stars and planets, human and animal bodies, and all the things that can be seen and touched. It is a dynamic, energy-filled medium in ceaseless fluctuation."[20]

This "infinite sea of energy [that] unfolds to form space, time and matter" is David Bohm's "implicate order."[21] What he terms the "holo-movement" is "the ultimately flowing nature of what is . . . the ground of everything, of all that is."[22]

It's the Hopis' "heart of all things."

And it records, conserves, and conveys information holographically.

For Bohm, exactly as for native peoples, "the whole is present in each part, in each level of existence. The living reality, which is total and unbroken and undivided, is in everything."[23] Therefore "all is one," "everything is alive," and "everything is enfolded in everything else."[24]

"Any part of one cell has information about the whole," Bohm explains. "The more cells you bring together the more detailed the information . . . the more of the hologram you take, the more detailed and the more ample the information is always going to be."[25]

According to Peat, the holomovement explains what his Blackfoot friend Sa′ke′j Henderson meant when he said that "a certain gourd contained the whole world." Bohm's "flowing movement throws out explicit forms that we recognize through our senses of sight, smell, hearing, taste, and touch," Peat says. "These explicate forms abide for a time and we take them as the direct evidence of a hard and fast reality. However . . . this explicate order accounts for only a very small portion of reality; underlying it is a more extensive implicate, or enfolded, order. . . . To take rocks, trees, planets, or stars as the primary reality would be like assuming that the vortices in a river exist in their own right and are totally independent of the flowing river itself." Therefore, he says, Henderson's gourd "is the explicate or surface manifestation of an underlying implicate order. Within that implicate order the gourd enfolds, and is enfolded by, the universe. Within each object can be found the whole and, in turn, this whole exists within each of its parts."[26]

HOW IT ALL MIGHT WORK

There is a group mind or collective intelligence working in every situation and if we can trust it, and sincerely support its natural movement, it will astound us with its ability to use whatever we give it.

SHAUN MCNIFF[27]

If the Akashic Field/implicate order is the source and repository of All That Is—including all the information that life on Earth requires—holography may explain not only how our ancestors obtained the information that native cultures have preserved, but also how collective intelligence works. Ervin Laszlo offers this explanation:

We know that holograms created with lasers or ordinary light beams are capable of coding, conserving, and conveying a stupendous amount of information in a minimal space—it is said that the entire contents of the Library of Congress in Washington could be coded in a multiplex hologram the size of a cube of sugar.[28]

Generations after generations of humans have left their holographic traces in the Akashic Field, and the information in these holograms is available to be read. The holograms of individuals integrate in a super-hologram, which is the encompassing hologram of a tribe, community, or culture.

The collective holograms interface and integrate in turn with the super-superhologram of all people. This is the collective in-formation pool of humankind.[29]

So how does this information reach us?

We find ourselves back at Pribram's holonomic brain theory, which describes how the brain's receptor and memory functions "operate essentially in a holographic mode."[30]

The brain isn't the only holographic information receptor. We reencounter the circle and its magical center point in the electromagnetic field produced by the heart, which forms a torus, a doughnut-shaped field that extends as far as twelve to fifteen feet from the body.

"This torus function is apparently holographic, meaning that any point within the torus contains the information of the whole field," Joseph Chilton Pearce tells us. As above, so below: not only is the Earth the center of such a torus, but "our solar system is apparently toroid in function, with the sun at its center as our heart is at our center. . . . We seem to live in a nested hierarchy of toroid energy systems that extend possibly from the minuscule atom to human to planet, solar system, and, ultimately, galaxy," says Pearce. "Because electromagnetic torus fields are holographic, it is probable that the sum total of our universe might be present within the frequency spectrum of any single torus. . . . One implication of this is that each of us centered within our heart torus is as much the center of the universe as any other creature or point, with equal access to all that exists," he adds.[31] Working with the circle's center point, our indigenous ancestors were well aware of this.

Tribal people, Laszlo says, are able to receive information not only from the consciousness of other people, but also from their environment, "almost as if they had developed some tiny celestial receiver through which they receive universal messages." A dramatic example of this occurred in December 2004, when tribespeople of the Andaman Islands in the Indian Ocean survived the Asian tsunami catastrophe by fleeing to the highlands before the wave hit. "Modern people seem to have lost access to this 'celestial receiver,' but laboratory experiments show that they have not lost the receiver itself," Laszlo writes.[32]

When a group is "thinking together" the way native people do, the conditions are right for its members to receive information through this receiver—from one another, from the environment, and from the infinite store of information in the field. According to David La Chapelle, "Any time you place a group of human beings together you have a possibility of field entrainment . . . the matching of vibratory capacity and action in such a way as to increase the overall energy of the system."[33]

Collective-intelligence researcher Renee A. Levi suggests that a group of people produces a "plate" that records the members' personal stories, whose intersection could act as a holographic "interference pattern."

"Assuming there is a force outside the individual, whether it be conceptualized as archetypal fields, morphic resonance, nature, or a spiritual domain—or all of the above and other—how might the interference patterns recorded onto the group plate through the intersection of personal stories open a window onto this larger domain, allowing whatever intelligence is needed by the group and its members to enter and dwell for a time, enriching them individually as well as collectively?" she wonders. "Might that happen even on a frequency level when the group energy entrains with the energy contained in the surrounding field(s)?"[34]

Interestingly, it appears that the celestial receiver that allows native people to bring in information from many sources also operates in dreams. As Jung's work revealed, individual dreamers tune in to the collective unconscious, and group dreaming is common among indigenous people. Américo Yabar told us the Q'ero masters often journey together in sleep; Hidden Wolf said that in his people's tradition, women who slept in the Moon Lodge during their menstrual periods had group dreams that would determine their tribe's next course of action.[35]

6

The Collective Intelligence of Health

Healing Ourselves and the World

Every organ, indeed every cell, in the human body contains an intelligence of its own and . . . each is informing the system every second of every day.

RENEE A. LEVI[1]

In native cultures, health is balance—the intelligent, cooperative mainte-nance of living energy within every being. What Deepak Chopra calls the "rich field of silent intelligence"[2] that fills our inner space is a form of col-lective intelligence, because, as Lipton and Bhaerman point out, each cell in a multicellular organism is an individual, yet all support each other.[3]

For the Andeans, a healthy body is proof that *ayni* is hard at work. As Fredy Quispe explains:

> In our bodies we have *[ayni]* too. For example, we have it in our heart: our heart doesn't have to overfeed itself. Your heart is not going to take everything for itself. There is a balanced way of sharing between all the different organs.
>
> In our body there is a lot of different *ayni*. Our kidneys are help-ing in some way or another for our heart to be. Our heart is helping in some way or another for our liver to be. Our brain is helping in some way or another for all these organs to be.[4]

Peat speculates that health is the maintenance of an intelligent "field of meaning" created by subtle energy that carries information among the body's systems and "brings together all the cells, organs, and biological processes within a coherent whole."[5]

ILLNESS IS DISHARMONY

When consciousness is fragmented, it starts a war in the mind-body system.

DEEPAK CHOPRA[6]

If health is the result of coherent, cooperative wholeness, illness is what Deepak Chopra calls a "distortion of intelligence."[7] As Fritjof Capra points out, this is "the shamanistic conception of illness . . . the belief that human beings are integral parts of an ordered system and . . . all illness is the consequence of some disharmony with the cosmic order."[8]

"Malays believe that the cause of any sickness is disharmony," writes Robert Wolff. "The particular form the disease takes may be the result of an invasion of some microorganism, but why this person becomes ill while the next person does not is a consequence of the kind and degree of disharmony in the patient's internal and external environment."[9]

Alternative-medicine specialist Dr. Julio César Payán de la Roche maintains that illness is "the vital process through which [the] being, composed of mind and body as a unit, seeks and maintains harmony with itself and its surroundings . . . it is the way an organism solves its conflicts at any given moment."[10] Capra says that temporary phases of illness "can be used to learn and grow. . . . Getting sick and healing are both integral parts of a system's self-organization."[11]

For Andeans, an accumulation of too much *hucha* (heavy energy) in one's energy bubble causes blockages in the body's energetic flow, leading to imbalances that eventually manifest in physical or psychological ailments. Healing happens when energetic harmony is restored and the body's collective intelligence is free to resume its work.

In many indigenous societies, this is a collective effort. According to

Sandra Ingerman, healing traditionally involved the whole community, because from the time a person was born, "the community saw your unique gift and was dependent on you shining. If one person is ill, it's a weak link in the community," she explains. "It's important for the whole community to show up [for the healing], not only because you are loved, but because your strength is really needed."[12]

Ingerman says she was surprised to learn from a Siberian shaman that when a shaman performs a soul retrieval for someone who is ill, he or she returns the missing soul part not to the person who lost it, as Western shamanic practitioners are taught to do, but to the whole community.

Lynne McTaggart describes the work of Elisabeth Targ, director of the California Pacific Medical Center's Complementary Research Institute, who assembled forty healers from a variety of traditions—Christian, Kabbalist, Native American, qigong—to do distance healing on half of a group of twenty people with advanced AIDS. After six months, she says, 40 percent of the control group had died, but all ten in the group chosen for healing were healthier.[13]

Targ's results were further validated by a twelve-month study carried out by the Mid-America Heart Institute on the effect of remote intercessory prayer for hospitalized cardiac patients. The study showed that patients "had fewer adverse events and a shorter hospital stay if they were prayed for."

Targ's studies and the work of psychologist William Braud suggested that "intention on its own heals, but . . . healing is also a collective force," and that "there may be a collective memory or healing spirit, which could be gathered as a medicinal force," says McTaggart.

She explains what might be happening at a quantum level:

If intention creates health—that is, improved order—in another person, it would suggest that illness is a disturbance in the quantum fluctuations of an individual. Healing . . . might be a matter of reprogramming individual quantum fluctuations to operate more coherently. Healing may also be seen as providing information to return the system to stability. It could also be that illness is isolation:

a lack of connection with the collective health of The Field and the community.[14]

This may help explain why illness remains rampant even in societies with technologically advanced medical care: according to author Sandra Ingerman, people in the United States today have 30 percent fewer friends than they did two decades ago, and one in four persons has no one to call in case of emergency. "We need each other," Ingerman stresses. "The community acts as a whole . . . healing the individual means healing the community."[15]

HEALING BY THE SPIRITS

I'm in a remote indigenous settlement 15,000 feet above sea level in the Peruvian Andes, and I'm sick. So are four of my companions.

We're part of a group of foreigners from various countries here to learn about the spiritual wisdom of the Q'eros, the legendary direct descendants of the Inkas whose isolation in the high Andes allowed them to preserve many of the Inkas' traditions.

After slogging through calf-deep snow over 17,000-foot mountain passes for two days, we barely had time to participate in the community's welcome for our group before we collapsed into our tents with high fevers and deep, rattling coughs.

This isn't altitude sickness. We'd acclimated over a week ago on the Bolivian *altiplano*. It's some kind of infection, apparently the result of the exhaustion and extreme cold we endured on our way here. Our unnecessarily difficult trek had been organized by a well-meaning but inexperienced guide called into service at the last minute, when Américo Yabar was unable to accompany us.

Everybody is really worried. None of us thought to bring antibiotics, and we're at least two days away by horseback from any kind of medical help—even if the sick ones could get on horses, which is clearly out of the question right now.

What to do? Shaman elders to the rescue!

Fig. 6.1. Q'ero shaman don Benito Machacca Apaza: conduit for spirit help. Photo by Jim Molloy.

Don Benito, don Pascual, and doña Bernardina had accompanied our struggling group of tenderfeet up the mountain, dancing ahead of us through the snow in their rubber-tire sandals, then encouraging us, with beaming smiles and words in Quechua, to catch up with them.

Now the three of them sweep into my tent waving a tray full of smoldering herbs (whose name I neglect to ask), thoroughly smudging me with fragrant smoke. Don Benito makes me sit up and brushes me carefully front and back with his woven wool *mesa,* a rosary, and the alpaca-fur bag containing his coca leaves, muttering prayers in Quechua with occasional words in Spanish: *"Jesucristo, Espíritu Santo."* Finally he blows forcefully several times into the crown of my head. I fall back into my sleeping bag and sleep deeply for the rest of the day and all night.

The others receive similar treatments. In the morning, miraculously, all of us are well! Though we feel a bit shaky, our fevers and coughs are gone, and we're able to rejoin the group and resume our adventure.

We're humbled and embarrassed. Here we'd been worrying about getting back to "civilization" and modern medical care, when all along we'd had this isolated community's veteran medicine people—the best possible healers—right there with us!

But a week later, on the airplane flying home, all of my symptoms suddenly reappear with a vengeance. I stagger from the airport to the hospital, where I'm diagnosed with pneumonia.

What happened? How did the shamans manage to keep me well just long enough for me to get home? And why didn't my miraculous healing last?

A bit of wild speculation:

Maybe those of us who fell ill were carrying too much *hucha* (heavy energy) in our energy bubbles, so we were already weakened and out of balance. The shamans may have changed the "field of meaning" in our bubbles, clearing out *hucha,* bringing in *sami* (refined energy), and restoring energetic harmony.

For me, this apparently held true only as long as I was inside the field of the *apus* (mountain spirits) and the beings of the Upper World who'd responded to don Benito's prayers by supplying the powerful refined energies he needed to "reprogram the quantum fluctuations" in our bodies. They also probably kept us filled with a steady supply of energizing, strengthening *sami.*

When I left the shamans' and spirits' protective embrace, my energy body apparently flipped back into its original "sick" configuration—no doubt aided (or maybe even caused) by my worries about returning to the stress of work and sadness at leaving my beloved Andes.

Refilled with *hucha,* my energy bubble likely became unbalanced again and could no longer resist the illness.

ANOTHER SCIENCE OF HEALING

F. David Peat notes that "in a very real sense, human beings create the conditions for their own illness, out of their dreams, beliefs, values, social structures, and thought." He contends that native populations

were relatively free of disease for thousands of years because they nego-
tiated alliances, compacts, and relationships with the powers of the
world such as the keepers of the animals, and with sacred plants and
medicines.

> Could it be that there is another science of healing, one that is
> profoundly different from our own? In times gone by, did The
> People possess a direct perception of the inner nature of the plants
> around them and enter into a dialogue with the spirits of the plants?
> Did the animals, birds, and insects exchange their knowledge with
> The People and teach them how to come into relationship with
> healing medicines?[16]

He's convinced that just such a reciprocal deal was made. "Just as
the gift of corn came about through a direct process of relationship,
acknowledgment, and obligation for renewal," he writes, "so, too,
exchanges may have been made and obligations entered into for the use
of medicine plants in healing ceremonies."

In other words, *ayni.*

These relationships linked humans to "active genetic and biological information that informs the processes of nature," Peat explains.
"This alliance between the molecular level and the world of powers and
energies is the practical side of indigenous science" and was regularly
renewed with sacred ceremonies.

When Europeans brought the sicknesses that ravaged native populations in the New World, Peat maintains, "the invasion of sickness was
at the level of concept, idea, and way of seeing. It was the clash between
an open system, a society that sought balance and harmony, that maintained a cyclic time of renewal, as well as an alliance of dreams and
spirits, and one that sought security through control—a society that
had accepted the sacrifice of disease in return for mastery over matter
and time and the accumulation of wealth."

Individualism, separation, and domination came to replace the
notion of working for the good of all. What happened next, says Peat,

was "a perturbation of balance, a virus in a field of meaning, the epidemic spread of an alien set of values"—a sickness that has persisted to the present, afflicting not only humans, but all beings.[17]

HEALING OURSELVES AND THE WORLD

Because they understand that each individual energy field is part of the field of everything else, traditional people know that if our world is sick, we are sick; if we are sick, our world is sick.

And there's no doubt that we and our world are sick. Modern humans have created a vicious circle: we've generated so much *hucha* that it has undoubtedly accumulated in our collective field, where it blocks the flow of divine wisdom, feeding our reality of violence and fear and threatening all life.

But we can do as the Andeans do, continuously and consciously releasing our *hucha* to Pachamama to help ourselves and our world. With this elegant act of *ayni,* we can begin to nourish Mother Earth again so that the flow of cosmic energy can resume and balance can be restored.

The Andeans tell us that we can go even further and practice *hucha mikhuy,* "eating" and channeling to Mother Earth the *hucha* of other people, groups, communities, and even entire populations—though they warn that one should not attempt this without first receiving instruction in the process, since one could inadvertently end up taking others' heavy energy into one's own bubble.[18]

Interestingly, this resembles *tonglen,* the Tibetan Buddhist practice of "sending and taking" in which one takes in the suffering of oneself and others and sends out relief and happiness. Notes Buddhist teacher Pema Chödrön, "After a while it becomes impossible to know whether we are practicing for our own benefit or for the benefit of others."[19]

As above, so below. As we cleanse our own and others' *hucha,* we help ourselves, others, and the Earth, cleanse the field for the good of all, and transform illness into health.

The process begins and ends with individual action by each of us—which requires awareness from all of us.

7

A New Kind
of Intelligence

Living, Listening, and Learning

*We educators have to remember that formal education is
only a very recent addition to a process of learning that has
taken place over hundreds of thousands of years of human
evolution. We must look for ways to connect learning as we
see it with those much older roots.*

ROBERT L. FRIED[1]

What David Bohm envisions as a "new kind of intelligence"[2] is in fact
ancient. It's the way our ancestors learned to live in the world before
the world became so complex that we needed schools and teachers to
interpret it for us.

We once experienced the world directly. Now we learn *about* it
from a remote vantage point many times removed from it. What we're
required to know comes packed in layers of information that only teachers trained in countless diverse areas can decipher.

Knowledge has become so specialized that it can be transmitted
only by a hierarchy of initiated intermediaries; in fact, most of us will
never be able to acquire even a fraction of the knowledge that makes
up our world. We've been cut off from our sources of knowing as
surely as we've been severed from our spiritual guidance. Tragically,

this reinforces the boxes in our brains through which we perceive the world, intensifying our feeling of separation from All That Is.

"Our education has taught us to separate, to compartmentalize, to isolate, and not to join notions together," say Edgar Morin and Anne Brigitte Kern. "Therefore, it makes us conceive of our humanity as an island, outside the cosmos that surrounds us, outside the physical matter of which we are constituted."[3]

For Bohm, civilization and the formal education that sustains it robbed us of our ability to perceive the "wholeness of existence."[4] "In early times man's activities were an undivided whole, in which art and science were not separate," he explains. "Similarly, young children do not tend, of their own accord, to separate such activities. What happens is that they are gradually trained to think, feel, perceive, and act in terms of this kind of separation (as happened to mankind in general with the growth of civilization)."[5]

Contemporary education serves the status quo. But is it equipping us to live in harmony with the Earth and our fellow beings? Is it helping us solve our most urgent problems, or is it simply perpetuating the Old Paradigm . . . and the old problems?

Confined by specialized straitjackets, our fragmented modern minds are simply too limited, their focus too narrow, to come up with anything but fragmentary solutions—which is undoubtedly why our problems are not only persisting, but growing. And it's why many new thinkers are taking a closer look at old ways of learning.

LIVING AND LEARNING

People in native cultures acquire knowledge that leads to wisdom. A lifetime endeavor that does not end with a diploma or a degree, learning in an indigenous society is spontaneous, open-ended, holistic, experiential, and spiritual.

For traditional people, according to James David Audlin, "education is not separated from other activities, but is integral to them."[6]

"For the People . . . knowledge forms a complete whole," says

F. David Peat. It includes the areas we call medicine, agriculture, history, geography, spirituality, law, and economics.[7]

"The teachings are a whole thing; they are a *sacred* whole," Audlin stresses. "They are not individual items among which you may choose as in a 'supermarket' of ideas. Rather, they are all connected in a nonlinear fashion."[8]

Peat adds that for a native person, knowledge cannot be accumulated "like money stored in a bank." Rather, acquiring it is an ongoing process, a "coming-to-knowing."

"Knowledge in the traditional world is not a dead collection of facts," he explains. "It is alive, has spirit, and dwells in specific places." For this reason, he says, in the indigenous world "you cannot 'give' a person knowledge the way a doctor gives a person a shot for measles." Instead, each person learns for himself or herself "through the processes of growing up in contact with nature and society, by observing, watching, listening, and dreaming."[9]

The open-endedness of coming-to-knowing suggests the "unfinishedness" that educator and philosopher Paulo Freire believes is essential to the human condition. "It is in this consciousness [of unfinishedness] that the very possibility of learning, of being educated, resides," Freire explains. "It is our immersion in this consciousness that gives rise to a permanent movement of searching, of curious interrogation that leads us not only to an awareness of the world but also to a thorough, scientific knowledge of it."[10]

LISTENING TO LEARN

We see *ayni* in indigenous listening: it's an active offering of attention and energy in exchange for wisdom.

"Coming-to-knowing arises out of silence," Peat stresses.[11] Audlin agrees: "We learn by observation, and we teach by example. In such teaching as this, hardly any words ever need be said." Hidden Wolf told me that he learned the healing powers of plants from his grandfather in total silence: his grandfather would point at a plant and indicate with a gesture what part of the body it would help. Hidden Wolf never learned the names of any plants; he was expected to remember each plant's medicinal purpose by feeling, smelling, and tasting it.

"I learned to consider carefully before asking my first teaching Grandfather questions," Audlin recalls. "He taught me that it was better if I was quiet and paid close attention, and that I would learn everything I needed to know in good time, provided only that I be patient."[12]

Learning from nature and from elders involves "a special quality of silence and alert watchfulness," Peat stresses. "The respect one shows to an Elder acts to create that area of quietness and creativity into which an Elder can speak."[13]

Nature, too, can speak most clearly when listened to actively. Her subtle messages are easily obscured by the clatter of modern life and the chatter of modern minds. "Nature itself is didactic," Audlin points out. "We are to pay attention, because reality is constantly speaking to us and teaching us."[14]

Peat notes that children in Western schools are often bored because they are passive consumers of knowledge. "The attention a child gives in a school is often not very different from what we all do in front of the television set," he says. "The watching that leads to coming-to-knowing may be closer to the active watching of a kingfisher who sits poised on a branch over a fast-flowing river."[15]

STORY MAGIC

Much of the active listening in native societies is directed at stories. Recounted by elders, traditional tales carry lessons from the ancestors that are eternal, immediate, and easily absorbed.

According to Joan Halifax, storytelling is the most ancient form of education. "[Stories] remind us that we do not stand alone," she says. "Through them we live in the body of coyote and crow, tree and stone, gods and heroes, Ancestral Mothers and Grandmothers. In this way, we confirm our relationship with all of creation."[16]

Great stories are transmissions of collective wisdom. They originate in the field and speak through metaphor directly to our souls. Like sacred geometric forms, they bypass our rational minds and express the metaphysical background of reality.

"The world around us, and every entity within it, is constantly telling us a story," says Audlin. "And we too are constantly participating in the unfolding of an infinite number of stories. These tales connect with each other in meaningful ways through space and time."[17]

According to Halifax:

> For Earth Peoples, real nature—storm and rushing waters, the silence of winter nights, and the greatness of protecting mountains—makes the story immediate and memorable, coded in geography and in the temper of the seasons. Stories like these are ecology. They make the landscape of the mind and the outer landscape one, thus protecting and enriching both.

For this reason, she says, storytelling is one of the most important ways we can "do the ancestral work that will reconcile us to Earth and Earth Peoples, to our true nature and unimpeded mind."[18]

WE CAN'T *NOT* LEARN

Curiosity killed the cat. . . .
Satisfaction brought him back.

OLD PROVERB

Everything is interesting, once you are interested in it.

HUMBERTO MATURANA[19]

Answers close us, but questions open us.

DAVID RICHO[20]

Modern educators struggle to teach. But traditional people and the new science insist that we can't *not* learn.

Watch a kitten, a puppy, a baby bird, a human child: they are driven by curiosity to know their world. Sometimes, as with the kitty in the old saying, their curiosity gets them in trouble—but if they manage to survive their more hazardous encounters with life, they always, inevitably, learn. David Bohm says:

> The ability to learn [something new] is a principle common to the whole of humanity. Thus, it is well known that a child learns to walk, to talk, and to know his way around the world *just by trying something and seeing what happens,* then modifying what he does (or thinks) in accordance with what has actually happened.
>
> In this way, he spends his first few years in a wonderfully creative way, discovering all sorts of things that are new to him. . . . As the child grows older, however, learning takes on a narrower meaning. In school, he learns by repetition to accumulate knowledge, so as to please the teacher and pass examinations.[21]

Education professor Robert L. Fried insists that the desire to learn "must surely be as strong as any impulse within the human soul. Children cannot *not* learn."[22]

Adults cannot not learn, either. Curiosity continues to drive human behavior throughout life, and when unfettered, it can lead the learner in unimagined directions. Curiosity leads naturally to the kind of group interaction that produces collective intelligence. When people come together in curiosity rather than certainty, magic happens. Sources of deep wisdom are tapped; totally new ideas and solutions emerge. Paulo Freire tells us that this permanent movement of searching creates a capacity for learning not only in order to adapt to the world but especially to intervene, to re-create, and to transform it. As he says:

> Curiosity as restless questioning, as movement toward the revelation of something hidden, as a question verbalized or not, as search for clarity, as a moment of attention, suggestion, and vigilance, constitutes an integral part of being alive.

There could be no creativity without the curiosity that moves us and sets us patiently impatient before a world that we did not make, to add to it something of our own making.[23]

GOOD NEWS, BAD NEWS

Discoveries in neurobiology confirm that we can't not learn. Biologist Humberto Maturana showed that all living organisms become "structurally coupled" to their environment at a cellular level;[24] we are hardwired to learn, easily, naturally, and continuously.

"We have ignored for half a century or more the studies that show some 95 percent of all a child's learning or 'structures of knowledge' form automatically in direct response to interactions with the environment," writes Joseph Chilton Pearce, "while only about 5 percent form as a result of our verbal teaching or intellectual instruction."[25]

"The way of life, the manner of living together, shapes and transforms people," says Maturana. "Teachers do not simply transmit some content, they acquaint their pupils with a way of living."[26]

Two examples bring this home dramatically. Maturana and Francisco Varela describe the case of two girls who were raised by a family of wolves in India. When they were "rescued (or snatched)" by missionaries in 1922, they continued to behave like wolves, and the missionaries were never able to make them completely human.

> This case—and it is not the only one—shows us that although they were human in their genetic constitution and in their anatomy and physiology, these two girls never managed to fit in with a human context. The behavior that the missionary and his family wanted to change in them, because it was unacceptable in a human context, was completely natural to their wolflike upbringing.[27]

The "Wolf Girls" were "structurally coupled" to wolf culture, which had created changes in their nervous systems. They learned their wolflike behavior naturally; nobody taught them how to become wolves. As the missionaries found out when they tried unsuccessfully to impose on the girls their beliefs about what human behavior should look like, nobody could teach them how to become human either.

On the other hand, using an approach based on curiosity, learning, and love, Anne Sullivan was able to reconnect Helen Keller with her humanity. David Bohm writes:

> When she came to teach this child, who was blind and deaf from an early age (and therefore unable to speak as well), [Sullivan] knew that she would have to treat her with complete love. However, on first seeing her "pupil," she met a "wild animal," who apparently could not be approached in any way at all.
>
> If she had seen only according to her preconceptions she would have given up immediately. But she worked with the child as best she could, with all the energies at her disposal, remaining extremely sensitively observant, "feeling out" the unknown mind of the child, and eventually *learning* how to communicate with her.[28]

The good news is that we can learn everything we need to know in spite of what Freire calls "the banking system of education" in the industrialized world, in which teachers are expected to stuff their passive students with material demanded by the system.[29]

The bad news is that some of what we're structurally coupling to may end up threatening our eventual survival. We'll be looking more closely at this in part 2.

ANCESTRAL LEARNING

There are no teachers—we are all learning.

DANIL MAMYEV

Native elder Danil Mamyev uses a cell phone and a computer. But he also rides his horse to sacred sites in the mountains, making offerings to the spirits. With one foot in each world, he is using the new to rescue the old, as he seeks to bridge the abyss that opened up when much of humanity lost the ability to learn from Earth and stars.

As our guide during our visit to the Altai region of Siberia, he was also our teacher, but not in the modern sense. He encouraged us to learn about this very ancient corner of the world in the way our ancestors did—with our senses and with our hearts.

Mamyev's life mission is to raise awareness of the need to preserve the Altai's land and its generations of unexplored secrets. But his manner is quiet, even shy. He watches us pensively, as if gauging how much we can absorb. At different times, whenever he feels we might be ready, he calls us together for spontaneous little talks—at the breakfast table, or around a fire at night.

Even offered through an interpreter, these tidbits—about his research, his people's traditions and spiritual beliefs, their past sufferings, and the threats they face now—rarely take longer than twenty minutes. He often weaves his words into the landscape, demonstrating the proper way to make offerings or encouraging us to pick out faces in rocks or trees.

Fig. 7.1. Learning from the land: students and teachers in Siberia's Altai.
Photo by Jim Molloy.

*Fig. 7.2. Sacred site overlooking Altai's Uch-Enmek Nature Park.
Photo by Jim Molloy.*

Mostly, he lets us learn from the land itself. It's a powerful way to expand our knowledge at a deep and lasting level—especially for people accustomed to being fed facts for our intellects to analyze, compare, accept, or reject.

The Altai's sweeping, pristine wilderness welcomes us with meadows waist-deep in wildflowers and the intoxicating aromatherapy of wild thyme and sage, sheltered by dramatic mountain peaks and dense evergreen forests and bathed by mighty rivers, sparkling streams, and serene, still lakes. The ancestors are present everywhere: in prehistoric stone monuments rising among the flowers, in stories told by ancient petroglyphs, and in springs, caves, and ribbon-festooned trees marking sacred sites.

In the villages, we are welcomed into six-sided, earth-floored log *ayils,* where we are given bowls of sweet creamy milk and listen entranced as each host or hostess draws us easily and naturally into the world of spirits and energies that has thrived in the Altai since the Stone Age.

Fig. 7.3. Arikem Lake: teacher of sacred wisdom.
Photo by Jim Molloy.

Mamyev leads us on horseback up a flower-carpeted mountain to sacred Arikem Lake, where we encounter a group of shining-faced young people and three of their teachers. They have been camping here as part of a special program in village schools.

The teachers proudly take turns telling us how the program, which combines ecology with indigenous wisdom and for which Mamyev serves as a consultant, seeks to reconnect students with their heritage by taking them to sacred sites in the wilderness.

Like Mamyev, the teachers are merely facilitators.

Like us, the young people are learning directly from the spirits of the land and the ancestors.

* * *

In Malaysia, Robert Wolff was offered the chance to learn from Ahmeed, a Sng'oi shaman, and eagerly accepted.

Later I realized that Ahmeed never used the word *teach;* he always said *learn.* Looking back, I am certain he saw his role as an opener of doors, never telling me what to do or what to think. What learning I did would be through my own effort—but at the time I did not know that.

Ahmeed invited Wolff on a series of long hikes, during which he

did not volunteer any information. He did not teach. When I asked him something, he barely answered, just grunted something.

I wondered whether this aimless silent walking would help me learn . . . whatever it was. Finally, in the evening, I asked him what I should learn from these walks. He laughed loudly, which was unusual for him.

"No, I am serious," I protested. "I need to know what it is I should learn." He chuckled and said, "It does not matter. You do not have to understand; you will learn."

I felt abashed. I did not understand his method of teaching. I thought about it all evening, and probably in my sleep as well. In the morning I woke up with the realization that we Westerners are so used to thinking of training, learning, and teaching as verbal activities that we forget that much—perhaps most—learning happens without verbal instruction.[30]

GROUPS ALSO HAVE MINDS

In *The Akashic Experience,* Ervin Laszlo compiles reports from numerous sources on the ways in which they receive information from the cosmic energy field. In the following section, religious studies professor Christopher Bache describes his awakening to collective intelligence.

When collective intelligence made its spontaneous appearance in his classroom, Bache was at first baffled, then intrigued.

It started with synchronicities: students would tell him that something in one of his lectures had expressed a thought, event, or dream from their own lives. Then he began to notice unexpected connections between his personal spiritual practice and his students' experiences.

"This was the beginning of a long odyssey with my students, a journey of discovery that lasted decades," Bache reports. "Eventually it led me to a new understanding of the dynamics of collective fields of consciousness and to recognize a true *collective intelligence* operating in the classroom. As an academic, I was so conditioned by the atomistic, Newtonian-Cartesian paradigm that it took years before I was able to admit what now looks to me to be the obvious and natural interpretation of these events—that beneath the appearance of separation, our lives are deeply intertwined with those around us, and that my spiritual practice was somehow triggering these incidents of resonance in my classroom. This was happening not through my conscious direction but involuntarily, through some sort of energetic resonance."

Bache's descriptions echo those of indigenous people using collective wisdom: "Sometimes insights surfaced in the room that seemed to come not from me or from any individual student but from the strength of our *collective awareness*. . . . I sometimes have the acute sensation that there is only one mind present in the room. . . . Individual persons melt into a softly glowing field of energy, and this unified energy thinks and feels and hungers to speak."

Bache also discovered that his students "began to periodically 'jump forward' in their learning en masse," obliging him to adjust his course material for each incoming group.

"Slowly I began to recognize that there was a *meta-learning* taking place behind the scenes, a pattern of learning that ran deeper than the learning of individual students. I began to recognize that there were *learning fields* growing around my courses, fields of consciousness that registered the learning taking place semester after semester . . . making it easier for subsequent generations of students to learn the same material." Bache credits Rupert Sheldrake's theory of morphic fields with helping him recognize that *groups also have minds.*[31]

"Central to Sheldrake's theory of morphic resonance is the notion that collective fields, once created, should begin to impact other groups engaged in similar activity around the world," Craig Hamilton explains. "Once one individual or group breaks through to new knowledge or capacities, it becomes easier for others to access that same knowledge or capacity."[32]

Holography once more sheds light on such experiences. Renee A. Levi suggests that it may hold a clue to how a group of people can learn "from a dimension outside of the space/time dimension," with each person's story acting as the "light" to produce a holographic image on a "group plate."

"This learning can be from two different sources, both reflecting holographic principles," she writes. "The whole of the group intelligence is contained within every member and every member's intelligence is contained in the group. . . . Listening to someone else's story might reflect a part of one's own reality and in such a way provide an answer to an unspoken question that influences one's own life. . . . Perhaps the troughs of the waves, when intersecting—or interfering—create a sudden unexpected energy and the spark from which learning can occur."[33]

Bache speculates that "if mind is a field phenomenon, if it registers not only as our particle-like sensory awareness but also as a wavelike, intuitive awareness that extends beyond our bodies, then teaching is more than just sending out information across an ontological chasm for students to catch. It is in addition *a direct energetic engagement of the mental fields of our students within the encompassing matrix of Sacred Mind.*" However, he stresses that these insights "don't cancel or negate the individuality that we prize so highly in the West. . . . Within this matrix, individuality is not suffocated but paradoxically liberated into deeper forms of self-expression."[34]

Significantly, Bache's recognition that his own spiritual practice seemed to trigger the energetic resonance necessary for collective intelligence also echoes indigenous spirituality: when people sense the sacred everywhere and in everything, the ability to think together isn't far behind.

THE "NEW INTELLIGENCE" IS COLLECTIVE

We are witnessing an evolution toward a planetary consciousness or global mind.

EDGAR MORIN AND ANNE BRIGITTE KERN[35]

> *Our spiritual ecology simply does not permit private awakening.*
>
> CHRISTOPHER BACHE[36]

The "new kind of intelligence" that will emerge if humanity can remember how we used to learn will be both creative—the way all learning starts out, according to David Bohm, before formal education gets into the act—and collective. He stresses that "intelligence does not . . . arise primarily out of thought. Rather . . . the deep source of intelligence is the unknown and indefinable totality from which all perception originates."[37]

Like Humberto Maturana, Bohm maintains that it is interaction with the whole that allows creation to happen.

> The implicate order implies mutual participation of everything with everything. No thing is complete in itself, and its full being is realized only in that participation. . . . We create a world according to our mode of participation, and we create ourselves accordingly.[38]

As Maturana and Varela put it, "We humans . . . exist in the network of structural couplings that we continually weave. . . . It is by languaging that the act of knowing . . . brings forth a world."[39]

To reach truly new inspiration, we need each other. In Bohm's words:

> We must be able to think together. That will create a new frame of mind in which there is a common consciousness. It is a kind of implicate order, where each one enfolds the whole consciousness.
>
> With the common consciousness we then have something new—a new kind of intelligence.[40]

8

Ceremony, Pilgrimage, and Initiation

No Free Lunch

Ceremony, pilgrimage, and initiation are all expressions of collective intelligence, and all involve reciprocity.

Native peoples' relationship with the energy flowing through all things is intensely conscious and actively participatory: as grateful

Fig. 8.1. Giving back: Q'ero shamans in Peru prepare a despacho for Mother Earth. Photo by Jim Molloy.

recipients of life's abundance, they acknowledge their obligation to contribute to it.

In other words, though modern people may not like to admit it, there's no free lunch.

"We owe to the cosmic order because we are individually and communally responsible for its maintenance," says elder, author, and teacher Malidoma Somé.[1]

This is why ceremonies, initiation rites, and pilgrimages are so important in traditional societies. When we look closely at these ancient practices, we find that initiation can be a pilgrimage, a pilgrimage can be a form of initiation, and both often involve ceremony. All usually are preceded by a strong calling of some sort—from elders, teachers, the community, or the spirits, or the pilgrim/initiate's own soul.

The pilgrim/initiate generally must undergo some ordeal or overcome a challenge, in exchange for which he or she receives energetic gifts and spiritual growth that benefit the entire community and the Earth itself. We *need* our initiates and pilgrims.

KEEPING THE BALANCE

We always pray for the harmony of the world. If we didn't do our ceremonies in the Longhouse, then this world would come to an end. It's our ceremonies that hold this world together.

LEON SHENANDOAH[2]

Ceremonies open sacred space—a place outside of time where participants can communicate with the spirit world, give thanks, and receive blessings. When people gather to engage the powers of nature, walls between individuals disappear and the group steps together into another dimension—a liminal space "between the worlds" where healing and transformation take place.

"A Native person is always part of a much greater entity and can never be separated from it," notes F. David Peat. "Each is an individual expression of the group, and in turn, the group comes together in ceremonies to draw upon a much greater energy."[3] For this reason, ceremonies are powerful acts of *ayni,* simultaneously helping not only the spirits and the Earth, but every participant.

"The forces aroused in a ritual function like a power plant into which every individual is hooked," says Malidoma Somé. "When one leaves the ritual space, the power of the ritual goes wherever the person goes."[4]

Ceremony is poetry for the Earth, speaking in the same language—metaphors, symbols—she uses to speak to us. Johanna Lambert draws an interesting analogy between the preparation of a homeopathic remedy, in which a substance is reduced to its energetic essence, and ceremony as celebrated by Australia's Aborigines: "It may take days, weeks, or even months in preparation for a ceremony," she writes. "During this time the performers refine their elaborate costumes and body painting. . . . This allows the vital essence of a particular ancestral or animal energy to emerge. . . . Then, each dancer begins to pound the earth in rhythm to clapsticks or a didjeridoo, entering into a repetitive rhythmic movement that may continue for days and nights." Lambert likens this to "the action of succussion [shaking] that a homeopathic substance undergoes in order to gain a healing power."

"Through the vibratory relationship developed from the dancer's feet pounding mother earth, the individual's ancestral imprint and connection with the Dreamtime is deepened," she explains. "This allows for an energetic transference of knowledge between the dancer and his ancestral spirits and can be seen as analogous to the process of information exchange in homeopathic healing."

"Entering into ceremony is, in Aboriginal thought, the ultimate healing process."[5]

In the Siberian region of Tuva near the Mongolian border, shamans have been desperately working to renew the energies in their land, which, they say, were severely disrupted during the Soviet era, when native rituals were banned and shamans persecuted. The shamans travel to sacred sites to celebrate ceremony with drumming, chanting, and sacred fires, imploring the spirits of each place to return. Wherever

Fig. 8.2. Healing the land: Tuvan shaman Herrell leads a fire ceremony.
Photo courtesy of Lucian Kragiel.

they go, they lecture the local community about the importance of ceremonies to restore balance.[6]

Interestingly, every indigenous group with which I have been lucky
enough to share ceremony has always expressed enthusiasm for the par-
ticipation of outsiders, apparently because of the energy they can contribute. The Tuvans were no exception: our group's arrival in June 2002
was heralded by a double rainbow, which they excitedly declared was
a sign that the spirits welcomed us and that we would be able to assist
the shamans in their ceremonial work. They were especially grateful for
help because huge wildfires had been raging through Tuva's forests. The
immense region is so isolated and sparsely populated that no effort was
being made to control the fires.

The shamans made the most of our visit. Three of them volunteered
to take us from one sacred site to another in the wilderness to celebrate

ceremonies. In each place they transmitted the urgency of their mission by chanting, wailing, and imploring as they drummed and whirled after instructing us to help drum or, depending on the site, to kneel or lie on the Earth in silent prayer. They also gave us prayer ties of different colors to attach to trees or shrines.

To their (and our) delight, the hard work paid off. During each ceremony, clouds would suddenly gather in the totally blue sky and a few drops of rain would fall. By the end of our trip, Herrell, the elder shaman, was relaxed and happy. He assured us that big rain was on its way.

The day after we returned home, torrential rains drenched the region for a week, finally quenching the fires.[7]

Ceremony is a perfect expression of collective intelligence, indicating, in Peat's words, "the way in which a powerful new action can come about when people sit together, working through consensus and coherence. They are able to draw upon energies that vastly exceed those that are accessible to an isolated individual."[8]

Elizabeth Jenkins learned this firsthand from many Andean ceremonies:

> Using the collective intention of a large group to move energy was one of the most exciting parts of the practice for me. Its effects were powerful, at times to the point of exaltation. And the spiritual and energetic merging of a group seemed to me the highest purpose and expression of human community.
>
> Rather than striving for individual enlightenment or mystical experience, the Inka tradition valued collective work with energy—eating *hoocha,* directing *sami,* using the potency of the community bubble—thus generating a spiritual power beyond the capacity of any one individual.
>
> Yet . . . the individual was empowered by the practice, and moved significantly forward along their personal path to wholeness.[9]

It's no accident, of course, that native ceremonies invariably take place in circles.

*Fig. 8.3. Chosen by the spirits: in the Peruvian Andes,
Q'ero shamans doña Bernardina and don Pascual, with sacred
Mount Ausangate in the background. Photo by Jim Molloy.*

LIGHTNING STRIKES

Not just anybody can become a shaman. Candidates are chosen by the spirits and must pass grueling tests before they can serve their communities as healers, ceremonialists, and visionaries with the extraordinary powers they are given.

The initiation of a shaman can be as dramatic and brutal as being struck by lightning—literally. In the Andes, surviving three successive lightning strikes is the fast track to receiving shamanic powers.[10] In every native culture, the summons to shamanic service takes the form of some kind of initiatory ordeal—a sudden or prolonged illness, physical or mental, or both; a near-death experience; a series of personal catastrophes.

The ordeal is necessary because the shaman-to-be must undergo dismemberment of every previously known structure in order to be put back together and reborn in his or her new role. The initiation process breaks down psychic walls, permitting the initiate to more easily perceive other dimensions, empathize more deeply with the people he or she will be helping, and align with the energies of nature.

In the Andes, according to Juan Núñez del Prado,

> The first [lightning] strike kills the initiate, the second strike dismembers the body, and the third strike fuses the body back together again, but in a new configuration.
>
> If we look at this ancient initiatory experience metaphorically, we see that the ego dies, is taken apart, and finally, is reconfigured into a more appropriate form that can hold more energy. The Andean masters also say that if you move the body of someone before they have been struck three times they will die.[11]

If the initiate answers the call, he or she is happier and healthier. But the future shaman must then undergo a long apprenticeship with a teacher, as well as additional trials, and make a lifelong commitment to serve the community, often at considerable personal sacrifice.

The shaman's initiation is vital, because the community needs his or her powers. Only after demonstrating the strength required to pass the many demanding tests and enter into relationship with the spirits in this and other dimensions can the shaman offer himself or herself as a conduit.

Though selected by the spirits, the shaman candidate is not wholly passive; even here, there is reciprocity. Joseph Chilton Pearce explains that "real lightning . . . strikes only a primed, fully charged target. When all conditions are present, the intelligence of field function breaks through to an intellect of a like order. Like attracts like."

He is referring to sudden insights that arrive out of the blue, like lightning bolts. But a similar process seems to take place with a shaman-to-be, who apparently has assembled the necessary qualities that make him or her a likely candidate, even though he or she may not be consciously aware of them.

Oddly and symbolically, the great mass of energy for a lightning bolt is built up in the clouds while a corresponding, opposite, but minor charge builds up in the ground. Eventually, the two charges seem to seek out each other, and when they reach the closest proximity to each other, the weaker ground charge makes a gesture up to the clouds through any medium that will offer it a bit of lift or passage, such as a tree. . . .

The earth has sowed a small wind and reaped a whirlwind from the skies. Or, we could say the earth asked a question and the sky gave its answer.[12]

In Linda Tucker's masterful exploration of the mysteries of South Africa's white lions, Lion Priest Credo Mutwa tells her about his initiation:

It was my grandfather, ma'am, who was the only person capable of curing me when I was struck down by an incurable sickness, which kept me bedridden and unconscious, for three years right here in Soweto. It was during this time that I had many terrifying visions, ma'am, some of which we *sangomas* [shamans] call the "sacred dreams" that occur before you become a *sangoma*. I had the vision of the earth stretched out like a lion skin pegged at all four corners—north, south, east, and west—with the four lion brothers tearing at it in four directions. . . . In our tradition we believe, ma'am, that the universe is sustained by four great forces and in the center is the fifth power, *Nxaca-Nxaca*, meaning "confusion" or "chaos." From this power comes order and from order again comes chaos—and so on for all eternity.[13]

Significantly, the images in Mutwa's vision included the universally held notions of the four sacred directions and mystical center point.

Joan Halifax notes that shamans chosen for initiation can be abducted by a predatory creature who takes them to the Underworld, where they encounter terrifying spirits and creatures; in many cases the shaman is dismembered and consumed by them. They then become the shaman's teachers, and he or she can embody their qualities.

"Losing the battle, the shaman becomes all-victorious," she writes. "This process is a kind of transmission between species. Those who were the shaman's enemies become Allies and Protectors."[14] Many native traditions hold that an animal whose spirit has chosen a human to serve as a totem often lets the human know by attacking, biting, or stinging him or her.

Mutwa goes on to tell Tucker about his subsequent shamanic training:

> After the process of healing, ma'am, my grandfather showed me how to control my powers of perception, and how to sharpen my senses and make them more accurate—like the arrow from a hunter's bow. He taught me the art of rhythm, and the secret of joining my consciousness to the great gods of the unseen world. He taught me not to fear them, but to work with them as helpful guides who would sharpen and broaden my perception, not only of this world, but of the whole cosmos.[15]

The passage that delivers a shaman to a life of service can, unfortunately, be perverted: some shamans stumble along the way, intoxicated by their newfound powers. Losing sight of the mandate to work for the whole and maintain balance, they're diverted to the dark side, driven by a lust for power, vengeance, or easy wealth. Black magicians exist in all shamanic cultures and range from simple scamsters to truly evil sorcerers who manipulate the energies of the Earth to cause harm. The law of *ayni* is meaningless for these lost souls, who also disregard the Law of Three respected by Wiccans and many other ancient Earth-honoring traditions: "what ye send out comes back to thee"—threefold. Many end up learning bitter lessons, but only after wreaking havoc.

Everyone who undergoes initiation to one degree or another experiences the shaman's ordeal—what Halifax calls a "sacred catastrophe."[16] She cites cultural historian Arnold van Gennep, who describes three distinct phases in the initiation process: separation, or severance; transition, or threshold; and incorporation, or return. Like ceremony, initiation takes the person into a liminal space where anything is possible, so great changes can occur.

"Initiation is equivalent to a spiritual maturing," says Mircea Eliade. "And in the religious history of humanity we consistently find this theme: the initiate, he who has experienced the mysteries, is *he who knows*."[17]

SAFE PASSAGE

Initiation was necessary to keep the Earth alive, which is why traditional people kept coming back to help the "New Ones" get through, because if those nestlings did not get through, the Earth would die and everybody with it.

MARTÍN PRECHTEL[18]

In traditional societies, the initiation of young people is everybody's business: the process is vital to the survival of the society and of the Earth itself.

Native cultures channel the passionate energies of adolescence into rites of passage involving the forces of nature. These rites are aimed at giving birth to young warriors, equipping them to do battle with the challenges awaiting them as adults.

Initiations are always conducted by elders, whose wisdom is essential to the process. Their task is to help young people begin to acquire wisdom, which involves introducing them to situations in nature—sometimes dangerous and frightening, always extremely challenging—from which they can learn.[19]

Blessed by the ancestors, the youths are welcomed into the sacred continuum of their society, which infuses their lives with meaning and mystery. Passing through the three phases mentioned earlier, they face their fears and discover that they can call on sources of strength and courage they never imagined they possessed.

The young initiates learn to trust—their elders, their peers, themselves, their world, the divine. Most importantly, when they meet and begin to work with the spirits of nature, they realize that they too are part of the Earth and, in exchange for loving care, will be allowed to use her powers. As Johanna Lambert writes:

> An important aspect of the initiation of a young Aboriginal girl is to develop the sensibilities and concentration that make her aware of the living and symbolic interrelatedness of the natural world. During her isolation she is instructed to listen to the first note that any bird sings throughout the day, to which she must respond with a particular ringing sound. The birds are believed to be inhabited by the spirits of her deceased female ancestors, and in this way a subliminal communication is maintained between the generations.
>
> Likewise, she is to focus her attention so that she is aware of every sound made by members of her tribe in their distant camp. This practice of turning full attention to, and filling herself with, the sounds, smells, and sights of her natural and social surroundings is believed to increase the life force and animation of her body.[20]

The new adults who emerge from the other end of an initiatory passage have begun to recognize their responsibility to the community and to the world and are on their way to acquiring the wisdom they need to become elders themselves.

"The madness of youth was enormously useful and was honored as the necessary magical consciousness needed by the culture to save its existence from disintegrating into a flat nothing," Martín Prechtel says, describing the initiation of Tzutujil Maya youths. "It kept the world flowering, but it needed the spiritual intelligence left by the ancestors and directed by the elders."[21]

The young people never participated willingly: Prechtel describes how the elders had to "kidnap them, forcibly dragging them away from their families in an elaborately staged severance ritual, which, even though expected and understood, was nonetheless fiercely resisted." The elders acted as agents of change and upheaval, sparking the crisis that forced the initiates to undergo their ordeals and grow—just as the spirits of nature disrupt the life of the shaman-to-be with illness or catastrophe.

Paradoxically, the elders were also the agents of continuity. Acting from collective wisdom, they perpetuated the ancient, sacred bond with All That Is that renewed every member of society while renewing the Earth itself.

Although it was the ripening of each initiate's soul that ultimately enabled the Earth to regain her fruitfulness, the Tzutujil initiation was a collective event. Prechtel stresses that "every year, everybody in the village was somehow getting a rite of passage simultaneously in different groups at different levels; but every size person, man or woman, was doing it to save the Earth, not to become initiated."[22]

I WON'T GROW UP

We are obviously failing to keep the Earth alive, in large part because we've abandoned our rites of passage. Denied the challenge of initiation with the guidance of elders and the support of their communities, too many young people in "developed" societies find themselves unable to safely navigate the perilous journey to adulthood and grow into their fullness as wisdom keepers. Seduced by consumerism, immobilized by addictions, or trapped in fanaticism, many Peter Pans of the modern world—and the crippled adults they eventually turn into—are incapable of participating in collective consciousness.

Robert Bly bemoans what he terms the "sibling society," in which "the parents regress to become more like children, and the children, through abandonment, are forced to become adults too soon, and never quite make it."[23] Again we see the fragmentation that plagues our modern vision: the circular continuum linking the generations and connecting us to our planet and one another has been broken, leaving everyone alone and adrift.

According to Edgar Morin and Anne Brigitte Kern, modern people don't realize that adolescence is "the weak link in the chain of civilization, that it concentrates within itself the problems, the hurt, and the aspirations elsewhere diffused and atomized," and that the rebellion and turbulence that accompany the teenage years point to what's missing in contemporary Western society.

"The search for autonomy along with community, the need for an authentic relationship to nature wherein we rediscover our own nature, and the rejection of the adulterated life of adults, reveals through negation the privations suffered by us all," they write. "The call for peace and love of Californian adolescents in the 1960s betrayed a deep distress of the soul."[24]

After listening to two Andean *paqos* describe their initiations, Elizabeth Jenkins says she was struck by how they "had found the cultural support to go through their ordeals. It made me realize how so many of us in the West lacked initiation rituals of any sort. In fact we were spiritually isolated, cut off from those sources that might help us to endure and digest our own unorthodox or visionary experiences, so that we might use them to guide our lives."[25]

As we will see in part 2, many of the roots of collective stupidity can be found right here. Without initiation, we've been losing our shamans as well as our elders. Those who might have responded to the spirits' call have either been medicated into deadened uselessness or driven by their suffering into rehab centers and mental institutions, never comprehending the gift they were offered or how they might have used it to benefit their communities.

Instead of providing kids with technotoys, Bly believes,

we need to reintroduce them to the dangerous energies of nature. The "body-soul" needs to be changed in order to receive what Joseph Campbell calls "the inexhaustible energies of the cosmos" that pour down toward human beings. Without gratitude to energies much greater than our own, there will be no new meanings.[26]

*Fig. 8.4. Power spot: Huayna Picchu, seen from the
sacred sanctuary of Machu Picchu. Photo by Jim Molloy.*

SACRED SITES AND POWER PLACES

*The earth contains places of exceptional power where the
human soul is infused with cosmic energy, places where the
soul of the person and the soul of the universe meet.*

Tom Cowan[27]

If everything in nature is supposedly sacred, why are some places
believed to be especially holy?

When we look at pilgrimage destinations around the world, we invariably find a spot in nature—a rock, a cave, a body of water, a tree, a mountain—that our ancestors sensed held mysterious power. Over eons, this unusual energetic vibration was confirmed and strengthened by repeated visits and ceremonies—often leading to the establishment of temples, tombs, or churches on the sites.

These spots reverberated with power from both Earth and Cosmos: they were places where portals opened to other dimensions and magical transformations were possible. Tom Cowan maintains that

> instinctively we sense the power of these places when we enter them, even though we cannot always articulate the reasons for the shift in our sense of well-being, the tingling sensation we might feel in our bodies, or the altered quality of consciousness that overtakes us there. We simply feel, as some describe it, more whole, more complete, more ensouled.[28]

According to Mircea Eliade, "Every sacred space implies a hierophany, an irruption of the sacred that results in detaching a territory from the surrounding cosmic milieu and making it qualitatively different."[29]

Such places exchange energy with those who come to them. Joan Halifax explains:

> People have traveled over this Earth with a heart of inquiry for millennia. They have sung through the land as a living being, offered themselves, their steps, their voices and prayers as acts of purification that opened them to an experience of connectedness.
>
> Whether it is Huichol peoples of Mexico who annually journey to Wirikúta, or Australian aborigines, whose song-lines connect dreamings across thousands of miles, or Hindu pilgrims who make their way to the Mother Ganges or Shiva's Abode, or Buddhist pilgrims who reconstitute the life of the Buddha by visiting the groves and mountains, towns and villages where his birth, realizations, teachings, and passage occurred; pilgrimage is a remembering in the passing through of sacred time and sacred space.[30]

Humans aren't the only ones drawn again and again to places of power; the migrations of many other creatures are also pilgrimages along ancestral pathways. In every such journey, human or otherwise, we can observe collective *ayni* at work, as the travelers feed and are fed by the energy of the holy site. The mass return each year of sea turtles, birds, and butterflies to nest in their birthplaces—traveling thousands of miles to reciprocate the gift of life by bringing them new life—are beautiful examples of this.

Credo Mutwa insists that human survival depends on animal migrations.

> What many people do not realise is that these huge, wild herds existed because the native people of Africa regarded them as a blessing from the Gods—as something unbelievably sacred and vital for the continued existence of human beings. No-one ever interfered with these great migrations because they really believed that wildlife was the soul, the very life-blood, of Mother Earth.[31]

Psychologist Roger Nelson, who for many years coordinated the experiments of the Princeton Engineering Anomalies Research (PEAR) laboratory at Princeton University, put twenty-seven sacred sites in North America and Egypt to the test with a random-event generator (REG)—a machine developed by Princeton engineering professor Robert Jahn to measure parapsychological phenomena.

According to Lynne McTaggart, Nelson found that "some resonance reverberated at the sites, possibly even a vortex of coherent memory." The group accompanying Nelson sometimes engaged in rituals such as chanting, which produced the strongest effects on the machine. "Both the type of place and the activity of the group seemed to play contributing roles in creating a kind of group consciousness," McTaggart reports. However, "in the sacred sites where chanting hadn't taken place, simple group presence, or perhaps even the place itself, held a high degree of resonating consciousness." When Nelson compiled the data from all twenty-seven sites, he found that "the spirit of the place itself appeared to register effects every bit as large as the meditating group."[32]

STAR TREKS

There are very sacred places of great energy. There are places of earth energy. There are places of water energy. And then, finally, there are places of star energy.

CREDO MUTWA[33]

Our ancestors in every culture believed that sacred sites all over the Earth are linked by energetic pathways, or ley lines. Australia's Aborigines call them *songlines;* Andean masters know them as *seques.* According to Fredy Quispe, every person's *qosqo* or spiritual stomach also contains a system of *seques* connected with the major power points on the planet and in the universe, as well as with "many, many people and things with whom we are in relation—all the people in your life."[34]

"Aborigines believe they can project their psyche or inner consciousness along these songlines as a means of communicating songs, stories, and knowledge over great distances," Johanna Lambert writes. "It is said that songlines were once a sacred tradition that stretched across the entire earth, and, in this way, cultural knowledge was shared worldwide."[35]

Pilgrimage routes frequently follow these pathways, which in many traditions coincide with the positions of stars. The famous pilgrimage across Spain to Santiago de Compostela ("Field of the Star") is said to follow the path of the Milky Way.[36] Jean Chevalier and Alain Gheerbrant say that

in all traditions the Milky Way is regarded as a roadway, built by the gods, linking their world with the Earth. It symbolizes the road taken by pilgrims, explorers and mystics from one plane to another on Earth, from one plane to another in the cosmos and from one level to another in the psyche. It also marks the boundaries between the busy world and the stillness of eternity.[37]

Mircea Eliade reports that the Kwakiutl people believe the Milky Way is the place where their *axis mundi* enters the upper world.[38] We've seen that for the Mayas, the Milky Way is the source of all life. Africa's shamans connect it to the birth of humanity.

All over the world, the stars' contact points on Earth are mountains, homes of spirits that embody the peaks' different powers.

"Since the sacred mountain is an *axis mundi* connecting earth with heaven, it in a sense touches heaven and hence marks the highest point in the world," says Eliade, adding that in Islamic tradition, the highest place on earth is the Kaaba, "because the Pole Star bears witness that it faces the center of Heaven."[39]

In Peru, the *apu* (mountain spirit) of the snow-covered peak of Ausangate summons pilgrims to receive their *estrellas* (stars)— expressions of the *apu* himself. These are spiritual gifts, which, carried in their hearts, will guide the pilgrims and keep them tethered to the mountain until they return them to the *apu* at the end of their lives.[40]

Pilgrimage, stars, and initiation come together in the Andeans' annual festival of Q'ollorit'i, a high, narrow valley in the range neighboring Ausangate, towered over by the Sinak'ara glacier. Teachers of shamans in training send initiates there to undergo further initiations, cleanse themselves in sacred lagoons, and make *despachos* to the Lord of Q'ollorit'i. Thousands of pilgrims from all over Peru and beyond also take part in the festival, which blends ancient beliefs with Christian legend.

According to the legend, in 1780 a mysterious boy befriended a young llama herder in the valley and helped him so much that his herd flourished. When the llama herder's father asked the boy how he could reward him, the boy asked for some cloth to make himself a new tunic.

The father agreed and took a piece of the boy's tattered tunic as a

Fig. 8.5. Link to the cosmos: the sacred peak of Ausangate in the Peruvian Andes. Photo by Dery Dyer.

sample to a shop in the city of Cuzco—the Inkas' "navel of the world" in the heart of the Andes, which the Spanish turned into an important colonial center—where he was told that the cloth was fine canonical material used only to make priests' robes.

When church authorities went to the valley to investigate, they found the llama herder and his friend standing near a large rock. As Juan Núñez del Prado recounts:

> The mysterious boy ran away and seemed to disappear into the rock itself in a blinding flash of light. It is said that the image of Christ appeared at that moment, etched into the stone. According to the myth, the young Indian llama herder died of shock and was buried beneath the rock.
>
> We know that [Q'ollorit'i] has been an important pilgrimage site since at least 1780, though we suspect that it was a sacred site long before that.[41]

Núñez del Prado tells us that the constellation that watches over the Q'ollorit'i festival is the Pleiades, "which emanates a powerful cosmic influence. This influence, of joining diverse living energies together into a collective whole, truly embraces the energetic and spiritual meaning" of the festival.

STONES AND BONES

The rock central to the Q'ollorit'i legend is only one of countless examples of stones drawing pilgrims to sacred places. In every traditional culture, rocks are considered living beings and repositories of information, power, wisdom, and magic.

Shamans the world over use stones for divination, healing, and energetic cleansing; ancient megalithic structures mark spiritually significant sites in alignment with the positions of celestial bodies.

"A stone is a field of energetic action, of magical action that you express . . . in the language that the stone is connected to—to the moon, or to Pachamama, or to Mama Qocha [ocean or large lake]," says Américo Yabar.[42]

Sioux holy man Frank Fools Crow says that "stones . . . have spiritual power. But this spiritual power must be stirred up by ritual use, so the stones work together with individuals like myself who are hollow bones. It is a very ancient way."[43]

A large egg-shaped rock sits inside the main doors of Cuzco's cathedral. In the syncretistic blend of native and Christian beliefs practiced by Peru's indigenous people, this smoothly polished stone is as holy as any of the Roman Catholic images in the church: it's the Wiraqocha Stone, a "heavy-energy eater," which absorbs people's *hucha* and channels it to Mother Earth.

According to Juan Núñez del Prado, the Wiraqocha Stone is a *khuya,* which "refers to the love energy infused into an object, usually a rock, and given to the student by his master. This love-gift transmits the power of the master to the student. This stone egg is the *khuya* of

Wiraqocha from the superior world," he says. "It is the love-gift to the people of the material world, from Wiraqocha, the metaphysical God of the Inkas, and the great master of the superior world."[44]

A rock is also the origin of the famous pilgrimage to Copacabana on the Bolivian shore of Lake Titicaca. Though pilgrims now make the journey to honor the Virgin of Copacabana, Robin Kazmier tells us that a large sandstone boulder on the Isla del Sol (Island of the Sun) in the lake off the Copacabana peninsula was a sacred site and pilgrimage destination for centuries before the Spanish arrived. According to Kazmier, the Inkas' pilgrimage "was rooted in the creation myth that tells how the sun—the divine being from which the Inka directly descended— was born on *Isla del Sol*," rising from the Sacred Rock after a prolonged period of darkness.[45]

Rocks play similar roles all over the world. According to Credo Mutwa, bladelike strips of ringing stone or "rock gongs" found in South Africa and the ancient ruins of Great Zimbabwe were used to communicate with the stars.[46]

Siberia's Altai people believe that much of their land's spiritual power resides in the mounds of stones known as *kurgans,* which house prehistoric tombs. These burial sites, many marked by tall standing stones that are thought to act as antennae, exchange energy with the cosmos, they say.

Honoring the spirits of the kurgans keeps them strong, while every desecration destabilizes their delicate energetic balance. Danil Mamyev sadly takes visitors to see tumbled piles of rock inexpertly "excavated" by Soviet archaeologists who knew and cared nothing about the tombs' spiritual and energetic significance.[47]

Mamyev has spent years studying these stone mounds, measuring their placement, magnetic fields, and radioactivity. He believes he has begun to uncover evidence to support his people's belief that the kurgans, which contain gold artifacts as well as mummified bodies, were carefully arranged to channel cosmic energy into the Earth.

"The rocks that make up the kurgans are not especially distinctive in appearance, but they contain magnetite," writes Altai Mir University

*Fig. 8.6. Ancient antennae: Bill Pfeiffer greets standing stones
in Siberia's Altai. Photo by Jim Molloy.*

founder Carol Hiltner. "In an undisturbed kurgan, each stone is mag-
netically oriented to enhance the specific magnetic function of the site."
Just as important energetically are the bodies and the gold interred with
them. "Altai lore claims that the bodies serve as crystals, with a function
similar to a quartz crystal in a radio—tuned to a certain frequency; to
adjust the 'life force' arriving in that place, and funneling it into the
planet," Hiltner writes. "However, the electromagnetic energy that
quartz crystals attune is a pale offspring of the 'life force' transmuted
by these 2,500-year-old human crystals. And gold, as all computer scientists know, is a 100 percent conductor."[48]

Such discoveries strengthen the universal native belief that ancient
burial grounds must never be disturbed—and may explain why gold
artifacts were so often buried with bodies.

The Altai people are particularly worried about the Ukok Princess, a shaman and warrior laid to rest on the Ukok Plateau near the Mongolian border some 2,500 years ago. In 1994 archaeologists dug up her mummified body, perfectly preserved under the permafrost and covered in beautiful tattoos depicting fantastic animal-like beings, and moved her to a vacuum chamber in a museum in the Siberian city of Novosibirsk. Since then, she has been taken on tour to other museums, and the Altai people believe this is depleting the energetic balance of their land.

According to shaman Maria Amanchina, the princess has been visiting her in dreams. "The Princess told me, 'It is of crucial importance that I get reburied because I am losing my power and my power is part of the power of the Altai.'"[49]

TURTLE MOTHER'S MESSAGE

Every year when de turtle come around, dat turtle rock turn. It turn and face de land, and when de turtle is over (meaning when the nesting season has finished) it turn back around to de sea.

FISHERMEN WHO LIVE NEAR CERRO TORTUGUERO,
ON COSTA RICA'S CARIBBEAN COAST[50]

If we save the turtle, we save the world.

JACK RUDLOE[51]

Turtle researcher Jack Rudloe first heard the legend of the Great Turtle Mother while working with famed turtle conservationist Archie Carr in Central America in the 1970s. As Rudloe recounts in his beautiful and fascinating book, *Search for the Great Turtle Mother,*

along the lower Caribbean, the old Caiman Island and Miskito Indian fishermen consistently described Turtle Mother as a three-foot-long black rock in the shape of a turtle that normally sat on the beach at the foot of a 500-foot-tall volcanic hill in Tortuguero, Costa Rica—

the last big green sea turtle nesting beach in the Caribbean. The rock sat facing the sea, not moving, until magically it turned.[52]

University of California geographer Bernard Neitchmann described a similar rock on the coast in Miskito territory to the north:

> This rock, called the Turtle Mother, had magical properties. According to the Miskito myth, the Turtle Mother was a benevolent spirit that acted as the intermediary between the world of animals and the world of humans. When the turtles were moving in close to the mainland to nest on the beach or feed in the shallows, the rock would swing around and point westward. When the turtles were to move out into deeper water around the cays, the rock turned and pointed towards the east.
>
> Besides foretelling the movement of turtles so that humans could more easily catch them, the Turtle Mother could also increase success by controlling both a person's luck and the movement of the turtles. . . . The Turtle Mother then symbolically balanced relationships between humans and turtles.
>
> The belief in the Turtle Mother made the Miskito responsible for maintaining prohibitions against overkill: individual greed would bring retaliation to all through the magical removal of the turtles.[53]

As the myth faded, the rock disappeared. Only a few old-timers remembered having seen it; some said it had been "broken." Its disappearance coincided with the diminishing numbers of turtles coming to nest on their ancestral beaches. Theft of eggs, pollution, beach development, and industrial fishing practices that killed turtles as bycatch had driven many sea turtle species to the brink of extinction.

"Legend says that the Turtle Mother rock vanished from the coast of Nicaragua after being harassed and reappeared in Tortuguero, where it was seen for a time before disappearing into a cave on the mountain Cerro Tortuguero," Rudloe writes. "The legend says that only when humankind comes to its senses will the rock return."[54]

Fig. 8.7. Mysterious beacon and Turtle Mother's home: Cerro Tortuguero.
Photo courtesy of Fran Vaughan Watson and Modesto Watson.

Local people have always considered the mysterious, jungle-draped Cerro Tortuguero, which rises incongruously out of the flat expanse of coastline, a magical beacon that served to guide the turtles back to their nesting grounds. According to veteran Tortuguero boat captain and naturalist guide Modesto Watson, people in the area said Mayan priests who came to Costa Rica from northern Central America originally brought the Turtle Mother rock, which they installed in a cave in the mountain. Old-timers told him they'd visited the cave, where the rock occupied a kind of platform flanked by two stone crocodiles.

Modesto and his wife, zoologist and nutrition expert Fran Vaughan Watson, recall that they took Rudloe and Neitchmann to try to visit the cave. Unfortunately, the 7.1 magnitude earthquake of 1991, which raised Costa Rica's Caribbean coastline, had collapsed the cave entrance, forcing the explorers to enter on hands and knees—until swarms of bats obliged them to turn back.

Rudloe was sure that the Turtle Mother legend "had some basis in fact, that it was somehow related to magnetic orientation and all the millions of submicroscopic ferromagnetic crystals that scientists had discovered in the brains of sea turtles." The first confirmation came from the discovery in 1975 by Dartmouth College geographer Vincent Malmstrom that an ancient pre-Olmec stone turtle head found in Izapa, on the Pacific coast of Mexico, had a magnetic nose. The rock had been carved "so that the magnetic lines of force came to focus in the nose. It was bizarre and preposterous—but if true, was the first tangible evidence of the obscure Turtle Mother myth that still scarcely survived on the Caribbean coast of Central America," Rudloe writes.

> There was no way the old turtlemen of the Miskito coast could know about biogenic magnetite, and yet, coincidentally or metaphorically, their nature spirit that manifested in the Turtle Mother rock turned like a compass needle.
>
> Dr. Malmstrom's discovery of the magnetic turtle head could indicate that the ancients knew what scientists and their advanced technology are just beginning to find out: that real flesh-and-blood sea turtles, using submicroscopic crystals concentrated in their nose, migrate across the oceans following the earth's magnetic field. . . .
>
> Submicroscopic bits of lodestone seemed to occur in migratory species almost everywhere scientists looked.[55]

Noting that sea turtles nuzzle the sand with their noses before emerging from the water to nest, Rudloe wonders whether they are

> scanning the organic molecular maps and charts of the area or reading the imprints of the earth's magnetic field on rocks beneath the sand. A mile or so beneath the sands, deep down in the crystalline bedrock formed back in the Mesozoic Era two hundred million years ago, there exists a very stable and constant magnetic field as distinct as your fingerprints. The rocks have their own individual paleomagnetic patterns created when the sea floor erupted and the north or south alignment of the geomagnetic field in existence at the time imprinted on the cooling rocks, creating invisible magnetic stripes. And these patterns, detectable to oceanographers pulling magnetometers from ships, at the sea surface, many thousands of feet above the sea floor, are even more detectable to the turtle.

He remarks, sadly, "It's tough being a sense-dulled human, unable to sense forces that we cannot see or touch, such as gravity, electricity, and magnetism."[56]

Yet it's only modern humans who are "sense-dulled": our ancestors, including the Siberians who built their burial grounds with magnetic stones and the early Americans who carved the Izapa stone and brought Turtle Mother to Tortuguero, were obviously keenly aware of such forces.

A stone turtle altar high on top of a mountain in Tonalá, Mexico, while not magnetic, also pointed to early people's understanding of the mysterious relationship between rocks and turtles. Rudloe recalls the work of Colin Limpus, PhD, Australia's foremost sea turtle biologist, who reported that his country's Aborigines "piled up cobbles and built effigies of turtles and depicted them in rock art to maintain their abundance. Somehow by piling those cobbles in the shape of a turtle and communing with spirits, the aborigines knew how to influence the turtles' behavior," Rudloe speculates. "Perhaps the stone turtle in Tonalá, and the magnetic turtle head in Izapa, tapped into those most ancient rituals which provided food and well-being for the community."[57]

Rudloe collected stones and soil from Cerro Tortuguero and sent them to the Cal Tech Rock Magnetism Laboratory and the physics department at Florida State University. Neither found any special magnetic qualities. But then he brought samples to Philip Callahan, a retired physics professor in Gainesville, Florida, whose magnetic susceptibility meter measures low-frequency electromagnetic fields emanating from rocks.

"Dr. Callahan was taking multiple readings when all of a sudden the machine seemed to go haywire. . . . The rock [from Cerro Tortuguero] was pulsing," Rudloe reports.

"This rock acts just like an antenna," he quotes the professor as saying. "You'll have to rewrite the physics book to explain the mountain's variation. The British talk about 'Ley Lines' and Chinese geomancers lay out their buildings and graves based on Feng Shui—wind and water forces charged with 'Chi' energy. Parts of the earth where 'chi' is intense—certain mountains or watercourses—are called 'dragon spines.' This is one of them."[58]

As his search led him deeper and deeper into the metaphysical mysteries of the natural world, Rudloe realized that Turtle Mother's message was much more profound—and universal—than he'd ever imagined. When he learned of a rock known as the "Mother of the Turtles" in Malaysia, he traveled there to see it and was taken to a stone carved in the shape of a sea turtle high on top of a hill. It was crumbling into pieces. The local people told him this was because the turtles were no longer coming to nest on their beaches—for the same reasons that the turtles' numbers were diminishing in Central America, where the vanished Turtle Mother rock was said to be "broken."

"A feeling of gravity came over me," he writes. "The ancient ways that respected nature were disappearing all over the world. . . . The decline came from our industrialized society, from our grasping the land and squeezing everything we could get out of the water. . . . Loss of spiritual awareness, greed, and ignorance of humanity caused the Turtle Mother spirit to withdraw her turtles and send them far out to sea, perhaps to another land."[59]

In Native American teachings, Turtle is the symbol of Mother Earth. "[Turtle] is the personification of goddess energy, and the eternal Mother from which our lives evolve," say Jamie Sams and David Carson. "In honoring the Earth, we are asked by Turtle to be mindful of the cycle of give and take, to give back to the Mother as she has given to us."[60]

Sea turtles making their annual pilgrimage for thousands of miles to nest on their ancestral beaches reenact the very appearance of life on Earth: from the primordial waters, they emerge onto the land to bury their Earth-shaped eggs in the womb that will both nurture and guide their offspring throughout their lives. The cycle embraces as well all the beings who live from the Mother's generosity, including humans—as long as the balance is kept.

The law of *ayni* is dramatically at work here. When the turtles' migrations/pilgrimages diminish, Turtle Mother no longer receives energetic nourishment from her returning children, nor from the humans who depend on them—and therefore can no longer nourish them in return. The sacred give-and-take is disrupted, along with the collective intelligence that guided it.

Turtle Mother's withdrawal is not punitive—it's simply what happens when sacred reciprocity is not maintained.

"Maybe Turtle Mother wasn't a physical thing but a part of our psyche, hidden in the inner recesses of our minds," Rudloe speculates. "And then again maybe she was manifest in the magnetite crystals that we, along with the turtles, the dolphins, the homing pigeons, and other creatures, possess in our brains, computer chips beeping out not just directional vectors, but also a message telling us that we must live with and not against nature if we are to survive."[61]

Fig. 8.8. Pilgrim: a green turtle heads back to sea after traveling thousands of miles to lay her eggs on the beach at Tortuguero, where she was born. Photo courtesy of Fran Vaughan Watson and Modesto Watson.

9
Black Madonnas and White Lions
Manifestations of Mystery

What could Black Madonnas and White Lions possibly have in common?

A lot more than meets the eye.

At first glance, both seem anomalous. But as Turtle Mother showed us, Gaia always speaks through persistent, compelling mysteries.

The madonnas and the lions emerge spontaneously and apparently inexplicably at specific places on Earth, powerful manifestations of the metaphysical background of the surface reality perceived by most of humanity.

In their blackness and whiteness, they embody the polar extremes—archetypes whose messages resonate deep within our psyches, revealing the continuous flow of information between Earth and Cosmos. Both have strong connections to indigenous wisdom. And their call is always to the collective, urging us to work together for the good of all.

HONORING LA NEGRITA

We're in a human river. We *are* a human river. Both flowing in it and forming it, shoulder to shoulder, feet moving rhythmically, in sneakers, hiking boots, sandals—or no shoes at all—the steady shuffling sound of feet on pavement punctuated by songs, prayers, and bursts of laughter as we flow up and over the Continental Divide on our way to La Negrita.

It's around 8 p.m. on the eve of August 2, and two million of us—close to half the population of this Central American country—are paying homage to Costa Rica's miracle-working patron saint, Our Lady of the Angels, who lives in the basilica in the colonial capital city of Cartago at the foot of Irazú Volcano. Some of us have been walking for days, from all over the country and beyond; the rest of us—families, singles, grandparents, teenagers, old people pushed in wheelchairs, babies pushed in strollers—are making the annual pilgrimage from San José, the nation's modern-day capital, to arrive at the basilica twenty-four kilometers away sometime during the night or the following day, Negrita's day.

Half of the divided highway to Cartago has been closed for the occasion, and we fill every inch of it. Along the way vendors hawk sodas, water, and rosaries; signs in front of houses offer "clean bathrooms." Billboards cheer the *romeros* (pilgrims) on, announcing how many kilometers we've covered; homeowners hand out free cups of steaming coffee or *agua dulce,* water sweetened with brown loaf sugar.

Brightly lit Red Cross posts provide first aid and massages for worn-out walkers daunted by the steady climb to the Continental Divide, five thousand feet above sea level. We are crossing from the Pacific slope to the Caribbean side, with accompanying shifts in wind and weather patterns.

The atmosphere is joyful and festive. Like the turtles guided through the ocean by Turtle Mother, we are moving along ancestral energetic pathways determined, perhaps, by the stars and kept vital by the collective energy of so many feet, so much hope, so much devotion to the little Black Virgin who gives so much to this country and its people. Many credit Negrita's love and protection with keeping Costa Rica a peaceful oasis in a turbulent, violent part of the world.

When our river finally pours down the other side of the divide and into the sea of humanity packing the broad plaza in front of the graceful white basilica, a Byzantine structure ablaze in lights, the flow abruptly halts. We stand pressed together front, back, and sides, grateful for the mass of bodies supporting our tired selves. Music and occasional announcements blare over loudspeakers.

Eventually we inch forward, one shuffled step at a time, dimly discerning rivulets in the distance that seem to be trickling out from the jumble, funneling people in the direction of two huge signs above the church entrances—one for those on foot, one for those who want to enter on their knees. We step carefully around exhausted pilgrims curled on the ground; some have set up tents to await the dawn and the official mass that will be attended by the nation's dignitaries.

Finally we are inside the cavernous sanctuary, which has been emptied of pews. Our river resumes its flow in two parallel channels moving steadily along the colorful tiled floors, and now, at last, we can see her: a tiny dark figure surrounded by a golden, jewel-encrusted corona, looking down on her weary and hopeful children from high above the main altar. Some pilgrims are in tears.

The Little Black One. Carved of dark greenish-gray stone—believed to be a mixture of graphite, jade, and volcanic rock—La Negrita is only six inches tall. Yet she and her miracles have drawn millions to this sacred spot for almost four hundred years.

Fig. 9.1. Miracle worker: La Negrita, Costa Rica's Black Madonna. Photo courtesy of the Tico Times.

Her story—with an added local twist—links her to countless other Black Madonnas throughout the world, all of whom embody a mystery that is eons old.

NEGRITA'S STORY

In 1635, Cartago was a segregated city. Blacks, indigenous, and mestizos lived on the fringes and were not permitted to mingle with the "pure" whites of Spanish descent.

One day a young mestiza girl named Juana Pereira went into the forest to gather firewood. Suddenly she spotted, perched atop a boulder in the middle of the woods near a spring that bubbled into a creek, a dark stone statuette of a woman holding a baby in her left arm.

Though crudely carved, mother and child wore serene expressions. The mother was leaning slightly over the child in a protective attitude; the baby's right hand rested against her heart. The simple little statue resembled depictions of the Virgin Mary with the baby Jesus, but the way the mother held the baby over the draped folds of her mantle also recalled the way indigenous mothers carry their children in their shawls.

Juana was delighted with her find and happily took the statue home. But the next day, it wasn't where she had put it. After looking everywhere for it, she returned to the forest for more firewood—and there was her figurine, on the rock where she had found it the day before.

Suspecting that somebody had played a trick on her, Juana took the statue home again. This time she hid it carefully in a box—only to have the same thing happen again.

Juana realized that something strange was going on and decided to ask the village priest about it. The priest placed the statue on the altar of the village's small chapel. But La Negrita disappeared again, showing up back on the boulder in the forest.

After this happened three times, despite his efforts to keep it under lock and key, the priest concluded that the statue was a manifestation of the Virgin Mary, who was indicating quite clearly that she wanted a church built on the site of the rock. And in a remarkably enlightened interpretation, he declared that because she was black, La Negrita was also telling the world that God loves all his children equally, no matter what their color.

A church was built over the rock. The spring became a source of holy water. The fame of Our Lady of the Angels as a powerful miracle worker quickly spread, attracting pilgrims from all over Central America.

Eventually the church evolved into a basilica, which today has rooms and cabinets filled with ex-votos and other testimonials—diplomas, trophies, models of houses, cars, airplanes, ships, medical certificates—left by grateful pilgrims in thanks for Negrita's miracles.

One of the most dramatic gifts of gratitude is an oar from a six-foot plastic raft presented to La Negrita by Bill and Simonne Butler, a Miami couple rescued by the Costa Rican Coast Guard in August 1989, sixty-six days after pilot whales sank their thirty-eight-foot sailboat in the Pacific Ocean. Simonne, 52, and Bill, 60, credited Negrita with their rescue when, exhausted and emaciated, their battered raft leaking and under continuous attack by sharks, they picked up a news report on their faltering radio of the annual pilgrimage to Costa Rica's beloved Black Virgin and decided to pray to her.

Shortly afterward—fortuitously, since it was not following its usual route—a patrol vessel spotted and rescued them.[1] The couple later published a book about their ordeal, *Our Last Chance,* which they also presented to Negrita.

People can still touch the rock beneath the church where the Virgin first appeared and fill bottles with holy water from the original spring to the north of the basilica, which flows continuously into pipes under the church. Tested regularly, the water is pure and untreated, despite the fact that the forest that once sheltered the spring is now a city.

NEGRITA'S GIFT TO ME

I was desperate. I'd been in the hospital with a broken hip for a month and there was no end in sight. The hip wasn't the problem. For some reason, after the surgery, my potassium levels remained stubbornly low every day, and doctors wouldn't let me leave unless they were normal.

It was August 1, the night of the Negrita pilgrimage. "Negrita, you are the only one who can get me out of here! Please help me!" I begged.

When one of the doctors appeared on his rounds later that evening, he was smiling—for the first time in weeks. "Your potassium is normal!" he announced.

The doctors agreed it was a miracle!

Thank you, Negrita!

AN ANCIENT PATTERN

La Negrita's story is far from unique. In fact, it's repeated throughout the world, wherever shrines dedicated to the Virgin Mary have become known as miraculous places of healing and pilgrimage. The statues documented in at least five hundred such places in Europe alone, and in at least thirty countries elsewhere in the world, are black.

"There are many Black Madonnas throughout Western Europe," writes Jean Markale in his exhaustively researched study, *Cathedral of the Black Madonna,* which sifts through the many layers of spiritual beliefs underlying Chartres Cathedral in France. "These objects of worship and even pilgrimage have been a source of much fascination, both for their black color and for the mystery of their origins. If a list were made of all the statues and statuettes in this category, the number would be staggering."[2]

The places where Black Madonnas appeared were considered holy long before Christianity, and the metamorphosis from pagan to Christian of statues believed to depict the Virgin and Child generally followed a well-established pattern. Markale explains:

During the first centuries of Christianity, and even long afterward, pagan images became Christian images because of an analogy of form or function. The sculpted pairs of Cybele and Attis, Venus and Adonis were easily transformed into Virgin and Child. . . . As for the countless *matronae* statues, the Gallic Mother Goddess holding a child on her knee, they were easy to pass off as the Virgin with the infant Jesus.[3]

Discoveries of such statues often involved the so-called "return," which Markale says was widespread throughout Europe, and which Negrita's story retells almost word for word.

E. Saillens, author of *Nos vierges noires* (Our black virgins), says:

The image having been discovered in some deserted, even uninhabitable if not outright inaccessible spot, the finder, who is never a priest, brings it back home. During the night it returns to the place where it was found.

The peasant then turns to the local priest, who carries it to the parish, but the next morning it is back in its original location. The priest goes in search of it with cross and banner, but it flees again. It proves necessary to build a chapel for it exactly where it was found.

According to Markale, this was the origin of a large number of sanctuaries dedicated to the Virgin. Saillens adds:

And, of course, whatever reality there may be to the marvelous events surrounding the finding of the magical image, the image itself is necessarily miraculous and cases can always be cited of miraculous healings or the granting of simple wishes to those who came to see it on pious pilgrimage.[4]

Given this pattern, it would be easy to dismiss La Negrita, her story, her pilgrimages, and her miracles as just another example of the Catholic Church opportunistically usurping native beliefs to exploit the credulous and perpetuate its own power: the blueprint having been successfully established in Europe, church officials had only to transfer it to Costa Rica, where it accomplished the additional task of promoting racial equality.

It would be easy . . . if we didn't know what we now know about the realities that underlie our surface perceptions, all of which point to something far more interesting going on here.

DEEPENING THE DARKNESS

To say that one is "longing for darkness" is to say that one longs for transformation, for a darkness that brings balance, wholeness, integration, wisdom, insight.

CHINA GALLAND[5]

Black Madonnas, and their dark counterparts in other traditions, are multilayered manifestations of the Divine Feminine. They come into our reality with a primordial mission: to restore unity. They operate through continuous sacred exchange, animated and sustained by collective intelligence.

With them, we find ourselves back in the realm of the Goddess. Ancient Black Goddesses—such as Egypt's Isis; the Sumerian-Babylonian Ishtar or Inanna, who eventually evolved into Astarte; Cybele and Artemis (who, we will recall, were bee goddesses)—continue to guide our lives as Kali, Green (which can also mean *dark* in Tibetan) and Black Tara, the Andeans' Princess of the Black Light, and the Black Virgin Mary. Jean Markale tells us: "Cybele is derived from the Neolithic goddess of life and death, of war and fertility, who is the origin of every creature, human and animal. She is the material representation of the generative principle that transmutes and transforms the world."[6]

Interestingly, according to Andrew Gough, Cybele was often worshipped in the form of a meteorite stone, or "a stone from heaven."[7]

Why are they black?

Because we need them to be. As an archetype, the Dark Feminine carries the power of the Earth and maintains our connection with it. It's significant that the madonnas are always found by indigenous people: farmers or peasants—folk with strong connections to the Earth. And they are often associated with rocks.

For those of us in the modern world who have lost our ancestors' "double vision," the Dark Feminine restores our psyches to wholeness by allowing us to again be comfortable with paradox. It helps us embrace the dual nature of the Goddess and accept that destruction and creation, darkness and light, are part of the same divinity, as expressed in the ever-changing nature of the moon: many Black Madonnas, such as Mexico's Virgin of Guadalupe, evolved from ancient moon goddesses and are often depicted with a crescent moon.

"It is more difficult for us to accept this contradictory nature than it was for primitive peoples," observes Fred Gustafson. "Our more rational mind cannot easily tolerate such a flux. Yet both the light and dark poles are always present, no matter how neatly one or the other may be covered. Both are always at work and indispensable to the mysterious round of life and death, growth and decay."[8]

For Andeans, the perilous and paradoxical power of the Divine Feminine is encountered in the essence of contradiction: Black Light. This is found, among other places, in the mighty Urubamba River, which roars and tumbles past all the sacred Inka sites from Cuzco to Machu Picchu, linking them physically as well as energetically. The waterway's ancient name was Willkañusta, which, according to Juan Núñez del Prado, means "Princess of the Black Light."

"*Willka* means at once 'sacred' and 'dangerous' and related with the power of the Black Light. *Ñusta* is the Inka word for 'princess,'" he explains. "The Black Light is the most sacred and most dangerous power in our tradition because the one who tames the Black Light has power over life and death. It is really the ultimate creative power which walks hand in hand with the power of destruction."[9]

According to *The Book of Symbols,* the color black contains both life and death:

> Black dirt can be the soil itself, the fertile covering of the earth from which life arises. In Ancient Egypt black evoked death but also life, as the black silt of the inundating Nile brought fertility; the resurrecting god Osiris was sometimes depicted with black skin, sometimes green.

. . . The "black" deities are ambiguous, chthonic, and fateful. Divine smiths are black with the soot of volcanic forges in Psyche's fiery, creative depths.

The dark ground of Kali, the Black One, absorbs the blood of sacrifice and nature's slaughter and nurtures the seeds of return. Black Mary, Isis, Persephone, Artemis, Hecate possess the black womb of uncanny darkness and new moon.[10]

MADONNAS AND MAGIC

The Black Goddesses, including the madonnas, are linked to the ancient Egyptian occult science of alchemy, again underscoring their connection with the primal powers of creation. Our word *alchemy* may be derived, through the Greek, from an old name for Egypt, *khem*, which means "land of black earth."[11]

According to Barbara Walker, "Mary the Jewess" was said to have been the first great alchemist. "Mary-Sophia was the Goddess of both Gnosticism and alchemy," she writes. "The Philosopher's Stone was sometimes called the Sophistical Stone. Alchemical writings called the hidden Goddess the Mother of Wisdom, combining elements of the Madonna with those of the pagan mother-image."[12]

Jean Markale and Fred Gustafson both mention the Shulamite in the Old Testament's Song of Songs, who is black because she was burned by the sun (Song of Songs 1:6). They note that the first stage of the alchemical process is the *nigredo* (blackening), when the *materia prima* (primordial matter) is tempered and blackened by fire. Explains Markale:

The Virgin Mary . . . is nothing other than the *materia prima* of the alchemical work, a series of metamorphoses that lead to the creation of the philosopher's stone, the crystallization not only of all knowledge, but also of all energies. Whether it is the Holy Ghost whose shadow covered Mary or the secret fire of the alchemists, the result of the operation remains the same: The primal matter turns black. But this is because, when impregnated by the Spirit, it can give birth to the One who will be the Light, Jesus in the evangelical scriptures, the philosopher's stone in alchemical treatises.[13]

SACRED SETTINGS

Like their pre-Christian predecessors, Black Madonnas emerge in natural settings and remain deeply part of them. The images are inseparable from their "birthplaces": they don't move around or appear anywhere else, and they draw people to them. The sites themselves are a vital aspect of the madonnas' power.

"At each site where a Black Madonna can be found, ancient legends surrounding the presence of a sacred fountain, a sacred tree, or a healing spring awaken the shadows of the past, including the worship of the Mother Goddess," writes Jean Markale.[14]

La Negrita, herself carved from stone, appeared on a rock.

Remember that rocks considered especially sacred, including the Wiraqocha Stone (which, interestingly, shares the Cuzco cathedral with Our Lord of Earthquakes, a Black Christ), apparently emit unusual energy. The rock at Q'ollorit'i had drawn pilgrims to its glacier valley long before the dramatic events that emblazoned Christ's image on it (the literal superimposition of Christian over pre-Christian belief), while the stone at Copacabana was a pilgrimage destination long before the Virgin arrived on the scene.

The rock where Negrita appeared happened to be located near a spring, in a forest. The Black Madonna of Einsiedeln in Switzerland appeared in the Finsterwald, the Dark Forest. Chartres Cathedral is home to two madonnas: Our Lady of the Pillar—a Black Madonna—and Our Lady of Under Ground, which Markale says may originally have been a petroglyph.[15]

Chartres was built over a well whose water was believed to have miraculous powers, on a mound in a *nemeton*—a circular clearing in the forest used by Druids for their rituals. Markale tells us that the Celts "thought there were places, symbolic or real, where the human world could open onto the world of the gods and vice versa; the *nemeton* is this place of sacred exchange . . . every *nemeton* is the center of the world."[16]

Significantly, the cathedral also houses an important symbol of circle magic and the Goddess: a labyrinth whose circular path is 666 feet long.[17] (Remember, 666 was Aphrodite's number.)

As we've seen in many ancient and indigenous traditions as well as the PEAR experiments, power places are spots where cosmic energies seem to concentrate and Mother Earth herself speaks. But they are also places that draw her children's collective consciousness to act in reciprocity and renew her energies with their own. Markale stresses:

> It is human beings who establish this center, through their intuition. The *nemeton* is never chosen at random. Most of the time, it is located at the site of a prehistoric sanctuary, because sacred tradition demands that certain privileged spots remain so even if the religious ideology changes.
>
> Sacred places are really privileged places, either because "supernatural events" occurred there that defy our understanding . . . or because the psychic strength of individuals practicing rituals there for centuries eventually permeated the site with what is called an *aura,* or an *égrégore* (this seems to be the case with Chartres).[18]

Philologist Peter Lindegger tells writer China Galland:

> The Black Madonna is the most contemporary form of the idea of a very old goddess, whether we are talking about our Madonna here in Switzerland or one in France. She had different names, forms, and functions in different cultures. The ground her shrine or temple was built on was itself holy.
>
> One cannot make the ground holy, it simply is. Knowing this, one culture would incorporate the sacred sites of the preceding culture, building one temple over another temple or calling the same statue by a different name. If you didn't do this, the people would worship there anyway.[19]

POWER AND POTENTIAL

Black Madonnas are mothers—or future mothers. The Madonna always appears carrying a child, or expecting one.

Mary's virginity refers not so much to her unsullied physical state as to her power. Jean Markale tells us that the word *virgin* "comes from an Indo-European root that means 'strength' and 'potency.' The Virgin is literally 'the Powerful One,' and that is all. But this gives sufficient indication of the *potentiality* she represents. . . . Mary represented a *perpetual maternity*. She is the one who regenerates, who allows transcendence. She is, like her son, the Resurrection and the Life. She cannot die because *she is life*. This is a fundamental idea inherited from the dawn of time, and it is clear that it is superimposed over the concept of the Great Goddess of the Beginnings."[20]

Alice O. Howell adds an interesting twist to this idea when she points out that there were other virgin births: "I had to find out for myself that Gautama Buddha's mother, though married to a king, conceived by the holy spirit through a vision of a white elephant; that Krishna had a virgin mother, Devaki; that Cuchullain, the Celtic hero, and Adonis, Attis, Osiris, Dionysus, Zoroaster, Herakles, and many others, be they solar heroes or human saviors, had virgin births," she writes. This, she believes, indicates that the notion of virgin birth enacts a powerful archetypal process—"a symbolically beautiful way of expressing a truth in the realm of the psyche. It is, perhaps, the closest way the collective can come to describing the Divine Child in us; the undiscovered Self," she explains. "Any such inner conception will by its very nature be a virgin birth and of a spiritual father. For the Spirit to incarnate in any of us, we have to have a body or a vessel or a grail."[21]

It reminds us that every Virgin thus blessed is expressing the power of the Great Mother—Mother Earth. This is what enables her to play out the age-old love story between Heaven and Earth, spirit and matter, giving life to the divine.

The Black Madonnas show us this again and again. Our Lady of Under Ground, located in a subterranean crypt next to Chartres's holy well, represents a *virgo paritura*—the "virgin about to give birth" wor-shipped by the Druids.[22] The Virgin of Guadalupe, who appeared to the indigenous farmer Juan Diego, "wore a black belt above her waist, traditional Indian style, indicating that she was pregnant."[23]

NEED FOR THE DARK

Jean Markale notes that "quite often the Black Madonnas were dark-ened intentionally, as if someone wished the color to signify something specific."[24] Fred Gustafson adds:

> It is not historic accident that popular demand had the Virgin [of Einsiedeln] remain black following her renovation in 1799. These were common people, peasants who reacted from what can simply be called a common or earth-oriented side of the soul.
>
> This common or natural side of every person has a wisdom beyond that handed down by traditional culture. Through their demand . . . they met their need for psychological balance.
>
> The attraction of the Black Madonna was felt unconsciously, and it is to this side of the psyche that she makes her greatest appeal.[25]

The need for Black Madonnas seems to spring from the collective understanding that the Dark Feminine, like nature itself, is part of us. Though fearsome, the Black Goddesses were a vital source of psychic power before they were sanitized and satanized. Robert Bly notes that "the Indians imagine Kali as the initiating, instigating, active, forceful divine energy in the universe. She starts things."[26]

"Whenever the wild diversity of experience is twisted into a sim-ple opposition between what's good and what's bad, whenever the heterogeneous multiplicity of life is polarized into a battle between a pure Good and a pure Evil, then the earth itself is bound to suffer at our hands," David Abram points out. "When the sacred is concep-tually stripped of its various shadows and idealized as a pure light, or Goodness without any taint of the dark, then those stripped-away shadows inevitably seem to gather into a concentrated and implacable gloom, or Badness."[27]

In demanding the right to be selective about nature, accepting only the domesticated and the light (loving Mother, gentle breezes, refreshing rain, cozy hearth fires, flowers) while rejecting the wild and the dark (devouring Goddess, tornadoes, tsunamis, forest fires, earthquakes), we lost our access to the life force that is available only by embracing the whole: nature's darkness and our own.

And so the Black Madonnas appear, even in our dreams. The Dark Goddess refuses to be forgotten or "whitened." According to Marion Woodman:

> In the dreams of contemporary men and women, there is appearing with increasing frequency the image of a sensual, sexual, earthy Black Madonna. This is not an idealized, chaste, detached Madonna, high up on a pedestal. This is a Madonna who loves her own body, her own flirtations, her own compassionate presence among human beings. . . . That she is beginning to surface in contemporary dreams suggests that as a race we are at last beginning to find in ourselves a vision of the feminine that has been buried in the unconscious for too long.[28]

Jungian analyst Dora Kalff tells China Galland that "when the Black Madonna comes [in dreams], I usually see this as the first impulse of the good feminine. When she appears, then we can guess that the psyche is beginning to grow in a spiritual direction, spiritual as together with everyday life, with the body, the earth. Not separate."[29]

We need her, and she is there, restoring balance. The Black Madonna "is a collective expression in image form which compensates the collective conscious mentality of our age . . . an expression of the need for psychic-spiritual wholeness in an age and culture that has far over-valued the place of reason and the need for causal explanation," Gustafson says. "Never before in history have we so sorely needed to reconnect ourselves with the earth, to find our place in the total ecological system, to reacquaint ourselves with Her mysteries, to revere Her giving and taking and to learn again that there is no spiritual life that is not rooted in the soil."[30]

MADONNAS AND MIRACLES

At one point in the Broadway production of *Peter Pan,* Tinkerbell is dying because people no longer believe in fairies. In desperation, Peter turns to the audience.

"Do you believe in fairies?" he asks. "Please! If you believe in fairies, clap your hands!"

The audience responds with thunderous applause, and Tinkerbell is saved.

Here the boy who refused to grow up shows us that it's important to keep seeing the world through a child's eyes: by believing in magic and miracles, we make them happen. The pilgrims who pay homage to the miracle-working Black Madonnas seem to know this. At some deep level, they understand that miracles require an energy exchange.

A 2015 survey by the Costa Rican Technological Institute found that 98 percent of the people who took part in the pilgrimage to La Negrita in 2014 said they believe in miracles. Most declared that they had experienced or knew someone close to them who had experienced a miracle thanks to Negrita, and more than half said they were making the trek in gratitude for prayers miraculously answered.[31]

Given that some two million people make the pilgrimage each year, that's a lot of miracles—and a lot of faith, all of it focused on a single tiny stone statue above a single rock.

The fact that Black Madonnas everywhere are renowned as miracle workers seems to unite the power of rocks and sacred sites with the power of belief and intention. Could we be drawn to these sites because the Earth needs us as much as we need miracles?

China Galland offers a possible answer when she asks the lama Tulku Chos Ki Nyima Rinpoche about an image of the Tibetan Buddha Tara that is mysteriously growing out of a rock in Nepal. The lama responds:

The power of devotion calls Tara out of the rock, yes? We have many occurrences like this in Tibetan Buddhism. We call it *rangjung,* it means "self-arising.". . . These things appear because of the power and blessings of enlightened beings. Such beings work through the power of mental substance and the power of concentration.

Western science has been working with the power of material substance for some time, but the power of mental substance and the power of concentration can accomplish incredible things as well. Under the right circumstances, the enlightened mind concentrated in a certain direction can even bring an image of the deity out of solid rock.[32]

The Dalai Lama agrees that Tara's appearance in the rock is an example of *rangjung,* a miraculous phenomenon that blends human and divine energy. He tells Galland:

There's a great sort of interrelationship between the appropriateness of the time, the place, and also a person intimately related to it. All these factors must be taken into account.

When suitable people remain there, the image remains. When there are no more suitable people there, the image also disappears.[33]

"*Rangjung* is a very precious thing," Tibetan scholar Tashi Tsering tells Galland. "The veil drops, another reality penetrates, and all the blessings of that deity are concentrated. To us it is natural, not amazing."[34]

Galland notes that "Buddha Tara, indeed all the Buddhas, are said to emanate in billions of forms, taking whatever form is necessary to suit the person. Who can say that Mary isn't Tara appearing as a form that is useful and recognizable to the West?"[35]

For that matter, who can say that Tara, Mary, and all of their dark predecessors aren't forms taken by Mother Earth to guide and aid her children according to the culture and the epoch they are living in?

No matter what her form, she calls us with her miracles, and we, collectively, answer with the energy that sustains her. Her message is clear: nourish me and you will be nourished; care for me and you will be cared for.

Ayni.

WHITE LIONS: LIVING ARCHETYPES

Like bees and turtles, the White Lions of South Africa are living archetypes. They exist in multiple dimensions of reality, asking us to relate to them not only as living animals, but as embodiments of the divine.

While Black Madonnas are expressions of the earth and the moon, White Lions are manifestations of the stars and the sun. Like the Madonnas, the lions are inseparable from their "birthplaces" and bring a vital message.

The mystery of the White Lions that unfolds in Linda Tucker's book of the same name weaves together many of the strands of wisdom preserved in other native traditions—fittingly, since Africa is likely their most ancient source on Earth—and gives them an intriguing new context. Tucker recounts how, under the guidance of two powerful shaman teachers, she uncovers the connection between White Lions and humanity's birth and future.

The snowy-coated, blue-eyed lions appear only in the Timbavati region of South Africa and, though considered sacred by tribal people, have been hunted almost to extinction. Tucker finds her destiny entangled with them after she and a group of friends blunder into the territory of an angry pride of tawny lions one night and are rescued by a shaman.

The shaman, Maria Khosa, becomes Tucker's teacher and connects her with Credo Mutwa, Africa's Lion Priest, who eventually initiates her into the mysteries of lion shamanism and helps her understand the White Lions' significance.

Fearing the ridicule of her academic colleagues, the Cambridge-educated Tucker initially struggles to fit her "paranormal" experiences and the information she is receiving from her native teachers into the accepted norms of Old Paradigm science. But finally she realizes that "I had to ake a stand—either for science or for sacred science." When she decides to accept the validity of the ancestral wisdom preserved in Africa's highly complex and secret shamanic tradition, she receives a sweeping view of the big picture totally missed by the old science, and the puzzle pieces fall into place in "one truly amazing hologramatic whole."[36]

LIONS R US

From Mutwa, Tucker learns that lions and early man carried out a "sacred exchange of souls," and the lions' gift to humanity was "lion-heartedness"—bravery, nobility, kingship, and the divine brilliance of the sun.

"In old Africa, ma'am, we believed that human beings could not exist without animals, birds, and fishes or trees," Mutwa tells Tucker. "We believed that the universe was not only all around us—but also within us. For this reason, many African gods were depicted as part animal and part human."[37]

The gift of animals' divine qualities is reflected in the many animal-headed or animal-bodied deities found in ancient Egypt, such as Sekhmet, Hathor, Horus, Anubis, Thoth, and the Sphinx. As we've seen, shapeshifting as practiced by ancient and indigenous shamans worldwide often involves exchanging powers with animals.

During a visit to Egypt, Tucker learns that the gods and goddesses associated with the Egyptian *zep tepi,* or "First Time," when humans first appeared on Earth, were leonine.

"Since the ancients believed that these leonine star gods were not only real and living figures, but arrived on earth at a specific leonine moment of time, the commencement of the Egyptian calendar of First Time leads to the idea that these lion gods were concurrent with a former Leo Age," she writes.[38]

When she realizes that the Southern Hemisphere, where the White Lions have appeared in our time, is a mirror image of the Northern Hemisphere, Tucker has the sudden insight that the Southern Hemisphere is entering a new Age of Leo—the mirror image of the

Age of Aquarius starting in the North—and a new cycle of time that could be marking the return of the lion gods.

LIONS, STARS, STONES, AND SOUND

The first lesson Tucker learns from Maria Khosa is that "if you kill a White Lion, you kill the world"—the lions are "supreme protectors of the land, sacred guardians of our earth."[39] Khosa also says that the name of the lions' "birthplace," Timbavati, means "river of stars" or "the river that never runs dry." The White Lions, she says, come from the Milky Way—the sacred star path in so many traditions.

Mutwa repeatedly tells Tucker, "Never forget that the story of the White Lions is connected to the stars." He says the Bushmen's sacred word for lion—*tsau!*—means "star beast."[40]

In Egypt, Tucker discovers a key connection between sound, stones, stars, and lions: she learns that some Egyptologists believe the pyramids in Egypt may have been built using sound frequencies.

> Judging from the current research of archeoastronomers on the sound emission frequencies of stone, and their proposal that the Egyptian obelisks were giant "tuning forks" used to "tune in" to the frequency of certain stars, Mutwa's point about the ringing stones of Timbavati and Great Zimbabwe being used for purposes of communication with the celestial bodies struck me as a fitting echo.
>
> The original meaning of "the Word" is identified with the notion of sound. In Bushman culture, the word *Tsau!*—the lion word— carries the same vibratory power as the beast itself, a sonic resonance befitting a sun god. . . .
>
> The ancient Egyptians viewed the energy of the sun—the solar Logos—as the cosmic law that linked lions, humans, and stars in our archetypal consciousness.[41]

Mutwa also refers to the "star power" harnessed by ancient lion priests, which enabled them to "move objects with sheer mind-power."[42]

This coincides remarkably with the Tibetan Buddhists' *rangjung*, as well as with the legend of Inkarí, the first Inka, who was believed to have power over stones.

How the Inkas built their sacred structures out of enormous stones weighing hundreds of tons and carved to fit together so perfectly that a knife blade can't be inserted between them has long baffled scientists. Not only did the Inkas not use the wheel, but many of their structures were built on sheer slopes, where wheels would have been useless.

Q'ero elder don Julián Pauqar Flores believes the legend of Inkarí, with its message of the power of love, holds the answer. As he recounts it to Joan Parisi Wilcox:

> God appeared as a man to Inkarí and told him, "Inkarí, I will give you more *munay* [capacity to love]," don Julián recounts. "But Inkarí said, 'What *munay*? I have my own *munay*.'"
>
> God saw out of the corner of his eye that Inkarí was herding rocks with a crop, like we would herd llamas. Inkarí built houses this way, not doing useful work but saying to the stones, "You must become a wall!" And the stones became a wall.
>
> But over time, the stones began to disobey Inkarí.
>
> Seeing this and wanting to restore the stones' abilities, Inkarí remembered the person who had offered him more *munay*. Inkarí now looked for this person, but the person had disappeared. And because of that, now men must carry stones only by the power of their own arms. We can no longer make the stones obey our will.
>
> If Inkarí had received that additional *munay*, we could today build houses by commanding the stones to move.[43]

Joseph Chilton Pearce notes that the ruins of Baalbek in Lebanon contain a structure composed of stones ranging in size from 750 to more than a thousand tons each, "cut and fitted so perfectly that at first the structure was thought to have been carved from a single immense rock bed."[44]

He believes that this ancient monument and similar ones around the world whose construction can't be explained are evidence that early humans used "concrete operational thinking, which a child begins to employ at about age seven and which is poorly developed in most of us. It involves the ability to operate on or change some or all characteristics of a physical process or material through the use of an abstract idea."

According to Pearce, most of humanity lost this ability because of the supposed traumatic event that he insists changed our brains in ancient times—the "calamity [that] shocked the species into a defensive recoil from which it hasn't recovered. Because of the self-replicating imprint a fear-based culture brings about in each new generation, we haven't yet regained our balance as a species on any functional, widespread level," he maintains. "We essentially lost our nerve and haven't regained it."[45]

In other words, for most of humanity, fear stifled the power of love—the *munay* God offered Inkarí. Only Tibetan Buddhists, with their ability to use love to draw holy images out of rock, seem to have retained this power.

SACRED GEOGRAPHY

Tucker gives us fresh insights into the significance of animal migrations and human pilgrimages when she learns that the Milky Way is believed to mark the route not only of the Nile River, but also of a vast underground river that, in Credo Mutwa's words, "is said to hold the continent of Africa together."

She discovers that the Nilotic Meridian, a longitudinal line that marks the center of the Earth's landmasses, also follows the Nile and directly connects Timbavati, the White Lions' "birthplace," with Giza in Egypt. The sacred site of Great Zimbabwe falls on the same line. And the meridian passes through the Rift Valley, "that geographical faultline now understood by modern scientists [and described by Hank Wesselman] as 'birth canal of the human species.'"[46]

"I began to visualize the notion of a 'river' in terms of waves, streams, frequencies," Tucker reports. "I began to suspect that what was meant was an energy line of sorts beneath the surface of the earth, whether one understood it in terms of a faultline of Western seismology, or the more ancient notion of ley lines, such as songlines (Aboriginal), dragonlines (Feng Shui), or chakras (Indian). . . . I knew that animals such as whales, elephants, and lions followed ancestral paths generation after generation. . . . For some reason, animals—like shamans around the globe—can tap subterranean energy currents. Similarly, the world's ancient tribes believe that walking these sacred paths is an act of creation."[47]

And let's not forget the ancient mystical connection of bees with both the Milky Way and Egypt's lion deities.

THE VITAL LINK

Tucker learns from Mutwa that the subterranean river "also appeared to be a vein of gold running beneath the African continent"—and that mining the precious metal has been causing severe energetic imbalances.[48]

We've seen that ancient and indigenous cultures that used gold to fashion their spiritual art frequently buried their dead with golden jewelry and artifacts. Remembering the Altai people's belief that gold and human bones interred in their stone *kurgans* draw cosmic energy to the Earth, one wonders: could early gold-mining cultures have been aware that gold taken from the Earth needed to be returned to it at regular intervals to maintain the planet's energetic balance?

Gold turns out to be the vital link connecting the White Lions to humanity's birth—and future. Tucker notices that gold-smelting sites

> seemed to cluster around the Nilotic Meridian, reminding me that this strip of the earth's geology appeared to have been the gold-producing center of the ancient world as far back as biblical and ancient Egyptian times (and very possibly further back in prehistory). Zimbabwe's secret word—*zim*—not only had to do with a lion, and the soul of a king, but also with gold. It intrigued me that lions and gold might be associated even at a geographical level, just as they were associated at a symbolic level.[49]

And then, "as if struck by lightning," she remembers that the South African gold-mining town of Barberton, positioned precisely on the Nilotic Meridian, "is the place where geologists believe life on the planet may have begun . . . the possible origin of the first organisms to use energy from sunlight to grow."[50]

And there's more. As we learned, a circle with a dot in the middle is the ancient symbol for both the sun and gold. Tucker points out:

> In ancient alchemical theory, as in many symbolic texts, gold is the image of solar light and, hence, of divine intelligence, both physical and metaphysical. The sun is also directly identified with the transmutation of prime matter (earth) into gold. In alchemy, the lion is often depicted "roaring" the sun, suggesting that the lion's roar issues forth the solar Logos, the Word of the sun.[51]

SACRED MESSENGERS

As above, so below.

Tucker realizes that the last Age of Leo in the Northern Hemisphere coincided with the end of the last Ice Age some 11,500 years ago. "The lions at that time would most likely have been white," she notes. "A white coat would naturally provide a selective advantage in glacial environs."[52]

Could their reappearance now mean that another Ice Age—literal, figurative, or both—is on its way? Tucker believes so—unless humanity wakes up. Fear, she says, "freezes consciousness"—precisely what Pearce believes happened to humanity in ancient times. "We tend to think of evolution as simply a physiological event," Tucker explains. "But if the shamans and lion ancestral spirits are anything to go by, humankind's challenge at this time appears to be in the nature of spiritual evolution: raising our consciousness. In its present course, our mass mind-set can only lead to disaster."[53]

The near-extinction of sacred messengers—White Lions, bees,

turtles—in our era is one of the ominous signs showing how fear in the form of collective stupidity can extinguish the light of awareness. The White Lions, Tucker insists, are an "early warning signal" to teach us "to overcome fear by summoning principles of courage, faith, and love."[54]

WHAT'S LOVE GOT TO DO WITH IT?

As we'll see in part 3, the new vision of our world that's emerging from current scientific discoveries includes the realization that love really does make the world go round. "Love, in shamanic understanding, is faith in a divine presence," Tucker says. "It is the knowledge that we are not alone, that we are all connected, we are all One."[55]

In their different ways, ants, bees, turtles, White Lions, and Black Madonnas are all bringing a remarkably similar message from Gaia. It's the message Inkarí ignored when he turned down God's offer of more *munay* and lost the ability to communicate with stones, and it's the principal message offered by native spirituality throughout the world: love is the force that fuels our true intelligence. Our hearts focus our "mind-power" so that we can live on our home planet in the way we were meant to: in harmony with All That Is.

Whether we'll be able to hear the message, overcome the fear that has crippled us, and reverse our deadly direction will depend on how successful we are in preventing collective stupidity from ambushing our awareness.

PART TWO

THE
CULTURAL TRANCE

10

The Descent into Collective Stupidity

Traveling on the Road to Nowhere

Only human beings have come to the point where they no longer know why they exist. They don't use their brains and they have forgotten the secret knowledge of their bodies, their senses, or their dreams. They don't use the knowledge the spirit has put into every one of them; they are not even aware of this, and so they stumble along blindly on the road to nowhere—a paved highway, which they themselves bulldoze and make smooth, so that they can get faster to the big, empty hole, which they'll find at the end, waiting to swallow them up. It's a comfortable superhighway, but I know where it leads to. I've seen it. I've been there in my vision, and it makes me shudder to think about it.

LAME DEER[1]

True story: two Native American "spiritual leaders" from the United States, one internationally famous, paid separate visits to Costa Rica a few years ago. Each brought drums, feathers, and messages of peace, love, and unity.

But to their hosts' surprise, it turned out that both were terrified of snakes, insects, and other inhabitants of the tropical wilderness. The first visitor opted to sleep on the bus rather than expose herself to possible creepy-crawlers in the humble accommodations prepared for her in a native village. The second, though housed in a luxury lodge, was so worried about the wildlife that she slept with windows tightly closed, lights on, and towels stuffed under the door.[2]

You can't blame them for failing to walk their talk. Raised in modern U.S. society, they, like most of us in the "developed" world, are suffering from *maya,* the cultural trance of fear and separation, which is so powerful that it overrides their own ancestral wisdom.

Like so many of us, they are victims of collective stupidity.

WHAT IT IS

A group won't be smart if its members imitate one another, slavishly follow fads, or wait for someone to tell them what to do.

PETER MILLER[3]

What could be stupider than working (and fighting wars) to perpetuate an unsustainable way of life that exploits and enslaves most of humanity, foments violence, daily becomes less livable, and threatens the existence of every species on the planet, including our own?

I confess: I wish I didn't have to write this section and you didn't have to read it. Acknowledging the power of collective stupidity can be disheartening and depressing. But it's important to ponder what we're up against. Collective stupidity is insidious and dangerous. And unfortunately, it's everywhere. So let's gird our loins and take a closer look at this human-made monster.

It's easy to recognize, because it

- is rooted in and feeds fear
- is devoid of empathy
- promotes separation

- often operates from the "lizard brain," characterized by mindlessness and the absence of critical thought
- is a human creation, kept alive by human sources—celebrities, gurus, politicians, the internet
- is lazy and passive, expecting others to do all the thinking
- is contagious
- results in addiction and enslavement
- requires continual, and increasing, stimulation and novelty
- encourages and perpetuates immaturity and narcissism
- by focusing on surfaces and stereotypes, discourages curiosity and the development of wisdom
- is destructive

Perhaps most obviously, you won't find much love in collective stupidity. What love there may be is fearful, constricted, behind walls, confined to what is *mine*—*my* family, *my* country, *my* group. Expansive, inclusive love for All That Is just isn't there.

If collective intelligence is a group's connection to an infinite source of wisdom, collective stupidity is the result of consistently failing to make that connection. Tom Atlee of the Co-Intelligence Institute believes it's the result of competition, conformity, or "poorly designed systems and feedback loops that reward people for doing—or punish them for not doing—actions that are destructive over the long term or endanger the life around them."[4]

As with collective intelligence, it starts with the individual and works through groups. But the great irony is that collective stupidity is driven by fear, which automatically causes division. The group, which should be a unifying force, reinforces the illusion of isolation and ends up becoming the problem.

Whenever we identify too strongly with *any* group—a species, a race, a gender, a religion, an ideology, a political party, a nation, a culture, a social or economic class, an occupation, a generation, even a football team—we're underscoring separateness. This identification opens the door to groupthink: the group takes over thinking for its members, setting the standards for their actions. Unlike collective intelligence, in which every member of a group consciously contributes his or her energy and talent for the good of all, collective stupidity requires no effort. Instead it expects each person to renounce or suppress his or her unique gifts to be part of the chosen herd, which invariably has a fixed and divisive agenda.

Implicit in groupthink is the belief that my group is better than yours, so I am better than you; you are the "other" and therefore not only inferior, but possibly dangerous as well.

Some contemporary scientists wonder whether collective evil could be the result of coherence created by group thought working negatively. Lynne McTaggart speculates:

> Maybe negative consciousness was also like a germ that could infect people and take hold. Germany had been depressed in every sense after the First World War. Could this dispiritedness have affected the Germans on a quantum level, making it possible for Hitler, that most intoxicating of speakers, to create a kind of negative collective, which fed on itself, and condoned the grossest of evils?
>
> Had a collective consciousness been responsible for the Spanish inquisition? The Salem witchcraft trials? Did collective evil also create coherence?[5]

Whatever the cause, collective stupidity is extremely scary. It ranges from the head-shakingly pathetic—the middle-aged woman who felt the need to post on social networks a photo of a $1,200 purse she had just bought—to just about every evil that plagues our world.

War, terrorism, genocide, racism, intolerance, discrimination, violence, and environmental destruction all start with collective stupidity.

THE DEMISE OF CRITICAL THOUGHT

Collective stupidity is our legacy from the patriarchy. When the masculine rational displaced the feminine intuitive, it paved the way ror stupidity, which is always characterized by the absence of critical thought.

The ability to think critically—the power of discernment—requires both brain hemispheres to work together. Intellect, collaborating with intuition, enables us to distinguish between truth and falsehood, rather than allowing others to think for us and dictate (often with painstakingly "reasoned" arguments) what they believe we should believe. Discernment is key on the Andean Path, where mastery depends on integrating the wild, untamed power of the left side (or right brain) with the ordering power of the right side (left brain).

Collective stupidity also owes its existence to a second brain imbalance—predominance of the survival or lizard brain, which is triggered by fear and puts us into flight-or-fight mode. If Joseph Chilton Pearce is correct, some ancient trauma may have been the cause of this overreaction.

One of the most dangerous dumbing-down effects of the patriarchy was the insertion of priestly hierarchies between humans and the divine—such as the ones that caused the degeneration of some indigenous cultures into fear-ruled societies sustained by war and bloody sacrifices. When we were no longer able to receive spiritual guidance directly, we became vulnerable to manipulation, and thus stupider.

Riane Eisler points out that the message we received from the priests—and from every despot and demagogue since—was: "Don't think, accept what is, accept what *authority* says is true. Above all, do **not** use your own intelligence, your own powers of mind, to question us or to seek independent knowledge."[6]

Unfortunately, our rigidly hierarchical educational system has reinforced this message. And in the Digital Age, we see it in the unquestioning dissemination of whatever nonsense comes along on the internet—most of it unsourced and aimed at promoting fear, hatred, and divisiveness.

The much-heralded "reason" of the eighteenth century ended up advancing collective stupidity by making sure the feminine stayed shackled and muzzled. Francis Bacon hoped to "torture nature's secrets from her,"[7] and the same attitude lives on today: theoretical physicist and futurist Michio Kaku voices his faith that, thanks to "an even more far-reaching scientific revolution," nature will eventually be "mastered."[8]

Eisler writes:

> "Rational man" now spoke of how he would "master" nature, "subdue" the elements, and—in the great twentieth-century advance—"conquer" space. He spoke about how he had to fight wars to bring about peace, freedom, and equality, or how he had to murder children, women, and men in terrorist activities to bring dignity and liberation to oppressed peoples.
>
> As a member of the elites in both capitalist and communist worlds, he continued to amass property and/or privilege. To make more profits or to meet higher quotas, he also began to systematically poison his physical environment, thereby threatening other species with extinction and causing severe illness in human adults and deformities in human babies.
>
> And all the while he kept explaining that what he was doing was either patriotic or idealistic and—above all—rational.[9]

Leonardo Boff describes what happened when the rational won out over the intuitive, bringing collective stupidity with it:

> The non-renewable resources of the Earth have been exhausted and the physico-chemical balance of the Earth has been broken. Sociability between humans has been torn apart by the domination of some peoples by others and by the hard-fought battle of the classes. . . .
>
> Two-thirds of humanity have been condemned to a life without any form of sustainability.[10]

Edgar Morin and Anne Brigitte Kern point out that "everywhere, and for decades now, supposedly rational solutions, put forward by experts convinced they were working for reason and progress . . . have

Fig. 10.1. Destroying our only home: rainforest giants succumb to human greed. Photo by Julio Laínez, courtesy of the Tico Times.

impoverished as much as they have enriched and have destroyed as much as they have created."[11]

Even worse, says Boff, the rise of "reason" damaged our very humanity, stripping us of "the notion of the human being as a being-of-relations, a being of creativity, tenderness, care, spirituality, and carrier of a sacred and infinite project."[12]

As collective stupidity steadily hijacks our brains and hearts, leading us to *rationalize* divisiveness and the continued devastation of the natural world that sustains life, humans morph into Earth's most terrifying menace.

STUPIDITY GETS A MEGAPHONE

The social networks give the right to speak to legions of idiots who once talked only in a bar after a glass of wine, without harming the community. They were rapidly

silenced, but now they have the same right to speak as a
Nobel Prize winner. It's the invasion of the imbeciles.

UMBERTO ECO[13]

The internet has given stupidity a megaphone and legitimacy it never before enjoyed—not only because glowing screens have kidnapped our consciousness, but also because the Web has turned into a redoubt for humanity's lowest common denominator. And our diminished powers of discernment assure exponential contagion.

What's even scarier is that those with nefarious economic or political motives have found the internet's credulous crowds fertile ground for mind control.

We now have access to more information from more sources than at any other time in history. How can we possibly be getting stupider?

Unfortunately, even unlimited quantities of information, if unquestioned and unexamined, can never translate into wisdom, the gift we need to live in peace with each other and our world.

Collective stupidity is both cause and continuing consequence of this ironic development. According to a survey by the Pew Research Center, nearly two-thirds of adults in the United States now get news on social networks. Pointing out that on social-media platforms, "anybody can be a publisher" with no need to establish credible sources of information or adhere to accepted ethical standards of journalism, the *Economist* notes that the internet makes "homophilous sorting" or "like-minded people forming clusters" much easier. The magazine quotes *The Wealth of Networks,* a book by Harvard University's Yochai Benkler, which explains that "individuals with shared interests are far more likely to find each other or converge around a source of information online than offline. Social media enable members of such groups to strengthen each other's beliefs, by shutting out contradictory information, and to take collective action."

One result of this is that opportunistic scam artists have found "a profitable niche pumping out hoaxes, often based on long-circulating rumors or prejudices, in the hope that they will go viral and earn clicks," the magazine reports. "Many share such content without even thinking twice, let alone checking to determine if it is true."[14]

Collective stupidity wins each time this happens. As they mindlessly spread false information, people become puppets, unwittingly placing themselves in the service of profit-hungry manipulators. And unscrupulous governments and politicians have been quick to take advantage of the legions of idiots thus enslaved.

Though none of this could have been foreseen, its consequences are ominous: people in supposedly free societies are becoming indistinguishable from those living under totalitarian regimes. Without access to reliable information, nobody can form an intelligent opinion. Stupidity reigns.

Philosopher Santiago Manzanal Bercedo calls the social networks "a multiplying factor of stupidity in the entire planet."[15] Even those who once believed in the platforms' glowing potential are coming to the same realization. Chamath Palihapitiya, a former vice president of Facebook, told Stanford Graduate School of Business students in November 2017 that he now feels "tremendous guilt" because "the short-term, dopamine-driven feedback loops that we have created are destroying how society works: no civil discourse, no cooperation, misinformation, mistruth."[16]

IT'S CLOSER THAN WE GROUPTHINK

When I started working on this book, I never imagined that world events would organize to illustrate collective stupidity to such stunning perfection. The *Economist* said that the United States election in 2016 was the result of "the power of groupthink" because it revealed how "most voters make political choices based largely on what people like them are doing, and rarely change their minds."[17]

In a TV interview following the election, filmmaker Michael Moore declared that many who voted for Donald Trump despite his shocking lack of any qualifications were so fed up with the status quo that they collectively chose to "throw a Molotov cocktail" into the U.S. democratic process.

This is classic collective stupidity: don't consider consequences, just destroy.

Moore failed to mention—possibly because its full extent had not yet been uncovered—the second part of the double whammy that made collective stupidity the biggest winner in the U.S. election: Russia's efforts to undermine U.S. democracy by secretly manipulating citizens' minds.

The fear-fueled symbolism in Trump's rhetoric—the need to build walls, debase the feminine, dehumanize and demonize the "other," devastate the environment—ignited mob mind. Simultaneously, citizens were being fed huge volumes of false, malicious, and divisive information manufactured by Russian troll farms. Unaware that they were being used, potential voters proceeded to fan the flames, sharing and spreading fear, aggression, hoaxes, conspiracy theories, and lies. Groupthink took over.

"The Kremlin deploys armies of 'trolls' to fight on its behalf in Western comment sections and Twitter feeds," the *Economist* reported in September 2016. "Its minions have set up thousands of social-media 'bots' and other spamming weapons to drown out other content."[18]

The extent of the disinformation campaign that gradually became known was hair-raising: in 2017, according to the *Washington Post,* Facebook disclosed that the "Internet Research Agency," a Kremlin-backed organization of Russian operatives that flooded the social-media platform with disinformation around the 2016 election, had operated 470 accounts and pages on Facebook's main platform as well as on its sister site, Instagram. Some 126 million people may have seen that propaganda, and similar efforts were under way to use social media to sow chaos, confusion, and hatred before the 2018 U.S. midterm elections, the paper reported.[19]

Even more horrific was the revelation in mid-2018 that since the beginning of the year, at least twenty-four innocent people had been killed in mob lynchings in India following the spread of fake reports of child kidnappings on WhatsApp, Facebook's messaging service.[20] Other hate crimes followed, including the 2019 massacre of fifty Muslims in a New Zealand mosque. All were linked to information spread on social media.

Like collective intelligence, collective stupidity bypasses the conscious mind. But collective intelligence opens to higher wisdom; collective stupidity blocks the wisdom available from the field. Those in its grip feed off each other, giving their power away to others whose vision is just as flawed.

At the same time, it's important to keep in mind that those who fall prey to collective stupidity aren't necessarily inherently stupid. Mob mind and groupthink can infect anyone.

THE STUPIDITY HARVEST

We must abandon the two major myths of the modern West: the conquest of nature-as-object by humans—the sole subjects of the universe—and the false infinite toward which industrial growth hurled itself, with its notions of development and progress.

EDGAR MORIN AND ANNE BRIGITTE KERN[21]

Humans are the only species on Earth actively working *against* Gaia's efforts to preserve the balance and beauty of our home planet. Stupidly, we stumble along toward suicide.

Joan Halifax tells a story about Huichol gods who have lost touch with their past:

We are like those gods, ill and disgruntled, alienated from the view that all of life is sacred. We are sitting around in our workplaces, in doctors' offices, in our churches and temples feeling out of sorts. Indeed, many of us are desperately sick. We complain about the state of the world and are fearful about the state of our bodies, our families, the economy, and the Earth. Over the years, we have become lazy, complacent, and depressed and, like the gods, have forgotten to tend the hearth of the Fire of our awareness and to enter the Waters of the Feminine.[22]

Social critic Jacques Sagot blames our current "propensity for 'ecocide'" on an "atavistic, ancestral resentment" against nature, "encysted in our genetic memory and in the world's collective unconscious. . . . We want to punish that force which inflicted on us—and continues to inflict—floods, earthquakes, hurricanes, volcanic eruptions. . . . That which so many times exposed our laughable defenselessness, humiliated and tormented us. Now, armed with the formidable arsenal of our technology, we hand it the bill for all the pain it has provoked. . . . So what if by doing so we destroy ourselves?"[23]

Halifax agrees: "In what appears to be an existential crisis of planetary proportions, our very existence is threatened as we destroy ourselves through the destruction of the Earth."[24]

So just go ahead and toss that Molotov cocktail.

Here's a further frightening thought: if, as we've speculated, the infinite supply of wisdom we need from the field has become blocked and blurred by the accumulation of *hucha* or heavy energy humans have manufactured and continue to spew out, could we be continuously downloading more and more of our own toxic detritus in a fatal feedback loop, growing stupider and more self-destructive by the minute?

MORE DUMB, MORE NUMB

Our growing inability to think critically has made it harder and harder to comprehend where we're headed or to chart a different course.

"We find ourselves in a vicious circle of increasingly multidimensional problems, increasing incapacity to think multidimensionally," Edgar Morin observes. "The crisis worsens as fast as the incapacity to reflect on the crisis increases; the more planetary our problems, the more they are left unthought."[25]

Because we can't conceive of solutions, we're unable to respond to problems; as we dumb down, we numb out. We become immobilized, no longer *response-able* for the fate of our world. We waste, pollute, and destroy, oblivious to the consequences of our actions—or, worse, aware of them but unable to change.

Morin and Kern lament the "laxity of indifference" resulting from "a closed and fragmented rationality," which they say "is obviously incapable of facing the challenge of planetary problems."[26]

As we grow more dumb and more numb, we risk transforming our world into the "flat nothing" Martín Prechtel says the initiation of young people is aimed at preventing. Collective stupidity, so rampant in our elder-starved, uninitiated societies, radiates self-absorbed immaturity. Much of the destructive mischief on the internet resembles nothing more than teenagers defacing newly painted walls—pointless acts of infantile nihilism carried out by those who feel powerless because they've lost contact with their power sources: Earth and Cosmos.

"Were we to have a society of true adults we would become responsible, self-organizing, and naturally tolerant of diversity," Elizabeth Jenkins observes. However, in what she terms the "adolescent state of awareness" of the modern world, "FEAR is the primary emotion, and the principal mind state is one of the victim/perpetrator. . . . This sadly adolescent power game . . . has nothing to do with integrity, goodness, altruism, sincerity, authenticity, or honor," she notes. "It is not the behavior of what my husband's grandmother would call 'grown folks.'"[27]

THE STUPIDITY COMMUNITY

In our stupefied world, "community" is one of those words that is so overused that it has become meaningless—and in fact has come to mean its opposite.

A "gated community" and a "retirement community" are not communities at all: they're artificial environments whose residents share a single feature—age or a desire for security—and are deliberately designed to isolate those who live there from natural interaction with the world around them.

The myriad groups that now call themselves "communities"—the "intelligence community," the "academic community," the "medical community"—have nothing in common but a label. They're not living, life-sustaining systems whose members are bound by complex networks of interdependent common needs and purposes that extend far beyond themselves.

"A corporate community is not a community," stresses Malidoma Somé. "It's a conglomeration of individuals in the service of an insatiable soulless entity."[28]

This perversion of the notion of community is symptomatic of our stupidity. Having lost true community and unable to replace it, we simply relabel and euphemize, ending up with grotesque imitations that we then unquestioningly accept as real.

The "communities" that aren't, the "communities" that are really just more groups that feel themselves different and separate from other groups, push all of us farther and farther apart and reinforce the illusion of our isolation.

11

A World out of Balance

To Take More than You Give

The world is too much with us; late and soon,
Getting and spending, we lay waste our powers:
Little we see in Nature that is ours.

WILLIAM WORDSWORTH[1]

The imbalance in our brains is reflected everywhere in our world, which is so critically out of balance that all beings on Earth are being held hostage by an economic system that relies entirely on the destruction of nature. Having forgotten how to practice reciprocity, we humans now live exclusively by taking: grabbing Earth's resources, accumulating wealth, acquiring goods, attaining a comfortable lifestyle, getting, buying, consuming.

The "developed" world's economic system—what Edgar Morin and Anne Brigitte Kern call "the infernal machine"[2]—has turned into a technology-driven monster with its own inhuman agenda.

In the view of Fritjof Capra, "The so-called 'global market,' strictly speaking, is not a market at all but a network of machines programmed according to a single value—money-making for the sake of making money—to the exclusion of all other values."[3]

Hazel Henderson, in her book, *Building a Win-Win World,* insists that human systems, like ecosystems, require balance: "Competition with cooperation, selfishness and individualism with community and social concern, material acquisitiveness with thirst for knowledge and understanding, rights with responsibilities and the striving for love, justice and harmony." Natural systems, she adds, "never maximize single variables, such as profit and efficiency."[4]

The imbalance relies on the arrogant belief that our scientific prowess will always save the day, so we are free to continue plundering, polluting, and paving over: we'll never run out of planet to exploit and denude. But because arrogance is rooted in fear, we are simultaneously gripped by the suspicion that there may not be enough to go around, so I'd better get (and defend) mine.

This doubly flawed perception is making us even stupider. As Morin and Kern explain, "Economic growth causes new disorders. Its exponential character not only created a multiform process of degradation of the biosphere, but equally a multiform process of degradation of the psychosphere . . . our mental, affective, and moral lives."[5]

Henderson sounds a similar warning: "When such ego-centered concerns become culturally reinforced, as in the Western development model, and dominate our awareness of society and nature, we can become mentally and physically sick and our societies can disintegrate."[6]

Our stupidity now threatens not only our societies, but all life on Earth. Capra declares that "the striving for continuing undifferentiated economic growth . . . is clearly unsustainable, since unlimited expansion on a finite planet can only be catastrophic."[7]

WAITING FOR THE TECHNO-FIX

The threefold race in science/technology/industry that has taken over the human adventure is now out of control: Growth is out of control, its progress leading to the abyss.
EDGAR MORIN AND ANNE BRIGITTE KERN[8]

At some point we shall use up all the technological fixes.
ROBERT THEOBALD[9]

Collective stupidity received an unexpected ally in the breathtaking rise of computer technology. The triumph of left-brain functioning, the technology revolution has produced unimaginable breakthroughs in countless areas. The trouble is, it's using a new vocabulary to lull us into the belief that we're progressing, when in fact it's furthering the very worldview that brought us to our near-catastrophic situation. Entranced by our ever-evolving electronics, most of us can't conceive of a future without them. Our machines lead; we slavishly follow.

"The logic of the artificial machine—efficiency, predictability, calculability, rigid specialization, speed, chronometric time—invaded everyday life," say Morin and Kern. "The notion of development that has imposed itself on the planet obeys the logic of the artificial machine."[10]

"Western Machine technology is the spirit of death made to look like life," adds Malidoma Somé. "It makes life seem easier, comfortable, cozy, but the price we pay includes the dehumanization of the self."[11]

The problem is not technology itself; it's our voluntary enslavement by it. New Paradigm economist Nicholas Georgescu-Roegen was the first to point out that what he termed "exosomatic organs"—"the seemingly endless variety of 'detachable limbs' humans have invented to extend the range and scope of their activity"[12]—caused and perpetuate our deadly dependence. Things like cars, computers, and smartphones have become human appendages, and detaching from them is almost impossible.

"Humankind's long history of utilizing these 'exosomatic organs' has created an 'addiction' to the comfort and pleasure they provide," explain authors John Gowdy and Susan Mesner. "The difficulty arises because their production is dependent on finite stocks of available energy and matter, bringing our species' obsession with more and better 'things' on a collision course with unavoidable biophysical limits."[13]

"Wherever there is technology, there is a general degeneration of the spiritual," Somé notes. "This is because the Machine is the specter of the Spirit, and in such a state, it does not serve because it can't serve. It needs servants. It is like having an elephant in your home as a pet. Would the energy spent to find 200 pounds of food every day compensate for what you get out of it?"[14]

Having given our power away to our machines, we can only wait, passively, stupidly, clinging to the hope that they'll end up saving us—that a techno-fix for the messes we've gotten into will surely come to our rescue before it's too late. Equally stupidly, we believe that technology's short-term benefits will somehow outweigh its long-term harm. It's undoubtedly significant that space travel, the apex of technological achievement, is aimed not at repairing our relationship with our home planet, but at eventually abandoning Earth once we've trashed it so thoroughly that it becomes uninhabitable.

Georgescu-Roegen's theory of bioeconomics, which relates economics to living systems, sees clearly the dangers of relying on technology to bail us out. "The favorite thesis of standard and Marxist economists alike . . . is that the power of technology is without limits," Georgescu-Roegen writes. "We will always be able not only to find a substitute for a resource which has become scarce, but also to increase the productivity of any kind of energy and material. Should we run out of some resources, we will always think up something, just as we have continuously done since the time of Pericles. Nothing, therefore, could ever stand in the way of an increasingly happier existence of the human species." However, he adds, "dinosaurs, just before they disappeared from this very same planet, had behind them not less than one hundred fifty million years of truly prosperous existence. (And they did not pollute the environment with industrial waste!)"[15] He calls for a fundamental change in values that will "take into account the finiteness of our unique planet, our dependence on the web of life which surrounds us, and the fragility of our species."[16]

SLEEPING WITH THE ENEMY

The unhappy findings are in. We are connected as we've never been connected before, and we seem to have damaged ourselves in the process.

SHERRY TURKLE[17]

Young people are especially vulnerable to becoming structurally coupled to machines, with consequent effects on brain function. As we've seen, the young in "developed" societies are steadily losing sensory perception and sensitivity to stimuli.

"Information is processed without evaluation, thus without reference to areas of knowledge or meaning and without emotional response," says Joseph Chilton Pearce, citing studies that show "new-brain functioning" in people born after 1969. "The new brain can tolerate extremes of dissonance or discord," he writes. This causes "a failure to recognize severe logical fallacies—which results in a young person meeting everything with equal indifference."

Pearce adds that fifteen years ago, people could distinguish 300,000 sounds; today "many children can't go beyond 100,000 and the average is 180,000. Twenty years ago the average subject could detect 350 different shades of a particular color. Today the number is 130." Verbal ability is declining as well. He says that U.S. high school students in 1950 had a working vocabulary averaging 25,000 words, while today "that level is 10,000." He blames these declines on "age-inappropriate use of electronic devices."[18]

It may be that our sensory and verbal skills atrophy when technology is available to do the work we once did. (Certainly our ability to remember even simple information such as telephone numbers and birthdays has suffered since our devices started remembering for us.) Far from repairing our already fragmented brain function, technology may be making it worse—and us stupider.

According to the *Economist,* smartphone users touch their devices somewhere between twice a minute and once every seven minutes—yet conducting tasks while receiving emails and phone calls, compared to working in uninterrupted quiet, has been shown to reduce a worker's IQ by as much as ten points. "That is equivalent to losing a night's sleep, and twice as debilitating as using marijuana," the magazine notes.[19]

Sherry Turkle, who has extensively studied human-machine relationships, cites a 2010 analysis of data from over fourteen thousand college students over the past thirty years, which shows that since 2000 young people have reported a dramatic decline in interest in other people and a growing lack of empathy. "Today's college students are far less likely to say that it is valuable to try to put oneself in the place of others or to try to understand their feelings," Turkle writes, adding that the study's authors blame "the availability of online games and social networking."[20]

As we saw in part 1, empathy is essential for wisdom.

Turkle sounds another alarm when she notes that "teenagers tell me they sleep with their cell phone, and even when it isn't on their person . . . they know when their phone is vibrating. The technology has become like a phantom limb, it is so much a part of them."[21]

A 2015 survey by the Comunidad Laboral Universia in Colombia revealed that 91 percent of 5,506 young people in ten Iberoamerican countries consider it "essential" to carry their smartphones with them at all times, while 54 percent describe themselves as "dependent" on their phones.[22]

"In interviews with young and old, I find people genuinely terrified of being cut off from the 'grid,'" Turkle reports. "People say that the loss of a cell phone can 'feel like a death' . . . whether or not our devices are in use, without them we feel disconnected, adrift. Connectivity becomes a craving," she explains. "When we receive a text or an e-mail, our nervous system responds by giving us a shot of dopamine. We are stimulated by connectivity itself. We learn to require it, even as it depletes us."

"A new generation already suspects this is the case," she continues. "I think of a sixteen-year-old girl who tells me, 'Technology is bad because people are not as strong as its pull.'"[23]

Turkle's research also reveals the disturbing irony that the craved connectivity is, in fact, pushing people apart.

"A thirteen-year-old tells me she hates the phone and never listens to voice-mail," Turkle writes. "Texting offers just the right amount of access, just the right amount of control. She is a modern Goldilocks: for her, texting puts people not too close, not too far, but at just the right distance. The world is now full of modern Goldilockses, people who take comfort in being in touch with a lot of people whom they also keep at bay."[24]

WORLD WIDE WEB OR WEB OF LIFE?

I have no interest in visiting Costa Rica. I hate nature.

U.S. TOURIST IN BUENOS AIRES

The more wedded to technology we become, the harder it gets to relate to the natural world. The supreme irony offered by the Web, spinning its illusion of connectivity, is that it has begun to replace the web of life in our awareness.

A sunset, a sky strewn with stars, or the tangled roots and branches of a centuries-old tree can't compete with the fantastic, fast-moving action and instant gratification offered by the virtual world. And as nature recedes into the background, it becomes ever more alien.

It's easier and safer to experience Earth's wonders on a screen, selected and digitally enhanced for dramatic effect, accompanied by appropriate music and easy to delete when we tire of them, than to engage with them in person and risk discomfort, danger, or boredom. And as our collective stupidity deepens, it becomes easier and easier to crush an ant, shoot an elephant, or clear a forest—never pausing to think about what we're actually doing.

"Accelerating technological 'progress' has only intensified the illusion of an isolated self," says Bill Pfeiffer. "This false perception considered normal by most people—'I'm in here and everything else is out there'—has led to an acute physical and psychological disconnection from the land. It's a negative feedback loop in which we retreat further and further from our core nourishment, the natural world."[25]

David Abram contends that the flatness of screens robs the world of its depth and us of our ability to participate in it. "The more we spend our days staring at screens, taking our dreams and directives from the signs and shapes that play across their smooth surfaces, the harder it becomes to make this transition," he argues. "Accustomed to peering at flat representations, we've begun to take the palpable world itself as a kind of representation . . . the land has now become something that we look *at.*"[26]

Pfeiffer quotes Richard Louv, who coined the term "nature deficit disorder," as pointing out that "our kids are actually doing what we tell them to do when they sit in front of that TV all day or in front of that computer game all day. The society is telling kids unconsciously that nature's in the past—it really doesn't count anymore—that the future is in electronics, and besides, the bogeyman is in the woods."[27]

But *ayni*—the giving and receiving of living energy—simply isn't possible with a screen.

* * *

Abram stresses:

> Despite all our giddy technological dreams, this vast and inscrutable land—drenched by rains and parched by the summer sun—remains the ultimate ground, and the final horizon, of all our science. It is not primarily a set of mechanisms waiting to be figured out, this breathing land. It is not a stock of resources waiting to be utilized by us, or a storehouse of raw materials waiting to be developed.
>
> It is not an object. It is, rather, the very body of wonder—a shuddering field of intelligence in whose round life we participate. . . .
>
> It is time to unplug our gaze from the humming screen, walking out of the house to blink and piss under the river of stars. There are new stories waiting in the cool grasses, and new songs.[28]

12

Two Paths

Artificial Intelligence
or Collective Wisdom?

Western man has come to believe that he is the master of all living things, and that nature is there to be tamed at best; despised, broken, and destroyed at worst. It has led to a very dangerous situation . . . the belief that humans can build a shining technological future without animals and trees and other life forms. Until this attitude is combated and erased from the human mind, Westernized human beings will be a danger to all earthly life, including themselves.

CREDO MUTWA[1]

We are facing a critical choice. Will we turn into cyborgs—human/machine hybrids—allowing collective stupidity to unfold to its catastrophic conclusion? Or will we rejoin Gaia's wondrous family, doing our part for the good of the whole? Most importantly, which path is more likely to hold the key to the survival of all the inhabitants of our planet?

A DEAD-END STREET

Obviously I believe that the technological path, so eagerly embraced by some contemporary thinkers as well as by most of the industrialized world, is in fact a dead-end street. By "technological path," I mean the zealous certainty regarding the supposed supremacy of computer technology—what computer philosophy writer Jaron Lanier calls "cybernetic totalism."[2]

Artificial intelligence is the holy grail of the cybernetic totalists. But it's actually the epitome of collective stupidity, because it narrows the definition of intelligence to that which can be replicated by machines, disregarding every form of knowing that can't be reduced to wires and circuits. The label itself says it all: if something is "artificial," it's ersatz, synthetic, fake. At best, it's a convincing imitation of the real thing, created to serve a limited purpose.

Is this the intelligence we want to entrust with our future?

The technologists' obsessive push toward an imagined future that sees us ever more severed from nature and from our spiritual selves leapfrogs over many technological breakthroughs that truly are benefiting the world, such as the innovative use of smartphones and robots to improve health care in Africa.[3] It's the reckless pursuit of new technology just because it's new, never pausing to wonder whether it's helping or hurting, that typifies collective stupidity.

The path of collective wisdom, on the other hand, takes us back to what our ancestors knew, inviting us to explore the ways in which it coincides with New Paradigm discoveries, in hopes of finding solutions for the increasingly complex problems the planet is facing.

"Machine-based technological solutions are often perceived to be the first and often sole response to human problems," Robert Kenny of the Collective Wisdom Initiative points out. "By contrast, the emergence of [collective wisdom groups] reflects a movement back toward a balanced, comprehensive worldview and approach to service, where human factors are seen as equally, if not more, effective in the sustaining of physical, emotional, mental and spiritual health."[4]

WE ARE NOT WHAT WE THOUGHT

On the technology path, we find that we are much less than we thought; on the collective wisdom path, we learn that we are much more than we suspected.

Both the technology and the wisdom paths are forcing us, in the words of futurist Ray Kurzweil, "to reevaluate our concept of what it means to be human."[5] They're also obliging us to take another look at the various definitions of intelligence.

For the technologists, "human" means cognitively supreme: the species with the brains to dominate nature. Intelligence is simply the speed at which this can be accomplished.

Machines speed up the process of acquiring information, so they're supposedly expanding human intelligence and becoming indispensable for our existence. "As human beings become increasingly intertwined with the technology and with each other via the technology, old distinctions between what is specifically human and specifically technological become more complex," Sherry Turkle tells us. "Our new technologically enmeshed relationships oblige us to ask to what extent we ourselves have become cyborgs, transgressive mixtures of biology, technology and code. The traditional distance between people and machines has become harder to maintain."[6]

Kurzweil predicts that humanity will "combine with its own creation. It will merge with its technology."[7]

Philosopher Andy Clark agrees. "We shall be cyborgs not in the superficial sense of combining flesh and wires," he writes, "but in the more profound sense of being human/technology symbionts—thinking and reasoning systems whose mind and selves are spread across biological brain and nonbiological circuitry."[8]

A cyborg, then, is a "value-added" human, deriving its worth from the machine it has become part of.

If "intelligence" means swift access to vast amounts of raw information, we can look forward to a future filled with genius cyborgs. As long as they can remain connected to their technology and their technology continues to work, the new machine-people will have all of humanity's information at their fingertips. (Of course, as we're already seeing, abundance of information doesn't necessarily imply the wise use of it.)

Traditional societies, on the other hand—many of them bypassed not only by the Digital Revolution but also by the Industrial Revolution—

have remained structurally coupled to nature, which has allowed them to preserve a very different kind of intelligence. Collective wisdom enables people to instantly tap into the infinite store of information in the field—and the wisdom itself ensures that whatever information they obtain will be appropriate, timely, and applied for the benefit of all beings.

JOHN HENRY IN THE TWENTY-FIRST CENTURY

In many ways, the current debate over the eventual reaches of technology revisits the legend of John Henry, the slave-turned-steel driver who came to epitomize the battle between man and machine during the Industrial Revolution.

John Henry was famous for his strength and speed in hammering rail spikes for construction of the railroad in West Virginia. When his bosses decided to acquire a steam-powered hammer, he resolved to try to save his job and those of his fellow workers. He challenged the machine to a race.

The bosses agreed that if John Henry could work faster than the steam hammer, the steel drivers could keep their jobs. John Henry beat the steam hammer. But he was so exhausted from the effort that he collapsed and died. The machine ended up winning after all.

In the Industrial Revolution, machines replaced humans because they could work faster. In our culture of relentless progress, faster is always better. John Henry's principal value for his bosses was his speed; no other qualities of his humanity mattered.

Today speed of computation is what matters. In the technologists' view, humans are human only to the extent that our brains can work faster, learn faster, develop and change faster, and create faster than those of other species—and those of machines. Since it's only a matter of time before the machines catch up and pass us on all counts, they'll soon be more "human" than we are—and thus equipped to determine our planet's fate.

"We can educate machines in a process that can be hundreds or thousands of times faster than the comparable process in humans," Ray Kurzweil enthuses. "It can provide a twenty-year education to a human-level machine in perhaps a few weeks or a few days, and then these machines can share their knowledge."[9]

By contrast, according to Robert Kenny, working with collective wisdom "requires regularly slowing down, instead of speeding up (even though decisions ultimately can be made more quickly)."[10]

Of course, lightning-fast machines may be able to compute some apparently intelligent short-term fixes. But can we rely on them having the necessary consciousness to see—and care about—the big picture in all its wondrous complexity?

ARE WE SCARED YET?

During the Industrial Revolution, machines replaced humans' bodies; now they are replacing our minds. The sense of fatalism is the same now as it was then; as Jaron Lanier notes, "Cybernetic eschatology shares with some of history's worst ideologies a doctrine of historic predestination."[11] Now, as then, the prevailing view is that people will inevitably be replaced by objects of our own creation.

"Here's where the fear factor kicks in," writes trend-spotter Faith Popcorn. "We're no longer merely dealing with mechanized body parts. We're re-engineering our minds, our spirit, our souls."[12]

Sherry Turkle introduces us to fifteen-year-old Howard, who believes that a robot would give him better advice than his dad would, because "its database would be larger than Dad's."[13]

The technologists also see "elder bots" and "nanny bots" as ideal solutions for elder and child care. But as Turkle points out, "When we lose the 'burden' of care, we begin to give up on our compact that human beings will care for other human beings. . . . Humans need to be surrounded by human touch, faces, and voices. Humans need to be brought up by humans."[14]

The Wolf Girls showed us what happens when they aren't (although in their case, they were better off with their wolf family than with their human one). And if our elders are handed over to robots, we—and our world—will end up the biggest losers. The machines will become the beneficiaries of our birthright: the wisdom our elders might have transmitted to us.

THE BOIDS . . .

Some artificial-intelligence researchers have focused on "lower" forms of intelligence, assuming, based on evolutionary theory, that "higher" intelligence must contain "lower" forms. Robotics expert Hans Moravec takes this approach when he states that "today's PC might be comparable only to the milligram nervous systems of insects or the smallest vertebrates." He predicts that the "path to machine intelligence" or the ultimate goal—"humanlike power"—will follow an evolutionary route through "mammal-like brainpower" and "a third generation [that] will think like primates."[15]

Of course, this Old Paradigm, hierarchical, anthropocentric view ignores the fact that, as evolutionary biologist Marc D. Hauser points out, "each species is intelligent in its own way"[16] and in fact may have access to essential wisdom that the world needs.

Collective intelligence as displayed by flocks and swarms of insects, fish, and birds has long attracted the attention of artificial-intelligence seekers because it apparently lends itself to computer simulation. Turkle cites early studies that seemed to show that flocking behavior was the result of "simple responses to a complex environment," or following "local rules" to create global behavior, much like the ant studies we looked at in part 1.

One such experiment sought to reproduce the behavior of a flock of birds. Each virtual bird, or "boid," "acted solely on the basis of its local perception of the world," and eventually "the flocks of boids on the screen [exhibited] realistic behavior."[17]

However, as with the ant studies, the boid experiment missed key connections with the big picture.

"Scientific models of emergent complexity feel a bit too reductionistic to explain collective intelligence among humans," notes Craig Hamilton, "and according to biologist Rupert Sheldrake, they don't really account for the group behavior of most other animals either."

Hamilton quotes Sheldrake as saying that "early attempts to create complexity-based computer models that simulated flock behavior, though initially impressive, ultimately failed because they tried to reduce the flock phenomenon to a few simple instructions followed by each individual. . . . The best state-of-the-art models of flock behavior are 'field models' where you treat the whole flock as if it's in a field, the field of the whole group. This is what I think of as a morphic field, a field that organizes systems where the whole is more than the sum of its parts."

As we've seen, this is the way humans experience collective intelligence.

"For most who have witnessed the emergence of collective intelligence, Sheldrake's notion of group fields seems to have some resonance," Hamilton observes. "Indeed, one of the most common ways people describe the experience of collective consciousness is as an increasing awareness of being in a field together, a field of knowing and seeing that unifies the group."

"But," he continues, "what makes this notion of collective fields particularly intriguing, in light of collective wisdom experiences, is the way it seems to account for one of the most remarkable phenomena of group experience: the sense that, once it emerges, the collective mind seems to take on a life of its own."[18]

. . . AND THE BEES

The astounding collective intelligence of bees has also been in the sights of artificial-intelligence researchers, but it too has defied efforts to use technology to explain it.

Marc D. Hauser describes a robotic honeybee, "programmed to dance in a certain way and replicate real honeybee behavior"—the way bees transmit information to other members of the colony.

"You can plop this robot in the middle of a colony, set it dancing in honeybee contra-dancing style, and the hive members will take the information and zip off to the designated location," he says.

This experiment undoubtedly proves that bees, like humans, can be bamboozled by convincing replicas of themselves. But in the end, no mystery is unraveled; the robot brings the scientists no closer to understanding bees' intelligence. As Hauser puts it, "When you step back and ask, 'What do we know about how the *brain* of the honeybee represents this kind of information?' the answer is, 'We know almost nothing.'"[19]

Maybe this is because the answers lie not in building a better mechanical bee, but in exploring bees' magical, mystical connections to collective wisdom.

BEYOND BRAINPOWER

Wisdom . . . is a sacred trust. It belongs not to you but to the ancestors.

JAMES DAVID AUDLIN[20]

The most beautiful and most profound experience is the sensation of the mystical. It is the sower of all true science. He to whom this emotion is a stranger, who can no longer wonder and stand rapt in awe, is as good as dead. To know that which is impenetrable to us really exists, manifesting itself as the highest wisdom and the most radiant beauty which our dull faculties can comprehend only in their primitive forms—this knowledge, this feeling is at the center of true religiousness.

ALBERT EINSTEIN[21]

It is possible to create a smart machine. But can anyone figure out how to build a wise machine?

The limits of artificial intelligence are nowhere more evident than when pondering this question, because as we've seen, wisdom is what extends intelligence beyond brainpower and gives all beings their place in the web of Earth and Cosmos.

Tom Atlee of the Co-Intelligence Institute reminds us that wisdom is

the ability to apply our intelligence with an extended perspective, especially the ability to keep in mind the big picture when we're handling the details, and to keep in mind the real lives of individuals today when we're handling the long-term fate of whole systems.

God is in the details—and in the whole. We are wise when we think historically and take into account future generations. We are wise when we think holistically and systemically and attend to the interconnectedness of everything.

We are wise when we recognize and creatively work with the ambiguity, complexity, paradox, mystery, and change that are inherent in life. We are wise when we can consider a situation from both inside and outside all relevant viewpoints. We are wise when we are humble and good-humored. There are many ways to be wise; all involve expanding our appreciation of what's involved, of our own limitations and of our place in the world.[22]

None of these ways, of course, is available to even the smartest machine.

"The first thing missing if you take a robot as a companion is *alterity,* the ability to see the world through the eyes of another," Sherry Turkle points out. "Without alterity, there can be no empathy."[23]

Without empathy, there can be no wisdom. Without wisdom, there can be no love. And without love, there can be no empathy. Empathy, wisdom, and love are vital links in the circular chain of consciousness that only we—not machines—have created, and which so urgently needs repairing in our techno-smitten age.

The sacred is also missing from the technology path. The cyber-enthusiasts actually resemble Old Paradigm scientists in their refusal to make a place for Spirit in their machine-dominated worldview.

This worries science writer Chris Anderson, who (although he says "religion" when he means "spirituality") wonders:

> How far can the revolution go without the "humanists" providing something to replace the role of religion? Suppose it turns out that religious instinct and consequent religious group behavior have been a part of our species since sentience first arose?
>
> While science, or at least the breathtakingly mysterious world unveiled by science, is potentially capable of filling that role . . . there is no venue for a group celebration of the mystery of our planet and the universe.[24]

How can there be, if cyborg wannabes, by casting their lot with machines, are devaluing and abandoning the part of themselves that is part of nature?

A NEW HUMILITY

We unlikely creatures known as humans, having arisen as one tiny manifestation of a massive, blind exploration of possible creatures, only imagine that the whole process was designed to lead to us.

JARON LANIER[25]

Group-wisdom researchers agree with technologists that humans no longer occupy the evolutionary pinnacle. But they argue that our new humility comes not from the fact that we are less competent than machines, but because we now understand that we are merely one part of an interdependent, lovingly woven whole that includes all of life.

To be human is not to be better than, but simply different from; it is to be just one expression of Gaia's incredible diversity. At the same time, to be human is to appreciate that we are more than speed, and that our awareness plays an important role in maintaining the balance of our world.

The technology path will always be limited by the reaches of technology itself and by our finite material resources; the collective wisdom path has no limits. But realizing this isn't enough. The modern human mind, cut off for so long from its sources of knowing, still faces the challenge of creating new synapses—of consciously relearning how to exchange living energy with the natural world—and structurally coupling to nature the way our ancestors did.

We can resist the siren call of the cyborg, the easy lure of the ubiquitous, ever-faster, ever-smarter computer, the suicidal tyranny of the omnipotent machine. We can develop and use our technology wisely, with an eye to building a better future for all inhabitants of our planet. As multidimensional beings, we certainly don't need to give the machines we've created the power to define our future.

Though they're following the more demanding path, collective wisdom groups are rediscovering that it's possible to download directly from the universe all the wisdom we need . . . all by ourselves.

* * *

Collective stupidity remains a serious threat to the survival of life on Earth, and when we look around us in almost any direction, it would seem to be in the ascendancy. Lest we despair, remember that the awareness of oneness is growing too, as ancestral wisdom and contemporary science continue to meet and merge.

More and more people are rebuilding their shattered perception, starting to see the big picture, and waking up to a much saner reality—many of them, ironically, shaken out of their slumber by witnessing the very horrors being wrought by collective stupidity.

There's hope. Collective intelligence is coming back, and every single one of us can do our part to hurry it along.

PART THREE

THE RETURN TO FORGOTTEN WISDOM

13
Reconnecting

A Vital Tool for
Restoring Oneness

What we forget we can also remember.

JOHN PERKINS[1]

We are simply laying the groundwork, or preparing the conditions through collective spiritual work, for the next steps in human evolution. . . . Each person must do their part. Nothing more. But nothing less. Let the energy world guide you. Do only what your heart tells you is right.

JUAN NÚÑEZ DEL PRADO[2]

The return of collective intelligence is a process of rediscovery. We all possess the deep knowing that makes it possible; it's simply a matter of reconnecting with it, awakening the ancient gift that sleeps in every modern person's heart. It takes no special skill or training; Gaia provides all the tools and instructions her children need to help her keep their beautiful world alive, balanced, and functioning.

We can start anywhere. Like the threads in an indigenous weaving or the strand of a spider web or the leaf on a tree, each individual action is part of the whole and ultimately leads to the same place.

Fig. 13.1. Weaving a new world: an "embroidery" spider adorns her web.
Photo by Jim Molloy.

The expanded awareness of every single one of us rearranges the field, making possible great changes in our collective perception—and the changes these can produce in our world.

So there's no particular order to the morsels of inspiration in the following sections, which, though separate, overlap and blend into each other. I offer them as food for thought—a smorgasbord of ideas to sample and, I hope, to savor and use. Together, they have the deliciousness of a satisfying meal, the textured beauty of a weaving, the glory of a many-voiced chorus: the epitome of collective wisdom.

Grab a thread—any thread—and see where it leads.

THE INDIAN AND THE CRICKET

Peruvian shamanic teacher, healer, and author Oscar Miró-Quesada Solevo tells the following story:

I was walking with my friend, an American Indian, on a crowded street in New York City when he suddenly exclaimed, "I hear a cricket."

"You're crazy," I said as I observed the crowded noontime street scene in Midtown. Cars were honking, construction crews working, planes flying overhead. "No, I hear a cricket," he insisted, and he proceeded to walk to a flower bed in front of a fancy office building. There, under a leafy plant, he showed me a cricket chirping with life.

"That's amazing," I responded. "You must have fantastic hearing."

"Not really. It all depends on what you're tuned in to," my friend explained.

"I find that hard to believe," I said.

"Watch," my wise friend offered, and he proceeded to drop a handful of coins onto the crowded sidewalk.

Instantly heads turned, eyes darted, and hands reached for pockets to see if they were the poor soul who'd lost his or her money.

"'See," his eyes twinkled, "it all depends on what you're tuned in to."[3]

RECONNECTING: THE PROPHECIES

Every single ill that modern humanity suffers from has only one cause: disconnection from Pachamama.

AMÉRICO YABAR[4]

Man must make two connections. . . . He must reconnect with the earth and he must reconnect with the stars.

CREDO MUTWA[5]

Native shamans the world over say that it's now time to share with the world the knowledge that traditional cultures have safeguarded for millennia. From indigenous people everywhere, we moderns are learning how to relate again to the Earth and our fellow beings in a healthy way.

The need to move from the individual to the collective is predicted with remarkable consistency in the prophecies of many spiritual traditions: the Mayas' Fifth Sun, "the Return to the Beginning";[6] the Hopis' Fifth World; the Hindus' Kali Yuga; the Age of Aquarius; the coming of Shambhala; the Andeans' *taripay pacha,* "the Age of Meeting Ourselves Again."[7] All describe a period of collapse of existing structures and worldviews, leading to a huge shift in awareness and the creation of a new reality based on long-forgotten wisdom.

In *The Turning Point,* Fritjof Capra notes that while "decline and disintegration" are part of every culture's evolution, simultaneously the seeds of a new reality are taking root. "During the process of decline and disintegration the dominant social institutions are still imposing their outdated views but are gradually disintegrating, while new creative minorities face the new challenges with ingenuity and rising confidence," he says.[8]

The return of collective intelligence—"our collective, collaborative interchanges with nature"—will be essential to this transformation.

"During the *Taripay Pacha,* an intricate web of interaction will be rewoven between the human and non-human, the physical and metaphysical, and the natural and the supernatural, an interaction that was once the ordinary state of being in the dim recesses of history," says Joan Parisi Wilcox.

This new age, she explains, is not so much the creation of a new form as the remembering of an ancient form, "when we lived in sync with the pulse of the cosmos instead of, as we do now, with the artificial rhythms of manmade time."

Echoing what the White Lions, bees, turtles, and Black Madonnas are telling us, she stresses that

> the prophecy suggests that all of humanity must help, that it is the collective consciousness that is important to this cosmic transformation.
>
> Therefore, whenever people anywhere or by means of any spiritual tradition raise their spiritual awareness, cleanse themselves of *hucha,*

and act from love rather than from self-interest, the energetic vibration is raised and the likelihood of a collective spiritual evolution is heightened. Consequently, each of us bears responsibility for the prophecy, and each of us has the ability to further its fulfillment.[9]

EXPANDING THE CIRCLE

There is, amidst the ruins of everything destroyed by progress—which is itself henceforth in ruins—a quest for lost truths.

EDGAR MORIN AND ANNE BRIGITTE KERN[10]

Chaos re-envisions ancient wisdom in a brand-new form. . . . Is it possible that we can shift our perception to embrace the self-organized and chaotic whole?

JOHN BRIGGS AND F. DAVID PEAT[11]

As it draws us back into its magical embrace, the circle expands to show us the circle of time linking not only elders to youths, but us to our distant ancestors and our future descendants.

Evolution could never happen without our ancestral anchor to the Earth, and it may be only an illusion anyway: what good are our highly developed intellects today if they've eclipsed our hearts and are being used to invent new ways to harm instead of heal?

If time is in fact circular, progress is illusory, and "back" is where solutions lie. And if the path to collective intelligence goes in a circle, it's no surprise that our remote ancestors should be the ones to usher us in to the era of "meeting ourselves again."

"We must take a great spiritual step backward," says Credo Mutwa. "We must embrace the original view of creation: that everything around us is part of one great and interconnected whole."[12]

According to Morin and Kern, "All that is essential in thinking punctures history, retroacts on the past all the way back to the point of origin, and carries us beyond the future."[13]

Fig. 13.2. Ancient enigmas: pre-Columbian stone spheres found in Costa Rica embody circle magic. Photo courtesy of the Tico Times.

Reaching to us with the primordial gift of the circle, our ancestors also hand our children a vital tool for restoring oneness. In the circle, nobody is better than, or worse than, anybody else. Teacher and student are interchangeable, each learning from the other.

The circle makes children feel welcome in their community, on Earth, in the universe. It's a place to learn their own and others' value and strengths, becoming aware of their sameness and their differentness, their deep connectedness with each other and all beings. Like the wombs that held them so recently, it's a place of comfort.

Morin believes that "teaching understanding of each other as the one necessary condition of humanity's moral and intellectual solidarity" is "the truly spiritual mission of education. Understanding what is human means understanding our unity in diversity. We must conceive the unity of the multiple, the multiplicity of the one."[14]

The circle fulfills this mission.

The mysterious pre-Columbian granite spheres found in Costa Rica embody the circle's recurring power. Nobody knows who made the perfectly round giants—some measuring over nine feet in diameter and weighing as much as twenty tons—how they were crafted, or their purpose.

Theories abound. One of the most convincing to date is Ivar Zapp's: he offers evidence that the spheres were navigational markers for an ancient seafaring culture, aligned with power points around the globe.[15]

Still, knowing what we now know about the magical and mystical power of both stones and circles, we may discover that the spheres hold an even deeper significance that has yet to be deciphered. Jack Rudloe recounts how he felt when he was drawn to embrace one of them. It "gave off a feeling of wholeness, of connectedness with the universe— the feeling defied words," he says. "No wonder Costa Rica never had a major war, I thought."[16]

RENEWING TRUST

Look deep into nature, and then you will understand everything better.

ALBERT EINSTEIN[17]

In wildness is the preservation of the world.

HENRY DAVID THOREAU

Be not afraid of the universe.

SILA[18]

Imprisoned inside every shattered, scattered modern human is a whole soul—what Martín Prechtel calls our "Indigenous Soul." This ancestral part, which refuses to succumb to what Prechtel terms "the ruined, depressed flatness left by the hollow failure of this mechanized, orphaned culture," remembers what it was like to be in continuous communication with the living universe and longs to live there again.[19]

And it can! But first we need to remember how to trust nature, and how to trust ourselves as legitimate, dues-paying members of the natural world. This can seem a bit overwhelming for many contemporary people, who may not be sure where to start. But all we have to do is become aware again of the world we are part of.

"Mystical, esoteric traditions understand the individual human's power to influence manifestation in this world," say Nan Moss and David Corbin. Citing the teachings of contemporary philosopher and mystic Eckhart Tolle, they note:

When we focus our attention on anything in Nature—a cloud, a breeze, or the plant that waves in the wind—we complete a circuit of awareness.

When we admire the beauty of the sky, the attention we offer becomes a catalyst for the sky's awareness of itself, which, in turn, sparks our own self-awareness.

Tolle asserts that Nature is waiting for us to wake up to this, and the beings of Nature are calling us to draw closer to them through our hearts and attention.[20]

It is the ever-present magic of *ayni.*

Bill Pfeiffer points out that "cultivating trust in the unfolding of the universe allows us to explore new, creative possibilities instead of being paralyzed by fear and despair."[21]

With this in mind, he created the Wild Earth Intensive (WEI), a ten-day spiritual experience that helps participants peel back layers of "civilized" learning and contact the wild souls that lie buried beneath the trappings of contemporary cultural brainwashing. His inspiring book, *Wild Earth, Wild Soul: A Manual for an Ecstatic Culture,* offers a blueprint for a return to a healthy, harmonious way of living.

"We can remember an ancient way of knowing that helped us humans thrive and develop for over a hundred-thousand years," he says, adding that the intensives enable the larger intelligence that is already within each of us—the wisdom and brilliance he insists are encoded in every human—to blossom and flourish. "Each participant is encouraged to trust this intelligence—his or her deepest knowing," he explains. "It is a wonderful paradox that a WEI, while providing a nurturing container where we don't lose our individual uniqueness and emotional stability, strengthens our sense of interconnection with each other and the universe. Participants come to recognize or develop their particular gifts and see how they enrich the group and eventually, the larger community."[22]

Magic can and does occur whenever we're able to move out of our brain-boxes.

Peruvian master and mystic Américo Yabar and his son Gayle take groups on powerful adventures in the Andean wilderness to experience the *salk'a* (wild, undomesticated) path. Through energy exchanges at sacred sites, communication with the elements, and ceremonies with native shamans, participants reawaken their awareness of the sacred in nature—and their own *salk'a* selves.

*Fig. 13.3. Américo Yabar with Q'ero shamans: breaking free from the tame.
Photo by Dery Dyer.*

"Gaia *is* wilderness," writes Stephen Harrod Buhner. "Gaia is the Earth ecosystem functioning with its wildness intact. . . . When you begin shifting your perception . . . [a] certain wildness begins to re-enter the self. Speech begins to change. A deep connection with the sacredness and intelligence of the Earth begins. Pagan sensibilities recur. You begin to become 'of the heath,' wild, once more."[23]

Says James David Audlin: "Ironically, it is in the place associated with chaos, the uncivilized region, where the sacred things are most safe."[24]

SEEKING NECTAR

"Nature is a profoundly important companion, mentor, and advisor, because it is our Ground of Being," Bill Pfeiffer says. "If you sit under a tree and observe its textures, listen to its surroundings, rub the fallen leaves on your palms, and be still, you will gain a sense of connection, gratitude, and awe. I can't explain how it works, but it does—and not just with trees, but almost anywhere 'out there' when we make the intention to connect."[25]

"Did you know that trees and plants not only produce oxygen for us but, according to the Q'ero Indians, they also produce a refined living energy, called *sami*—meaning nectar?" asks Elizabeth Jenkins. "This could be the explanation for why we instinctively feel the need to go outside for a walk when we are grumpy. We are seeking *sami,* nature's nectar. This may also be the reason we feel better after we **do** go for a walk. Not only are we taking in oxygen but also a form of refined living energy that refreshes our whole being, our living energy system. How do we know this? Because the original scientists of the earth have taught us that it is so."[26]

The Andean masters also say that connecting with Pachamama can be as simple as releasing our heavy, toxic *hucha* to her through our feet and bringing light, refined, healing *sami* into our energy bubble. According to Américo Yabar (giving a nod at how disconnected modern people have become), we can do this even on the top floor of a high-rise building.[27]

Both Jenkins and Yabar stress that communicating with nature the way the Andeans do is "simple and natural." Jenkins emphasizes:

The Andean Path wasn't about nature meditations, nature exercises, or even rituals or prayers to nature. It was about cultivating a state of contemplation that made absorption into the very power of nature, and a subsequent life transforming exchange of living energies between nature and human beings, possible.

The essence of this path was at once so simple, natural and ordinary, yet so utterly mystical. And this contemplation was like a kind of spiritual breathing that easily conducted these miraculous energy exchanges.[28]

HEARING THE EARTH

Peruvian shaman Rosa María Alzamora gave author Alfonsina Barrionuevo this teaching, based on her own experience:

I learned to silence my thoughts so I could hear the voices of the water. There are moments when the river is young, is old, has the voice of a woman, voice of a male. The creek, no matter how much water it has, is sometimes an old man.

The only way to listen to it is to be silent, but not to silence one's words, but rather be silent within, and the way to be silent is to know how to listen. Then nature begins to speak to you. You begin to receive the message of the winds, young and old, and even the winds that are bad.

You can hear the message of the Earth with your hands, your body, your womb. When I was a little girl I remember they told me that I should put my belly on the earth, that I should embrace Mother Earth, that I should ask her why she had sent me. I did it many times and she never answered me.

Until one day when I was crying for some reason and needed consolation. My mother wasn't nearby, my grandmother wasn't there, nobody. I threw myself on my belly and felt that the earth embraced me, that our hearts were beating together.

She told me why I had come. For the same purpose as the other Rosa, my grandmother. I listened to her with my throat, with the mouth of my stomach, with my bare womb.

For a moment I felt fear. I stood up. Shortly afterwards I became aware of her tenderness, that the air was sweet, it was warm, and I threw myself on the earth again, and fell asleep.

It was the strongest contact I had, I sought and finally found her answer. It's what we need to learn. What is called the triple harmony, with ourselves, with that which surrounds us, in other words, nature, and also with those who have accompanied us.

Coexistence in harmony with many people is a coexistence of fertility, because it produces. These three harmonies produce what, in Western terms, is known as health.[29]

14
Rebuilding
Wholeness Can Heal Us

In the course of our planetary journey we have gone through positive disintegration countless times. The life living through us repeatedly died to old forms and old ways. We know this dying in the splitting of the stars, the cracking open of seeds in the soil, the relinquishment of gills and fins as we crawled onto dry land.

JOANNA MACY AND MOLLY YOUNG BROWN[1]

The shamans teach us—the indigenous people teach us— once you change the mindset, then it's pretty easy to have the objective reality change around it.

JOHN PERKINS[2]

Reconnecting with the Earth is simple. But just as initiations in traditional cultures demand some kind of dismemberment, staying reconnected requires breaking down the walls we've built inside and outside of ourselves, toppling old secure structures—as the native prophecies say needs to happen in the world—so that we can replace them with new (for us) configurations. Of course, this must include being on the lookout for collective stupidity in all its guises and consciously unplugging from its insidious reach whenever possible. Anodea Judith writes:

Breaking the old form is necessary. It creates the fertile ground for a new emergence, much as plowing prepares the soil, or decaying compost fertilizes a garden. But the passage itself—the liminal state between the loss of the old and the beginning of the new—is a frightening and mysterious process. . . .

Breakdown is usually required before breakthrough can occur. . . . We must undo who we think we are and get down to our basic essence in order to build a new structure.[3]

Elizabeth Jenkins points out:

If you change your beliefs you have to change your actions. So if we truly began to live from this higher paradigm of harmony with nature, respecting the sacredness of all life and setting the needs of the whole before those of ourselves or our particular group, we would have to endure an ordeal of growth, develop a generosity of spirit, that would test us at every level. . . .

But ahhh, the benefits! Waking up HAPPY every day with a sense of freedom and belonging, knowing I am part of a great and glorious creation, feeling a magnificent life force flowing through me, seeing the world from a perspective that at last made sense to my mind *and* satisfied my soul.[4]

REMEMBERING GENEROSITY

Altruism appears to serve an evolutionary function in living creatures. In its inventiveness, nature—including human nature—may be on our side.

MARILYN FERGUSON[5]

It's hard to believe that we might have to remember how to give. Generosity, an essential part of nature, was essential in our ancestors' world and remains essential for ours. But giving was one of the skills many of us lost on our way to our contemporary me-mine culture of scarcity and selfishness.

As Morin and Kern point out, "The effect on civilization produced by the commodification of everything . . . is the disappearance of the gift freely given."[6]

We take our cue, of course, from Mother Earth.

"The ground of being is generosity," says Brian Swimme. "The root reality of the universe is generosity of being. That's why the ground of being is empty: every thing has been given over to the universe."[7]

"If we look at nature as a whole . . . it is, if nothing else, not selfish," Joan Halifax observes, adding that elder cultures imitate Earth's generosity in many ways.[8]

Antonio García of the San Juan Pueblo recalls how each morning his parents would "take sacred cornmeal, they'd blow their breath on it so the gods would know who they were and they'd feed the gods and they'd ask for good weather, they'd ask for rain, and they'd ask for good fortune for everybody, not only people of the Pueblo, but everybody in the world."[9]

"There are many ways to reconnect," says Linda Tucker. "Our totem might be the doves that we feed at Trafalgar Square, or the stray cat that we rescue along the road, or the vegetables that we plant in our garden, or even the crystal that we cherish as a light-radiating stone in our house. There are many ways to give something back for what we have received. The important thing is to start making the connections, and the interconnections."[10]

GIVING WITH WORDS

David Abram underscores the importance of what he calls the "animistic style of speaking," which, he says,

> opens the possibility of interaction and exchange, allowing reciprocity to begin to circulate between our bodies and the breathing earth.

If we speak of things as inert or inanimate objects, we deny their ability to actively engage and interact with us. We foreclose their capacity to reciprocate our attentions, to draw us into silent dialogue, to inform and instruct us.

How monotonous our speaking becomes when we speak only to ourselves! And how *insulting* to the other beings—to foraging black bears and twisted old cypresses—that no longer sense us talking to them, but only about them, as though they were not present in our world. . . .

Yet if we no longer call out to the moon slipping between the clouds or whisper to the spider setting the silken struts of her web, well, then the numerous powers of this world will no longer address *us*—and if they still try, we will not likely hear them. . . .

We can no longer avail ourselves of their perspectives or their guidance, and our human affairs suffer as a result.[11]

GIVING WITH CEREMONY

Sacred ceremony is a big part of recovering one's Indigenous Soul. According to Malidoma Somé, "The soul of any man or woman craves for this touchstone to the inner self that puts us back in touch with our primal selves."[12]

"Just as a river irrigates the landscape, the love within each of us needs to give back to the universe from which it sprang," Bill Pfeiffer reminds us. "Our love, expressed in myriad creative ways, feeds the unseen energies (the spirits) that give rise to the manifested world. During ceremony, we make a conscious and deliberate effort to honor and embrace these energies."[13]

"A person's life is ritualized who accepts the fact that everything he or she does is the work of the hands of the Divine," adds Somé. "Everyone can do this. Anyone can, before going out in the morning, send a little prayer to the ancestors on the hills or in the river. It takes a word or two, or at most a few sentences."[14]

RECIPE FOR RECIPROCITY

Once upon a time, a traveler arrived in a village that had been suffering from hard times. Bad weather had caused the crops to fail, and there was hardly any food.

The traveler knocked on the first door he came to and asked for food and drink.

"Go away!" he was told. "We don't even have enough for ourselves!"

He went from house to house, but everywhere the answer was the same.

"Very well, then," declared the traveler. "I'm hungry, so I guess I'll have to make some stone soup. I might as well make enough for everybody." He asked if someone could lend him a big pot.

One of the villagers brought a pot and the rest watched curiously as the traveler built a fire, then carefully selected some large stones from the side of the road, washed them off, and placed them in the pot. He filled the pot with water, covered it, and put it over the fire.

"The stones have to boil for a while," he explained. "It improves the flavor."

He rubbed his hands together happily. "There's nothing like a good stone soup!" he exclaimed, lifting the cover of the pot and peeking inside. "I wonder if anyone has a little salt? That always makes it better."

"I do," said one villager.

"Wonderful!" said the traveler, as the man handed him a pinch of salt for the soup. "You know, I wish we had a little piece of onion. That would make this soup really delicious!"

One of the women spoke up. "I have an onion," she said. When she came back, she was also carrying two cloves of garlic, which she threw into the pot too.

"Oh, this is marvelous!" exclaimed the traveler. "This will be the best soup I've ever made! Although," he added wistfully, "stone soup is even better with a little cabbage. It's too bad we don't have any cabbage."

"I have a cabbage!" yelled an old man, and he hurried home to get it.

"I was saving a couple of carrots in my pantry," the lady standing next to him volunteered. "Maybe they'd be good in the soup."

"Carrots? Of course!" cried the traveler.

"How about a potato?" asked another villager.

"Yes, yes!" The traveler clapped his hands excitedly.

One of the villagers remembered he had a stalk of celery in his kitchen. Someone else brought a handful of rice. Somebody even came up with a hambone with some meat still on it.

Everything went into the pot, and as the aroma of the bubbling soup filled the air, more and more people found something they could add to it: some herbs, a turnip, a few beans, a bit of chicken.

The traveler carefully stirred the soup, tasted it, and finally pronounced it ready. The whole village gathered to enjoy the feast, many returning again and again to fill their bowls with the tasty broth.

For the first time in many months, their bellies were full, and everybody agreed it was the most delicious soup they had ever eaten.*

* * *

Stone soup is rich in more than flavor. Like all great stories, this old tale speaks in metaphors and holds meaning on multiple levels.

When he arrives in the village asking for food, the traveler—a trickster figure whose role is to enlighten by shaking up the status quo—finds a people who have forgotten their interconnectedness. Hoarding their scraps of food, they're incapable of sharing: they can perceive only scarcity.

The traveler then asks to borrow a pot. Cooking is an act of creation. It takes place in a cauldron, the circular magical "womb," using fire, the element of transformation. The villagers provide this container for the changes to come.

Stones—the most ancient form of Mother Earth and repositories of magical power—are the basis for the healing soup. As "soul food"—the catalyst for the alchemical transformation the traveler is

---

*The origin of the Stone Soup story is unknown. Many different versions exist throughout Europe, including one that served as the basis of a 1904 play by Irish poet W. B. Yeats, *The Pot of Broth.*

bringing—the stones remind the villagers that they can trust Mother Earth to nourish them.

The traveler covers the stones with water, another womb image and symbol of purification. Now the villagers must complete the creation.

As the fire transforms the ingredients in the pot into the magical soup, the villagers themselves become transformed. They realize that they have much more than they thought, and they start remembering how to give. Making their contributions to the pot, sharing their individual energies and gifts, they reconnect with their oneness. Eventually they are able to transcend their individual egos, overcome their fear, and work together for the good of all.

In making stone soup, the villagers end up practicing not only *ayni*, but collective intelligence: the final product is much greater than the sum of its parts.

REDISCOVERING COMMUNITY

We can wait for a thousand years, barring a calamity, or we can have it all now. Not by competing but by joining forces—as persons, as professions, as communities, as nations.
MARILYN FERGUSON[15]

Perhaps we humans already know how to build a win-win world where we share the earth equitably and peacefully with each other and with all species.
HAZEL HENDERSON[16]

It's every one of our unique individual talents contributing to the whole that will produce the inspired genius our world needs. This is how communities are born, and how they thrive.

As always, nature is our teacher.

"In an ecosystem, no being is excluded from the network," Fritjof Capra points out. "Every species, even the smallest bacterium, contributes to the sustainability of the whole." The blueprint for sustainable human communities already exists; all we have to do is follow it. "Since the outstanding characteristic of the Earth household is its inherent ability to sustain life," Capra says, "a sustainable human community is one designed in such a manner that its ways of life, businesses, economy, physical structures, and technologies do not interfere with nature's inherent ability to sustain life."[17]

The world's indigenous people followed nature's example and can show us how they did it. Malidoma Somé lists some of the characteristics of a life-giving community, based on what he observed in his Dagara village:

1. **Unity of spirit.** The community feels an indivisible sense of unity. Each member is like a cell in a body. The group needs the individual and vice versa.

2. **Trust.** Everyone is moved to trust everyone else by principle. There is no sense of discrimination or elitism. This trust assumes that everyone is well-intentioned.

3. **Openness.** People are open to each other unreservedly. This means that individual problems quickly become community problems. Being open to each other depends upon trust.

4. **Love and caring.** What you have is for everybody. There is a sense of sharing, which diminishes the sense of egotistic behavior. To have while the others don't is an expression of your making up a society of your own.

5. **Respect for the Elders.** They are the pillars and the collective memory of the community. They hold the wisdom that keeps the community together. They initiate the young ones, prescribe the rituals for various occasions and monitor the dynamics of the community.

6. **Respect for Nature.** Nature is the principal book out of which all wisdom is learned. It is the place where initiation happens. It is the place from where medicine comes. It nourishes the entire community.

7. **Cult of the Ancestors.** The ancestors are not dead. They live

in the spirits in the community. They are reborn into the trees, the mountains, the rivers and the stones to guide and inspire the community.

Somé adds, "A community that doesn't have a ritual cannot exist."[18]

Sioux medicine man Fools Crow always urged his patients "to emphasize in their prayers that they wished to be well so they could help others. The need for curing had to transcend personal wishes if a lasting success was to be achieved. Fools Crow emphasized that what was being done was being done for the sake of the community."[19]

In the Andes, "if you claim to have a power, it means absolutely nothing until it has been demonstrated in a way that benefits your community," says Elizabeth Jenkins.[20]

When two Andean *paqos* meet, it's customary for them to challenge each other to determine how much power each has. The winner is then obliged to help the loser learn everything the winner knows.[21]

"This philosophy applies to group competitions as well and ensures the uplifting of the collective to the highest level through the required sharing of best practices," Jenkins points out. "It is the precise opposite of our current corporate model of competition that strives for the advancement and enrichment of the few at the expense of the collective."[22]

"What we need is to be able to come together with a constantly increasing mindset of wanting to do the right thing," Somé stresses, "even though we know very well that we don't know how or where to start."[23]

HUMPTY-DUMPTY'S LESSON

Humpty-Dumpty sat on a wall.
Humpty-Dumpty had a great fall.
All the king's horses and all the king's men
Couldn't put Humpty together again.

NURSERY RHYME

There is a level where all—where you, I, God—are one, and are trying to respond to the need that Earth has to heal herself.
RABBI ZALMAN SCHACHTER-SHALOMI[24]

We have to open the way to a fifth dimension that could be called the dimension of universal consciousness.
JULIO CÉSAR PAYÁN[25]

Until we heal our planet, we can never have lasting health. Our efforts to "conquer" disease by attacking it with Old Paradigm weapons—one cell at a time, one germ at a time, one organ at a time—are increasingly futile: we may win a spectacular short-term skirmish here and there, but the fragmented approach can have only fragmentary results in the long run.

Like Humpty-Dumpty on the wall, we placed ourselves high above nature. Now our hubris is presenting us with the bill. We have shattered into smithereens. Each broken piece requires a specialist to attend to it. And as long as all we can see are the pieces, we're as doomed as Humpty-Dumpty.

But the good news is that we are so much more than our splintered parts. There's hope for Humpty, and for us. Far from being separate bits of matter that, once broken, are beyond repair, we are energy, part of All That Is—expressions of spirit suffering, like Humpty, the illusion of fragmentation. We contain the intelligence of the cosmos—wisdom that transcends time and space. We're remembering that we can make and unmake illness.

It's a collective challenge: the perceptual awakening that must precede our restoration to health may be where relearning collective intelligence can help us the most.

The *taripay pacha* prophecy predicts the emergence of twelve "supreme healers" who will be recognized by their ability to heal infallibly, "any ailment every time," and will open the way for humanity to enter the new level of consciousness. But as Parisi Wilcox stresses, "it is the collective consciousness that is important to this cosmic transformation."[26]

Julio César Payán maintains that just as our "wise organism" creates disease in order to evolve, it has "the power, the strength or the knowledge to disappear it, modify it or modulate it when it discovers a new order that no longer makes [it] necessary."[27]

Herein, the great paradox: the global disease we've created is potentially fatal to all beings on Earth. But it may also be the imperative that will finally oblige us to come together and fashion a reality that will heal not only the disease itself, but the fragmentation that caused it.

Larry Dossey predicts that what he calls "Era III" or "nonlocal" medicine will include the perception of One Mind: "Health and healing are not just a personal but a collective affair."[28] The Maharishi Effect, in which transcendental meditators were able to reduce crime, confirms that such individual actions as meditation, prayer, releasing *hucha,* and practicing *tonglen* can have impressive collective consequences.

The Andean prophecy seems to be telling us that if we can regain oneness, we will restore health in our world and ourselves and will no longer need to generate illness in order to evolve. By healing "any ailment every time," the "supreme healers" will open us to a reality in which sickness has no part to play.

"During this period, when our healing capacities are fully harnessed, we can begin to move out of the deterministic stream of physical evolution and into the more creative stream of conscious evolution," says Parisi Wilcox. "The emphasis of life begins to shift from a physical expression to an energetic one."[29]

Separation made us sick; wholeness can heal us. As Payán puts it, "The process of personal transformation begins with one's own searches as a singularity and with one's relationship with the whole universe. From this point of view it is personal and universal at the same time, it is what allows us, as certain societies called primitive do every day, to 'enrhythm' ourselves or vibrate with all that lives: the hill, the river, the tree, the clouds, the sea, the stars."[30]

Adds Joan Halifax, "The Earth is imperiled. It is suffering. Living as part of its body, we suffer with and through it. Awakening through this suffering, we might be able to help the Earth and ourselves, heal it, and thus heal ourselves."[31]

WELCOMING BACK THE GODDESS

She may be down, but she's not out. The Black Madonnas show us that the Sacred Feminine remains a potent force in our consciousness and our world.

Leonardo Boff and Rose Marie Muraro hold the optimistic view that the human being "is not definitively the hostage of the institutions of the past, especially of the patriarchy . . . that which was historically constructed can also be historically deconstructed."[32]

"A new paradigm is emerging seminally, a paradigm of re-connection, of re-enchantment about nature and of compassion for those who are suffering," Boff believes. "One sees the dawn of a renewed tenderness for life and an authentic feeling of belonging to the loving Mother Earth."[33]

He stresses that "the most important thing is not to know, but to feel,"[34] which places care—the essence of the Divine Feminine—back in its rightful place.

"To give centrality to care . . . means bringing down the dictatorship of cold and abstract rationality," Boff says. "It means putting the collective interest of society, of the whole biotic and earthly community, above the interests that are exclusively human."[35]

What he hopes will become a "culture" of care will give rise to "a new state of conscience and connection with the Earth and everything that exists and lives in the Earth."[36]

Care, of course, implies responsibility. Mircea Eliade observes that "primitive" man "courageously assumes immense responsibilities—for example, that of collaborating in the creation of the cosmos, or of creating his own world, or of ensuring the life of plants and animals, and so on."

But, he stresses, "it is a *responsibility on the cosmic plane,* in contradistinction to the moral, social, or historical responsibilities that are alone regarded as valid in modern civilizations. . . . Existentially, the primitive always puts himself in a cosmic context."[37]

And now, so do we. Says Ervin Laszlo, "The Akashic experience . . . inspires solidarity, love, empathy, and a sense of responsibility for each other and the environment."[38]

"We are citizens of the Earth and, thus, we share the same fate as the Earth," say Morin and Kern. "This shared destiny imposes a telluric responsibility on humankind. . . . A partnership is required: a partnership of humanity and nature, of technology and ecology, of conscious and unconscious intelligence."[39] Riane Eisler agrees, calling for "a new science of empathy, a science that will use both reason and intuition 'to bring about a change in the collective mind.'" The new world, she says, "will be much more rational, in the true sense of the word: a world animated and guided by the consciousness that both ecologically and socially we are inextricably linked with one another and our environment."[40]

15
Rediscovery
Seeing with Our Hearts

Love is the activity of evoking being, of enhancing life.
BRIAN SWIMME[1]

We have only the world that we bring forth with others,
and only love helps us bring it forth.
HUMBERTO MATURANA AND FRANCISCO VARELA[2]

We don't need anybody else
To tell us what is real
Inside each one of us is love
And we know how it feels
PAUL McCARTNEY[3]

Creation is an act of love; love is an act of creation. Love and creativity spring from the same source—the ground of being that Tibetans call the Void and Navajos call—appropriately—Beauty.[4] Creation and love are interchangeable at every level: in the cosmos, in the tiniest particle, in the human heart.

The conscious, intelligent, responsive universe that interacts continuously with all beings is responsible for creative inspiration. And its driving force is love. The flow of loving energy from the cosmos—David Bohm's "holomovement," the unfolding of reality from the implicate order[5]—materializes in the glorious diversity of nature's forms as well as in human artistic creation. Whenever we create, we are expressing the universe's love. And whenever we express love, we are making manifest the cosmos's creative power.

A symphony, a poem, and a baby all obey the same need to be expressed—the "inner need" that Wassily Kandinsky called the basis of art.[6] This need is encoded in our souls and is not limited to human beings.

Love creates life. Its energy is generous, bountiful, joyous. The dynamic is a limitless outpouring, like a gushing fountain. It shares freely, unconditionally—a mother nursing her child. According to Brian Swimme, love "begins as allurement—as attraction," because "alluring activity is the basic reality of the macrocosmic universe . . . the basic binding energy found everywhere in reality."[7]

"Love is a manner of relating . . . that occurs spontaneously practically in all living systems," says Humberto Maturana. "Love is the fundamental relational domain in which human beings exist, and constituted the relational conditions for our evolutionary origin. . . . It opens up the possibility of reflection and is based on a form of perception that allows the other to appear legitimate. In this way, a space arises in which cooperation seems possible and our loneliness is transcended: the other is given a presence to which we relate with respect."[8]

In acting as a conduit for the universe's love, human creation ultimately creates love. As author Maxine Greene puts it, "Imagination is what, above all, makes empathy possible. It is what enables us to cross the empty spaces between ourselves and those . . . we have called 'other' over the years."[9]

When Kandinsky lamented that "art has lost her soul," he might well have been referring the loss of our ability to love our world. Now that we're in danger of losing our only home, we're realizing that every being in it has the ability to manifest the loving power of the universe: each of us is a creator, and each of us *must* contribute our love and our creations if life on our planet is to survive.

SEEING WITH OUR HEARTS

Look around. Better yet, let your heart look around. Are we happy with the way we interact with one another? Are we creating or destroying the world given to us? I suspect our hearts may hold some of the answers.

RENEE A. LEVI[10]

Certainly we are not taught to see with the heart, and yet the instinct is there. Ask anyone quickly to identify himself, and he will point to his heart, not to his head.

ALICE O. HOWELL[11]

It is only with the heart that we can see rightly; what is essential is invisible to the eye.

ANTOINE DE SAINT-EXUPÉRY[12]

The eyes of love are the eyes of the heart. They offer a secret escape route from the prison of our brain-boxes—a way to connect directly with the essence of everything, with no interference from our so very limited "rational" vision.

For most of us, the eyes of the heart offer a new way of seeing—the expanded perception that our ancestors used.

As John Perkins recalls, Shuar elder and shaman Tampur told him the following:

"Do as your spirit, your heart, directs. Don't think too much, the way my grandchildren are taught to do in the mission schools.

"Thinking is fine when we have to figure something out, like how to place a pole to help us get fruit from the spiny chonta tree that is impossible to climb. But when it comes to most things in life, the heart has the voice to listen to, because the heart knows how to follow the advice of the spirits. So I listen to my heart a lot. . . .

"Your heart is part of the universe. If you listen to your heart, you hear the Voice of the Universe. . . . Great wisdom is spoken every moment by the Voice of the Universe. You only need to listen. Your heart is always listening.

"Crossing your hands over your heart may help you to remember." Slowly he raised his hands and laid them across his heart. Do this sometimes.[13]

Sioux holy man Fools Crow explains:

If I decide with my mind I am influenced by all kinds of thoughts that fight against one another. If I try to decide with my eyes, even though I see with love, it is hard not to be influenced by what I actually see—how people look, react, and what they are doing.

If I decide with my heart, my judgments are never harsh. My heart takes into account the things that have hurt people—what they have had to deal with just to stay sane and alive. I guess this can be applied to most of the people in the world.

My heart thinks about fairness, comfort and hope.[14]

Renee A. Levi maintains that the intelligence of the heart brings in messages of empathy, connection, and love from both local and nonlocal energy fields and communicates with other hearts through entrainment.

"Perhaps . . . the individual human heart or the amplified heart resonance in groups can entrain with yet greater energetic forces in the universe, listening for messages that might help us live together more effectively than we seem to have been able to do with our brains solely in charge," she suggests.[15]

Interestingly, a 2013 study by Sweden's University of Gothenburg published in *Frontiers in Neuroscience* revealed that when people sing in unison, their heartbeats automatically synchronize, reminding us of the way our ancestors used chanting and drumming in their spiritual practices.[16]

Stephen Harrod Buhner claims that the kind of imagination that allows humans to comprehend and communicate with their environment "occurs not through or in the brain but through and in the heart."[17]

Citing numerous recent studies of the heart's hitherto-unsuspected role in perception, Joseph Chilton Pearce points out that "the heart, earth and sun furnish us the fundamental materials for our reality-making. . . . Heart radiation saturates every cell, DNA molecule, glia, and so on, and helps determine their function and destiny," he explains. "From this viewpoint the heart seems a frequency generator, creating the fields of information out of which we build our experience of ourselves and the world." It is the heart, he says, entraining with the brain, that will enable us to see again—to "see all things as 'holy' or whole, as William Blake did, or 'see God in each other,' as Muktananda did, or find God in the 'least of these our brothers,' as Jesus did," and which "offers us a dominion over our world that we have not yet accepted or exercised"—the same dominion, born of love, that may have permitted our remote ancestors to move gigantic stones.[18]

The eyes of the heart see the big picture, helping us understand that every one of us is a victim of humanity's mistakes, and love is our only hope of dissolving the fear that drives collective stupidity.

Robert Wolff gives us a dramatic description of the way he learned to use the eyes of the heart. He had been hiking in the Malaysian jungle with Ahmeed, his Sng'oi shaman teacher, and was getting thirsty. Finally he decided to try to find some water.

> "Do not talk," Ahmeed said—I knew he meant do not think. "Water inside heart," he said next, with a gesture of his hand on his heart. I knew he meant I should sense *inside*—not with my mind, but from the inside. . . .
>
> As soon as I stopped thinking, planning, deciding, analyzing—using my mind, in short—I felt as if I was pushed in a certain direction. I walked a few steps and immediately saw a big leaf with perhaps half a cup of water in it. . . .
>
> My perception opened further. I no longer saw water—what I felt with my whole being was a leaf-with-water-in-it, attached to a plant that grew in soil surrounded by uncounted other plants, all part of

the same blanket of living things covering the soil, which was also part of a larger living skin around the earth.

And nothing was separate; all was one, the same thing: water—leaf—plant—trees—soil—animals—earth—air—sunlight and little wisps of wind. The all-ness was everywhere, and I was part of it. . . .

Standing over a leaf with a little water in it, somewhere in the jungles of Malaysia, I did not think in words. I did not think. I bathed in that overwhelming sense of oneness. I felt as if a light was lit deep inside me. I knew I was radiating something—love, perhaps—for this incredible world, this rich, varied, and totally interconnected world of creations that, at the same time, gave love to me.

And with the love, I also felt a very deep sense of belonging.[19]

AN UNCOMMON LOVE STORY

In a cave in Borneo, a love story unfolds every day. The BBC's *Planet Earth* documentary series has captured a horrifically creepy sequence: thousands of bats roosting inside a huge cave have produced a mountain of dung, upon which a living carpet of cockroaches feeds continuously, in a crawling, gobbling frenzy.[20]

A love story???

When seen from our usual modern human perspective, this nightmarish scene undoubtedly elicits instant fear and loathing. But what if we were to view it as a living system, whose components are working together in perfect, harmonious cooperation and reciprocity? What if we were to imagine what the bats and cockroaches might be experiencing? What if, instead of automatically recoiling with repulsion, we paused for a moment and tried to see the scene with the eyes of the heart—the loving eyes of Mother Earth?

Here's what we might see: The bats, flocking together in synchronized flight, soar out of the cave each evening to feed—and occasionally, to offer themselves as food for waiting birds of prey. When the survivors return to roost and deposit their droppings, they bring the cockroaches food that the cave-dwelling bugs could never otherwise obtain.

In exchange, the cockroaches, also swarming in unison, clean the bats' home, recycling their waste. Each species, and each individual being, is in service to another; all are acting together for the good of the whole.

Who can say what kind of love binds this cave's creatures? What allurement brought them together in the first place?

Viewed archetypally, this love story has a message for us. A cave is a womb, a place of gestation and transformation "where the germinating powers of the earth are concentrated, where oracles speak, where initiates are reborn in spiritual understanding, and where souls ascend to celestial light."[21]

The bats, symbols of shamanic death and rebirth, roost head-down, resembling fetuses preparing to be born. In the Tarot, the Hanged Man is suspended head-down, representing the mystic who serves by placing heart above head.

The bats venture forth on their perilous journey and then return to the womb, enacting the hero's transformational quest and life's eternal cycles.

The dung is *hucha,* the heavy energy we must release and offer as food to Pachamama for recycling; the cockroaches are a manifestation of Mother Earth's generosity in helpfully digesting that which we don't need.

Love stories are happening all around us, all the time. Imagination can help us expand our limited vision and start seeing all of them as part of the big picture.

We can reframe our reality—sometimes even transform what we once viewed with horror into something necessary and beautiful—simply by looking at it with the eyes of the heart.

LOVING AS ONE

The universe would never bother to create two Shakespeares. That would only reveal limited creativity. The Ultimate Mystery from which all beings emerge prefers Ultimate Extravagance, each being glistening with freshness, ontologically unique, never to be repeated. Each being is required. None can be eliminated or ignored, for not one is redundant.

BRIAN SWIMME[22]

People come to see each other in a very different way, with different eyes. . . . They find themselves able to look beyond appearances—dress, stature, skin color—to see a deeper reflection in, and connection with, one another. They begin to notice the myriad forms in which people offer their gifts.

CENTERED ON THE EDGE[23]

When we relearn how to "think as one," we rediscover how to love as one. Group magic gives us a way to plug into the loving, creative energy of the cosmos.

This process needs every single one of us, with our unique configuration of energies, stories, and gifts, each one channeling cosmic energy in a way that has never been done before and will never be done again. It asks us to see, hear, and accept each other in all our glorious diversity.

For Maxine Greene, telling our stories—as she puts it, "naming our lived worlds," as art does, as literature does—is a powerful way to bring our worlds, and our hearts, together, forming "an expanding community that takes shape when diverse people, speaking as *who* and not *what* they are, come together in both speech and action to constitute something in common among themselves." She adds, "We are all the same, that is, human, in such a way that nobody is ever the same as anyone else who ever lived, lives, or will live." She quotes Hannah Arendt, who noted that "even though we are on a common ground, we have different locations on that ground, and 'each one sees or hears from a different position.'"[24] Each of our viewpoints, shaped by our personal joys and heartbreaks, is necessary to create a truly new vision—and from it, a new world. This is the creative power of the group. Together, we create a new configuration—a new, unique channel for the endless out-pouring of energy from the field.

"If we [like the Tibetans and Navajos] can awaken to the profound reality of our sacred world and develop a responsible relationship with it, we, too, may realize our connection with this living, pulsating universe of totally interconnected forms, energies, and ideas," writes Peter Gold. "Knowing this, how can one help but develop a sense of wonder, comfort, responsibility, and—in its purest expression—compassion for all beings and objects with which we coexist and interpenetrate in this amazing reality? Is not this awareness true love?"[25]

16
Rebirth

Love Will Replace Fear

To see the World in a grain of sand,
And a Heaven in a wild flower,
Hold Infinity in the palm of your hand,
And Eternity in an hour . . .

WILLIAM BLAKE[1]

Spiritual experience is an experience of aliveness of mind
and body as a unity. . . . The central awareness in these
spiritual moments is a profound sense of oneness with all, a
sense of belonging to the universe as a whole.

FRITJOF CAPRA[2]

The sacred has always been with us. It's right there outside the window.
It's right there outside the walls we've built around ourselves, right there
outside the doors of perception made opaque by the human ego.

Modern people have allowed our religions to follow our egos' lead
and divide us into competing fragments. But as we've learned, the sacred
is unlimited, all-pervasive, everywhere: it's in every being, accessible to
all. Every faith is rooted in it.

Indigenous people have always found ways to incorporate the
religious beliefs imposed on them by dominant cultures, producing a

syncretistic marriage that preserves their ancient bond with the sacred while honoring the new. Should we have a personal religious heritage, we don't need to defend or disown any cherished teachings. All of us have the ancestral memory we need to reawaken our spiritual sensibilities and restore our relationship with everything that animates the living universe, allowing what we've lived in the past and what we can now experience every day to enrich each other.

John Briggs and F. David Peat maintain that "an understanding of wholeness is already woven deep within us";[3] Leonardo Boff notes that the feeling of veneration for Mother Earth "has never been totally lost in humanity."[4]

We can have it all—because we are part of All That Is.

The sacred speaks through Gaia; Gaia speaks through the sacred. "Thinking together" enables us to hear her voice again.

"The individual nexus of pathways which I call 'me' is no longer so precious because that nexus is only part of a larger mind," notes Gregory Bateson. "The ideas which seemed to be me can also become immanent in you."[5]

For Briggs and Peat, "Experiencing solidarity with the whole universe . . . is about moving from . . . the consciousness of what we only know individually, to the consciousness of what we also know together."[6]

Rupert Sheldrake writes:

As soon as we allow ourselves to think of the world as alive, we recognize that a part of us knew this all along. It is like emerging from winter into spring. We can begin to reconnect with our own direct intuitive experiences of nature. We can participate in the spirits of sacred places and times.

We can see that we have much to learn from traditional societies who have never lost their connection with the living world around them. We can acknowledge the animistic traditions of our ancestors.

And we can begin to develop a richer understanding of human nature, shaped by tradition and collective memory, linked to the earth and the heavens, related to all forms of life, and consciously open to the creative power expressed in all evolution.

We are reborn into a living world.[7]

The sacred is right there, waiting for us.

As Bateson puts it, "A certain humility becomes appropriate, tempered by the dignity or joy of being part of something much bigger. A part—if you will—of God."[8]

Fig. 16.1. Photo by Jim Molloy.

WHAT A RELIEF!

We've stretched separateness as far as we can stretch it. And we've learned the gift of it, because it clearly is a gift. And now we're coming back to the realm of oneness and collectiveness.

RED PELE[9]

Henceforth we have to learn to be, to live, share, communicate, commune as humans of Planet Earth. Not to be in our culture alone, but to be earth people as well.

EDGAR MORIN[10]

The global heart is awakening, calling us . . . into the possibility of a world beyond our wildest dreams. . . . What we are birthing is far too large for any one person, organization, or country. Can we do it?

ANODEA JUDITH[11]

For me, one of the most wonderful things about the return of collective intelligence is that it frees us from having to figure everything out ourselves—not that we could do this even if we wanted to, the world's problems having become so unutterably complex.

Nor do we have to give our power away to leaders as clueless as we are. Collective intelligence allows us to trust the wisdom of the group to act in the best interest of every being that shares our planet. We can be confident that together we'll recognize and select the people most able to govern us wisely and well, because they too will be using collective wisdom to guide them. We can relax, knowing that everything self-organizes and all we have to do is our part, offering our unique gifts—whatever and however humble they may be—to the whole. The magic of the group will take care of the rest, bringing the solutions Mother Earth needs for her children to thrive.

Gradually, inexorably, love will replace fear on and among all levels of existence, and the great family of life on Earth will resume functioning the way it was meant to. With the return of collective intelligence, the promise of an incredibly exciting new world is real. And it's doable. In spite of the disastrous legacy humans have left up to now, there's hope!

"The wrecked landscape of our World House could sprout a renewed world, but a new language has to be found . . . to grow from the indigenous hearts we all have hidden," says Martín Prechtel.[12]

As the future reaches back to rescue the wisdom of the past and the past delivers us into the future, we can watch Gaia's genius at work. As always, she labors in mystery and paradox: the reality under construction is so much bigger than all of us, yet every single one of us is utterly vital for its creation.

We may have abdicated our responsibility to the miraculous living tapestry that supports us, but it continues to offer us its best and most beautiful promise every moment. We may have abandoned Gaia, but she hasn't abandoned us.

"The transformation of the human species has begun," declares Ervin Laszlo. "A new epidemic is spreading among us: more and more people are infected by the recognition of their unity. The fragmentation of human communities and the separation of man and nature were but an interlude in human history, and that interlude is now coming to a close."[13]

Sheila and Marcus Gillette predict that "our common external world . . . will be a reflection of the internal process that leads to the collective consciousness achieved by humanity."[14]

Joanna Macy and Molly Young Brown believe that this new consciousness will manifest "in an unpredictable array of spontaneous actions, as people step out from their private comforts, giving time and taking risks on behalf of Earth and their brother-sister beings." And given the dynamics of self-organizing systems, they say, "it is likely that as we reflect and act together, we will soon find ourselves responding to the present crisis with far greater confidence and precision than we imagined possible."[15]

"We believe that the power of our thinking can lead to a silent revolution that suddenly won't be silent anymore," the Gillettes insist. "We will move mountains and make a difference in ways that we have not yet begun to imagine, and express our love for our planet and our brothers and sisters while writing new history."[16]

To achieve this, says Prechtel, "we need all peoples: our poets, our shamans, our dreamers, our youth, our women, our men, our ancestors, and our real old memories from before we were people. We can't make the old world come alive again, but from its seeds, the next layer could sprout."[17]

Brian Swimme sums it up it this way:

We are now restructuring our fundamental vision of the world. The new cosmic story overwhelms all previous conceptions of the universe for the simple reason that it draws them all into comprehensive fullness.

And most amazing of all is the way in which this story, though it comes from the empirical scientific tradition, corroborates in profound and surprising ways the ecological vision of the Earth celebrated in every traditional native spirituality of every continent.

Who could learn what this means and remain calm?[18]

Notes

CHAPTER 1.
AN ANCIENT GIFT

1. Wolff, *Original Wisdom*, 7.
2. Miller, "Swarm Theory," 130.
3. Laszlo, *Quantum Shift*, 3.
4. Laszlo, *Quantum Shift*, 3.
5. Personal teachings.
6. Cowan, *Fire in the Head*, 48.
7. Jenkins, *Journey to Q'eros*, 168.
8. Dychtwald, "Commentaries," 110–11.
9. Capra, *Turning Point*, 309.
10. Swimme, *Universe*, 133.
11. Swimme, *Universe*, 59.
12. In Boldt, *Tao of Abundance*, 21.
13. Audlin, *Circle of Life*, 72.
14. Capra, *Turning Point*, 266, 267.
15. Macy and Brown, *Coming Back*, 42.
16. Briggs and Peat, *Seven Life Lessons*, 35, 145.
17. Laszlo, *Quantum Shift*, 52.
18. Quoted in Eves, *Mathematical Circles*.
19. Capra, *Turning Point*, 277.
20. Halifax, *Fruitful Darkness*, 156.
21. Halifax, *Fruitful Darkness*, 162.
22. McTaggart, *The Field*, 96.

23. Wan Ho, "The Entangled Universe," in Pearce, *Biology of Transcendence,* 75.
24. Chopra, *Quantum Healing,* 219.
25. Quoted in a speech by Robert A. Millikan to the American Physical Society, April 29, 1947, reported in the *New York Times.*
26. Hamilton, "Come Together," 10.
27. Cowan, *Fire in the Head,* 105–6.
28. Abram, *Becoming Animal,* 277–78.
29. Gallegos Nava, *Holistic Education,* 141.
30. Hamilton, "Come Together," 2–3, 5.
31. Capra, *Turning Point,* 292, 297.
32. Sheldrake, *Rebirth of Nature,* 198.
33. McTaggart, *The Field,* 226.
34. Gordon in Miller, "Swarm Theory," 130.
35. Johnson, *Emergence,* 30.
36. Gordon in Johnson, *Emergence,* 31.
37. Johnson, *Emergence,* 74–80.
38. Johnson, *Emergence,* 31.
39. Audlin, *Circle of Life,* 123.
40. Johnson, *Emergence,* 31.
41. Buhner, *Plant Intelligence,* 78–92.
42. Buhner, *Plant Intelligence,* 28.
43. Margulis and Sagan, *What Is Sex?,* 55. Quoted in Buhner, *Plant Intelligence,* 101.
44. Buhner, *Plant Intelligence,* 101–13.
45. Wohlleben, *Hidden Life of Trees,* 10–17.
46. Bohm, *On Dialogue,* 45.
47. Hock, *Chaordic Age,* 71.
48. Hock, *Chaordic Age,* 305.
49. Buhner, *Plant Intelligence,* 433.

CHAPTER 2.
WE CAN'T SEE

1. In Barrios, *Book of Destiny,* 132.
2. Frost, "Mending Wall," 200.
3. Bohm, *Wholeness,* 9.
4. Morin and Kern, *Homeland Earth,* 130.

5. Bohm, *On Creativity,* 30.

6. Galland, *Longing for Darkness,* 158.

7. Halifax, *Fruitful Darkness,* 166.

8. Pfeiffer, *Wild Earth,* 27.

9. Quoted in Briggs and Peat, *Seven Life Lessons,* 145.

10. Peat, *Blackfoot Physics,* 47.

11. Bohm, *On Creativity,* 110.

12. Briggs and Peat, *Seven Life Lessons,* 145.

13. Dossey, *Recovering,* 37.

14. Audlin, *Circle of Life,* 71.

15. Laszlo, *Akashic Experience,* 6.

16. Bohm, *On Creativity,* 99.

17. Ingerman, *Practice of Shamanism* (audio).

18. Peat, *Blackfoot Physics,* 276.

19. Buhner, *Plant Intelligence,* 19.

20. Bohm, *On Creativity,* 99.

21. Kenny, "Calling Out," 29.

22. Kenny, "Calling Out," 29.

23. Morin and Kern, *Homeland Earth,* 128.

24. Abram, *Becoming Animal,* 42–44.

25. Hock, *Chaordic Age,* 225.

26. Peat, *Synchronicity,* 226.

27. Hock, *Chaordic Age,* 225.

28. Laszlo, *Science,* 3.

29. Boff and Muraro, *Femenino y masculino,* 59. Quotations from this book are my translations.

30. Perkins, *Shapeshifting,* 41.

31. Boff, *Essential Care,* 74.

32. Perkins, *Shapeshifting,* 41.

33. Morse and Perry, *Where God Lives,* 159.

34. Pearce, *Biology of Transcendence,* 118.

35. Pellegrino, *Unearthing Atlantis,* 16.

36. Pearce, *Biology of Transcendence,* 118, 116.

37. Quoted in Cowan, *Fire in the Head,* 178.

38. In Powell, *Tao of Symbols,* 224.

39. Abram, *Becoming Animal,* 179–80.

40. Eisler, *Chalice & Blade,* xxiii, 53.

41. Boff and Muraro, *Femenino y masculino,* 46.

42. Pearce, *Biology of Transcendence,* 110, 112.

43. Buhner, *Plant Intelligence,* 83.

44. Buhner, *Plant Intelligence,* 31.

45. Buhner, *Plant Intelligence,* 434.

46. Peat, *Synchronicity,* 59–84.

47. Peat, *Blackfoot Physics,* 44.

48. Perkins and Chumpi, *Spirit of the Shuar,* 57.

49. Cowan, *Fire in the Head,* 30.

50. Men, *Secrets of Mayan Science,* 81.

51. Bohm, *On Creativity,* 110.

52. Blake, "To Thomas Butts," in *Selected Poems,* 147.

53. Audlin, *Circle of Life,* 60, 62.

54. McTaggart, *The Field,* 84, 85.

55. McTaggart, *The Field,* 91.

56. Peat, *Synchronicity,* 4.

57. Audlin, *Circle of Life,* 72, 70.

58. Peat, *Synchronicity,* 114, 221.

59. Wolff, *Original Wisdom,* 4.

60. Wolff, *Original Wisdom,* 120–21.

CHAPTER 3.
SUBTLE ENERGY

1. In Audlin, *Circle of Life,* 136.

2. Men, *Secrets of Mayan Science,* 81.

3. Wilcox, *Masters,* 43.

4. Audlin, *Circle of Life,* 136.

5. Chopra, *Quantum Healing,* 126.

6. Bohm, *Wholeness,* 9.

7. Bohm, *Wholeness,* 9.

8. Laszlo, *Quantum Shift,* 111.

9. Men, *Secrets of Mayan Science,* 81.

10. Wilcox, *Masters,* 24, 26.

11. Lambert, *Wise Women,* 6, 8.

12. Laszlo, *Science,* 103.

13. McTaggart, *The Field,* 21, xviii.

14. Villoldo, *Shaman,* 41.

15. Castaneda, *Separate Reality,* 49.

16. Villoldo, *Shaman,* 42–43.

17. Wilcox, *Masters,* 45, 53, 51.

18. Jenkins, *Journey to Q'eros,* 210.

19. Barrios, *Book of Destiny,* 89.

20. Halifax, *Fruitful Darkness,* 82.

21. Harner, *Way of the Shaman,* 50.

22. Buhner, *Plant Intelligence,* 386.

23. Peat, *Blackfoot Physics,* 143.

24. Chopra, *Quantum Healing,* 249, 251.

25. Beresford-Kroeger, *Global Forest,* 107–8.

26. Prechtel, *Secrets,* 278.

27. Kalweit, *Dreamtime,* 152.

28. Peat, *Blackfoot Physics,* 143.

29. Halifax, *Fruitful Darkness,* 84–85.

30. Lambert, *Wise Women,* 11–12.

31. Chevalier and Gheerbrant, *Penguin Dictionary,* 79.

32. Beresford-Kroeger, *Global Forest,* 108.

33. Chopra, *Quantum Healing,* 250.

34. Redmond, *When the Drummers,* 65, 72.

35. Walker, *Woman's Encyclopedia,* 401, 407.

36. Redmond, *When the Drummers,* 113, 114.

37. Gough, "The Bee," 24, 66.

38. Buxton, *Shamanic Way,* 50, 52.

39. Men, *Secrets of Mayan Science,* 31, 32.

40. Heid, "You Asked."

41. Humphrey, "'Killer' Bees."

CHAPTER 4.
THE MAGIC OF THE CIRCLE

1. In Schneider, *Beginner's Guide,* 1.

2. In Macy and Brown, *Coming Back,* 50.

3. Halifax, *Fruitful Darkness,* 137.

4. Morin and Kern, *Homeland Earth,* 24.

5. Morin and Kern, *Homeland Earth,* 143.

6. Lipton and Bhaerman, *Spontaneous Evolution,* 330.

7. Bear Heart, *Wind Is My Mother,* 190.

8. Schneider, *Beginner's Guide,* 2.

9. Cunningham, *Mandala Book,* 6.

10. Gold, *Navajo and Tibetan Wisdom,* 135.

11. Powell, *Tao of Symbols,* 185.

12. Halifax, *Fruitful Darkness,* 176.

13. Harner, *Way of the Shaman,* 28.

14. Jung, *Red Book,* 206.

15. Jung, *Memories, Dreams,* 367.

16. In Audlin, *Circle of Life,* 6.

17. Audlin, *Circle of Life,* 6.

18. Audlin, *Circle of Life,* 331.

19. Bear Heart, *Wind Is My Mother,* 190.

20. Cowan, *Fire in the Head,* 87.

21. Howell, *Jungian Symbolism,* 23.

22. Howell, *Jungian Symbolism,* 35.

23. Redmond, *When the Drummers,* 114, 170.

24. Men, *Secrets of Mayan Science,* 90.

25. Sarangerel, *Chosen by the Spirits,* 49.

26. Eliade, *Sacred and Profane,* 37.

27. Heaven, *Voudou Shaman,* 73, 75.

28. Perkins, *The World Is,* 30.

29. González Chaves and González Vásquez, *La casa cósmica,* 147.

30. Magee, *Peruvian Shamanism,* 42.

31. Cowan, *Fire in the Head,* 81.

32. Schneider, *Beginner's Guide,* 139.

33. Cunningham, *Mandala Book,* 192.

34. Barrios, *Book of Destiny,* 89.

35. Personal teachings.

36. Sarangerel, *Chosen by the Spirits,* 51.

37. Curott, *Witch Crafting,* 112–13, 257.

38. Magee, *Peruvian Shamanism,* 26.

39. Laszlo, *Science,* 71.

40. Briggs and Peat, *Seven Life Lessons,* 28.

41. Eisler, *Chalice & Blade,* 194.

42. Chevalier and Gheerbrant, *Penguin Dictionary,* 956.

43. Kharitidi, *Master of Lucid Dreams,* 120.

44. In Seed et al., *Thinking like a Mountain,* 71.

45. Jenkins, *Journey to Q'eros,* 23.

46. Magee, *Peruvian Shamanism,* 47.

47. Wilcox, *Masters,* 236.

48. Lambert, *Wise Women,* 108.

49. Jenkins, *Fourth Level,* 10.

50. Audlin, *Circle of Life,* 249.

51. Jenkins, *Journey to Q'eros,* 41.

52. Men, *Secrets of Mayan Science,* 26.

53. Jenkins, *Fourth Level,* 112.

54. Eisler, *Chalice & Blade,* 27, 193.

55. Murdock, *Heroine's Journey,* 181.

56. Murdock, *Heroine's Journey,* 129.

57. Schneider, *Beginner's Guide,* 32.

58. Stevens, *Awaken,* 148.

59. Men, *Secrets of Mayan Science,* 78.

60. Curott, *Witch Crafting,* 114.

61. Bateson, *Sacred Unity,* 301.

62. Eisler, *Chalice & Blade,* 111.

63. Chevalier and Gheerbrant, *Penguin Dictionary,* 728.

64. Janine Fafard, personal teachings.

65. M. Esther Harding, *Women's Mysteries, Ancient and Modern,* quoted in Gustafson, *Black Madonna,* 93.

66. Bly and Woodman, *Maiden King,* 47.

67. Boff, *Essential Care,* 52.

68. Gustafson, *Black Madonna,* 120.

69. Cowan, *Fire in the Head,* 171.

70. Quoted in Pellegrino, *Unearthing Atlantis,* 84.

71. Peat, *Blackfoot Physics,* 203, 204.

72. Audlin, *Circle of Life,* 5, 77.

73. Sarangerel, *Chosen,* 48–49.

74. Prechtel, *Long Life,* 364.

75. McTaggart, *The Field,* 164.

76. Briggs and Peat, *Seven Life Lessons,* 126.

77. Peat, *Blackfoot Physics,* 231.

78. Bohm, *On Dialogue,* 17.

79. Bennett, *Spirit Animals,* 130.

80. Bohm, *On Dialogue,* 203.

81. Bohm, *Enfolding-Unfolding Universe,* quoted in Wilber, *Holographic Paradigm,* 78.

CHAPTER 5.
COLLECTIVE INTELLIGENCE

1. Bohm, *On Dialogue,* 19.

2. Lipton and Bhaerman, *Spontaneous Evolution,* 330.

3. In Briggs and Peat, *Seven Life Lessons,* 59.

4. Perkins and Chumpi, *Spirit of the Shuar,* 133.

5. Prechtel, *Long Life,* 169.

6. Audlin, *Circle of Life,* 48.

7. Briggs and Peat, *Seven Life Lessons,* 54.

8. Sheldrake, *Rebirth of Nature,* 111, 119.

9. Morse and Perry, *Where God Lives,* 158.

10. Macy and Brown, *Coming Back,* 64.

11. Kenny, "Calling Out," 2.

12. La Chapelle, "What Supports?," 1.

13. Levi, "Holographic Theory," 2.

14. Kenny, "Calling Out," 4.

15. Peat, *Blackfoot Physics,* 140.

16. Pearce, *Biology of Transcendence,* 70.

17. Cowan, *Fire in the Head,* 48.

18. Powell, *Tao of Symbols,* 182.

19. Laszlo, *Akashic Experience,* 5.

20. Laszlo, *Science,* 76, 77.

21. Bohm, "The Physicist and the Mystic," in Wilber, *Holographic Paradigm,* 198.

22. Bohm, "The Physicist and the Mystic," in Wilber, *Holographic Paradigm,* 187.

23. Bohm, "The Physicist and the Mystic," in Wilber, *Holographic Paradigm,* 192.

24. Bohm, "The Physicist and the Mystic," in Wilber, *Holographic Paradigm,* 72, 194, 195.

25. Bohm, *Enfolding-Unfolding Universe,* quoted in Wilber, *Holographic Paradigm,* 45.

26. Peat, *Blackfoot Physics,* 140, 141.

27. McNiff, *Trust the Process,* 24.

28. Laszlo, *Akashic Experience,* 248.

29. Laszlo, *Science,* 115.

30. Laszlo, *Akashic Experience,* 249.

31. Pearce, *Biology of Transcendence,* 57–59.

32. Laszlo, *Science,* 150–51.

33. La Chapelle, "What Supports?," 1.

34. Levi, "Holographic Theory," 7.

35. Personal teachings.

CHAPTER 6.
THE COLLECTIVE INTELLIGENCE OF HEALTH

1. Levi, "Sentient Heart," 2.

2. In Levi, "Sentient Heart," 2.

3. Lipton and Bhaerman, *Spontaneous Evolution,* 249.

4. In Wilcox, *Masters,* 236.

5. Peat, *Blackfoot Physics,* 136.

6. Chopra, *Quantum Healing,* 257.

7. Chopra, *Quantum Healing,* 254.

8. Capra, *Turning Point,* 307.

9. Wolff, *Original Wisdom,* 62.

10. Payán de la Roche, *Lánzate al vacío,* 16.

11. Capra, *Turning Point,* 327.

12. Ingerman, *Practice of Shamanism* (audio).

13. McTaggart, *The Field,* 188–92.

14. McTaggart, *The Field,* 194.

15. Ingerman, *Practice of Shamanism* (audio).

16. Peat, *Blackfoot Physics,* 115, 120.

17. Peat, *Blackfoot Physics,* 120–22.

18. Wilcox, *Masters,* 51, and personal teachings.

19. Chödrön, *Places That Scare You,* 58.

CHAPTER 7.
A NEW KIND OF INTELLIGENCE

1. Fried, *Passionate Learner,* 56.

2. Bohm, *On Creativity,* 118.

3. Morin and Kern, *Homeland Earth,* 30.

4. Bohm, *On Creativity,* 93.

5. Bohm, *On Creativity,* 80.

6. Audlin, *Circle of Life,* 90.

7. Peat, *Blackfoot Physics,* 47.

8. Audlin, *Circle of Life,* 153.

9. Peat, *Blackfoot Physics,* 55, 59.

10. Freire, *Pedagogy of Freedom,* 85.

11. Peat, *Blackfoot Physics,* 75.

12. Audlin, *Circle of Life,* 150.

13. Peat, *Blackfoot Physics,* 74.

14. Audlin, *Circle of Life,* 70.

15. Peat, *Blackfoot Physics,* 72.

16. Halifax, *Fruitful Darkness,* 103.

17. Audlin, *Circle of Life,* 71.

18. Halifax, *Fruitful Darkness,* 107, 109.

19. Maturana and Poerksen, *From Being to Doing,* 129.

20. Richo, *When the Past,* 16.

21. Bohm, *On Creativity,* 4.

22. Fried, *Passionate Learner,* 7.

23. Freire, *Pedagogy of Freedom,* 38.

24. Maturana and Poerksen, *From Being to Doing,* 85.

25. Pearce, *Biology of Transcendence,* 259.

26. Maturana and Poerksen, *From Being to Doing,* 128.

27. Maturana and Varela, *Tree of Knowledge,* 128, 129.

28. Bohm, *On Creativity,* 5.

29. Freire, *Pedagogy of Freedom,* 32.

30. Wolff, *Original Wisdom,* 143–49.

31. Bache, "The Living Classroom," 83–92.

32. Hamilton, "Come Together," 12.

33. Levi, "Holographic Theory," 1–7.

34. Bache, "Living Classroom," 93.

35. Morin and Kern, *Homeland Earth,* 24.

36. Bache, "Living Classroom," 90.

37. Bohm, *On Creativity,* 61.

38. Bohm, *On Creativity,* 106.

39. Maturana and Varela, *Tree of Knowledge,* 234.

40. Bohm, *On Creativity,* 111, 118.

CHAPTER 8.
CEREMONY, PILGRIMAGE, AND INITIATION

1. Somé, *Ritual,* 13.
2. In Halifax, *Fruitful Darkness,* 114.
3. Peat, *Blackfoot Physics,* 301.
4. Somé, *Ritual,* 42.
5. Lambert, *Wise Women,* 128.
6. Expedition with Dream Change Coalition and Sacred Earth Network, June 2002.
7. A series of articles in the *Tico Times,* Aug. 30–Nov. 8, 2002, gives a full account of this trip. See the *Tico Times* website.
8. Peat, *Blackfoot Physics,* 301.
9. Jenkins, *Journey to Q'eros,* 183.
10. Américo Yabar, personal teachings.
11. Jenkins, *Initiation,* 212.
12. Pearce, *Biology of Transcendence,* 192–94.
13. Tucker, *Mystery,* 37.
14. Halifax, *Fruitful Darkness,* 179.
15. Tucker, *Mystery,* 37.
16. Halifax, *Fruitful Darkness,* 15.
17. Eliade, *Sacred and Profane,* 188–89.
18. Prechtel, *Long Life,* 259.
19. Peat, *Blackfoot Physics,* 70.
20. Lambert, *Wise Women,* 78.
21. Prechtel, *Long Life,* 241.
22. Prechtel, *Long Life,* 259.
23. Bly, *Sibling Society,* 132.
24. Morin and Kern, *Homeland Earth,* 65.
25. Jenkins, *Journey to Q'eros,* 167.
26. Bly, *Sibling Society,* 83.
27. Cowan, *Fire in the Head,* 178.
28. Cowan, *Fire in the Head,* 178.
29. Eliade, *Sacred and Profane,* 26.
30. Halifax, *Fruitful Darkness,* 52.
31. Credo Mutwa, *Isilwane,* 15–16, in Tucker, *Mystery,* 78.
32. McTaggart, *The Field,* 200–207.

33. In Tucker, *Mystery,* 83.

34. In Wilcox, *Masters,* 208.

35. Lambert, *Wise Women,* 47.

36. Frey, *Pilgrim Stories,* 35.

37. Chevalier and Gheerbrant, *Penguin Dictionary of Symbols,* 656.

38. Eliade, *Sacred and Profane,* 35.

39. Eliade, *Sacred and Profane,* 38.

40. Yabar, personal teachings.

41. In Jenkins, *Journey to Q'eros,* 81–82.

42. Wilcox, *Masters,* 272.

43. Mails, *Fools Crow,* 127.

44. Jenkins, *Initiation,* 135.

45. Kazmier, Pilgrimage, 7.

46. In Tucker, *Mystery,* 88–89.

47. Sacred Earth Network expedition, July 2008.

48. Carol Hiltner, "What Is a *Kurgan?*"

49. Pfeiffer, "Leon and Maria."

50. In Rudloe, *Search,* 15.

51. Rudloe, *Search,* 181.

52. Rudloe, *Search,* 15.

53. Bernard Neitchmann, *Caribbean Edge,* quoted in Rudloe, *Search,* 7.

54. Rudloe, *Search,* 75.

55. Rudloe, *Search,* 16.

56. Rudloe, *Search,* 148.

57. Rudloe, *Search,* 68–69.

58. Rudloe, *Search,* 108–10.

59. Rudloe, *Search,* 226–27.

60. Sams and Carson, *Medicine Cards,* 77.

61. Rudloe, *Search,* 84.

CHAPTER 9.
BLACK MADONNAS AND WHITE LIONS

1. Daly, "Couple Credit" and "Ticos Join Shipwrecked Pair."

2. Markale, *Cathedral,* 171.

3. Markale, *Cathedral,* 139.

4. In Markale, *Cathedral,* 140.

5. Galland, *Longing for Darkness,* 152.

6. Markale, *Cathedral,* 120.

7. Gough, "The Bee," 60.

8. Gustafson, *Black Madonna,* 93.

9. Jenkins, *Initiation,* 206.

10. Ronnberg and Martin, *Book of Symbols,* 658.

11. Online Etymology (website).

12. Walker, *Woman's Encyclopedia,* 18.

13. Markale, *Cathedral,* 193.

14. Markale, *Cathedral,* 171.

15. Markale, *Cathedral,* 265.

16. Markale, *Cathedral,* 214.

17. Walker, *Woman's Encyclopedia,* 401.

18. Markale, *Cathedral,* 215.

19. Galland, *Longing for Darkness,* 146.

20. Markale, *Cathedral,* 157, 269–70.

21. Howell, *Jungian Symbolism,* 45, 46.

22. Markale, *Cathedral,* 70.

23. Galland, *Longing for Darkness,* 247.

24. Markale, *Cathedral,* 185.

25. Gustafson, *Black Madonna,* 109.

26. Bly and Woodman, *Maiden King,* 48.

27. Abram, *Becoming Animal,* 304.

28. Bly and Woodman, *Maiden King,* 146.

29. Galland, *Longing for Darkness,* 142.

30. Gustafson, *Black Madonna,* 60, 116, 122.

31. Cerdas, "El 98% de los romeros cree en milagros."

32. Galland, *Longing for Darkness,* 65–66.

33. Galland, *Longing for Darkness,* 94.

34. Galland, *Longing for Darkness,* 120.

35. Galland, *Longing for Darkness,* 310.

36. Tucker, *Mystery,* 205–6.

37. Tucker, *Mystery,* 73.

38. Tucker, *Mystery,* 187–88.

39. Tucker, *Mystery,* 17.

40. Tucker, *Mystery,* 167–68.

41. Tucker, *Mystery,* 73, 180.

42. Tucker, *Mystery,* 179.

43. Wilcox, *Masters,* 95.

44. Pearce, *Biology of Transcendence,* 229.

45. Pearce, *Biology of Transcendence,* 232.

46. Ingerman and Wesselman, *Awakening to the Spirit World.*

47. Tucker, *Mystery,* 131, 132, 210.

48. Tucker, *Mystery,* 133.

49. Tucker, *Mystery,* 205.

50. Tucker, *Mystery,* 217.

51. Tucker, *Mystery,* 218.

52. Tucker, *Mystery,* 249.

53. Tucker, *Mystery,* 240.

54. Tucker, *Mystery,* 251.

55. Tucker, *Mystery,* 251.

CHAPTER 10.
THE DESCENT INTO COLLECTIVE STUPIDITY

1. Lame Deer, John Fire, and Richard Erdoes, *Lame Deer: Sioux Medicine Man,* 157, in Kalweit, *Dreamtime,* xvi.

2. Eyewitness accounts and personal experience.

3. Miller, "Swarm Theory," 130.

4. Atlee, "Co-Stupidity," 1.

5. McTaggart, *The Field,* 213.

6. Eisler, *Chalice & Blade,* 105.

7. See Capra, *Turning Point,* 56.

8. Kaku, *Visions,* 10.

9. Eisler, *Chalice & Blade,* 101.

10. Boff, *Essential Care,* 66.

11. Morin and Kern, *Homeland Earth,* 127.

12. Boff, *Essential Care,* 66.

13. *La Nación* (San José, Costa Rica), May 8, 2017, 29. My translation.

14. See "The Post-Truth World," *The Economist,* Sept. 10, 2016, 19.

15. *La Nación* (San José, Costa Rica), May 8, 2017, 29. My translation.

16. Wang, "Former Facebook VP."

17. *The Economist,* July 1, 2017, 5.

18. "The Post-Truth World," *The Economist,* Sept. 10, 2016, 20.

19. Dwoskin and Romm, "Facebook Says."

20. *La Nación* (San José, Costa Rica), July 29, 2018, 15A; *Washington Post* online edition, July 30, 2018.

21. Morin and Kern, *Homeland Earth,* 72.

22. Halifax, *Fruitful Darkness,* 40.

23. Sagot, "Desazón de una sospecha." My translation.

24. Halifax, *Fruitful Darkness,* 166.

25. Morin, *Seven Complex Lessons,* 35.

26. Morin and Kern, *Homeland Earth,* 70.

27. Jenkins, *Fourth Level,* 66–67.

28. Somé, *Ritual,* 53.

CHAPTER 11.
A WORLD OUT OF BALANCE

1. Wordsworth, "The World Is Too Much with Us," 338.

2. Morin and Kern, *Homeland Earth,* 49.

3. Capra, *Hidden Connections,* 141.

4. Henderson, *Building,* 90.

5. Morin and Kern, *Homeland Earth,* 49.

6. Henderson, *Building,* 189.

7. Capra, *Hidden Connections,* 146.

8. Morin and Kern, *Homeland Earth,* 72.

9. Theobald, *Reworking Success,* 43.

10. Morin and Kern, *Homeland Earth,* 69–70.

11. Somé, *Ritual,* 65.

12. Gowdy and Mesner, "Evolution," 149.

13. Gowdy and Mesner, "Evolution," 149.

14. Somé, *Ritual,* 66.

15. Georgescu-Roegen, "Energy and Economic Myths," 2–3.

16. Gowdy and Mesner, *Evolution,* 153.

17. Turkle, *Alone Together,* 293.

18. Pearce, *Biology of Transcendence,* 111–13.

19. "Paying No Mind," *The Economist,* Dec. 9, 2017, 77.

20. Turkle, *Alone Together,* 293.

21. Turkle, *Alone Together,* 17.

22. "Teléfono es vital para 9 de cada 10 jóvenes," *La Nación* (San José, Costa Rica), Oct. 13, 2015.

23. Turkle, *Alone Together,* 227.

24. Turkle, *Alone Together,* 15.

25. Pfeiffer, *Wild Earth,* 107.

26. Abram, *Becoming Animal,* 92.

27. Pfeiffer, *Wild Earth,* 107.

28. Abram, *Becoming Animal,* 80.

CHAPTER 12.
TWO PATHS

1. In Tucker, *Mystery,* 73.

2. Lanier, "One Half of a Manifesto," in Brockman, *New Humanists,* 234.

3. "Technology in Africa," 3–14.

4. Kenny, "Calling Out," 14.

5. Kurzweil, "The Singularity," in Brockman, *New Humanists,* 229.

6. Turkle, *Life on the Screen,* 21.

7. Kurzweil, "The Singularity," in Brockman, *New Humanists,* 225.

8. Clark, "Natural Born Cyborgs?," in Brockman, *New Humanists,* 68.

9. Kurzweil, "The Singularity," in Brockman, *New Humanists,* 221.

10. Kenny, "Calling Out," 8.

11. Lanier, "One Half of a Manifesto," in Brockman, *New Humanists,* 262.

12. Popcorn, "Humanoid Condition," 112.

13. Turkle, *Alone Together,* 51.

14. Turkle, *Alone Together,* 292.

15. Moravec, "Making Minds," in Brockman, *New Humanists,* 183, 185.

16. Hauser, "Animal Minds," in Brockman, *New Humanists,* 90.

17. Turkle, *Life on the Screen,* 163.

18. Hamilton, "Come Together," 12.

19. Hauser, "Animal Minds," in Brockman, *New Humanists,* 81.

20. Audlin, *Circle of Life,* 150.

21. Einstein, *Merging of Spirit and Science.*

22. Atlee, "Collective Intelligence," 2.

23. Turkle, *Alone Together,* 55.

24. Anderson, "Responses," in Brockman, *New Humanists,* 399, 400.

25. Lanier, "One Half of a Manifesto," in Brockman, *New Humanists,* 246.

CHAPTER 13.
RECONNECTING

1. Perkins, *The World Is,* xx.
2. In Jenkins, *Initiation,* 121.
3. Miró-Quesada Solevo, *Path.*
4. Personal teachings.
5. In Tucker, *Mystery,* 73.
6. Barrios, *Book of Destiny,* 116.
7. Wilcox, *Masters,* 72.
8. Capra, *Turning Point,* 418.
9. Wilcox, *Masters,* 75–76.
10. Morin and Kern, *Homeland Earth,* 67.
11. Briggs and Peat, *Seven Life Lessons,* 6, 162.
12. In Tucker, *Mystery,* 73.
13. Morin and Kern, *Homeland Earth,* 86.
14. Morin, *Seven Complex Lessons,* 45, 78.
15. Zapp and Erikson, *Atlantis in America.*
16. Rudloe, *Search,* 117.
17. In Pfeiffer, *Wild Earth,* 107.
18. In Cowan, *Fire in the Head,* 47.
19. Prechtel, *Secrets,* 281, 283.
20. Moss and Corbin, *Weather Shamanism,* 137.
21. Pfeiffer, *Wild Earth,* 49.
22. Pfeiffer, *Wild Earth,* 12.
23. Buhner, *Plant Intelligence,* 446.
24. Audlin, *Circle of Life,* 17.
25. Pfeiffer, *Wild Earth,* 12–13.
26. Jenkins, *Fourth Level,* 5.
27. Personal teachings.
28. Jenkins, *Journey to Q'eros,* 132.
29. Barrionuevo, *Poder en los Andes: La fuerza de los cerros,* 150. My translation.

CHAPTER 14.
REBUILDING

1. Macy and Brown, *Coming Back,* 45.
2. Interview in *Yes!* magazine, March 18, 2016.
3. Judith, *Waking,* 46.

4. Jenkins, *Journey to Q'eros,* 59.

5. Ferguson, *Aquarius Now,* 13.

6. Morin and Kern, *Homeland Earth,* 49.

7. Swimme, *Universe,* 146.

8. Halifax, *Fruitful Darkness,* 215–16.

9. Halifax, *Fruitful Darkness,* 200.

10. Tucker, *Mystery,* 251.

11. Abram, *Becoming Animal,* 70–71, 175.

12. Somé, *Ritual,* 97.

13. Pfeiffer, *Wild Earth,* 157.

14. Somé, *Ritual,* 98.

15. Ferguson, *Aquarius Now,* 198.

16. Henderson, *Building,* 24.

17. Capra, *Hidden Connections,* 152, 230.

18. Somé, *Ritual,* 52–53.

19. Mails, *Fools Crow,* 160.

20. Jenkins, *Fourth Level,* 144–45.

21. Personal teachings.

22. Jenkins, *Fourth Level,* 156–57.

23. Somé, *Ritual,* 53.

24. In Briskin et al., *Centered on the Edge,* 29.

25. Payán, *Lánzate al vacío,* 16. My translation.

26. Wilcox, *Masters,* 75.

27. Payán, *Lánzate al vacío,* 9. My translation.

28. Dossey, *Recovering,* 260, 265.

29. Wilcox, *Masters,* 73.

30. Payán, *Lánzate al vacío,* 129. My translation.

31. Halifax, *Fruitful Darkness,* 202.

32. Boff and Muraro, *Femenino y masculino,* 201.

33. Boff, *Essential Care,* 10.

34. Boff, *Essential Care,* 80.

35. Boff, *Essential Care,* 70.

36. Boff, *Essential Care,* 81.

37. Eliade, *Sacred and Profane,* 93, 94.

38. Laszlo, *Akashic Experience,* 7–8.

39. Morin and Kern, *Homeland Earth,* 146.

40. Eisler, *Chalice & Blade,* 191, 202.

CHAPTER 15.
REDISCOVERY

1. Swimme, *Universe,* 57.
2. Maturana and Varela, *Tree of Knowledge,* 248.
3. McCartney, Paul, from "Somedays," in *Flaming Pie.*
4. Gold, *Navajo and Tibetan Wisdom,* 5.
5. Bohm, *On Creativity,* 77–79.
6. Kandinsky, *Concerning the Spiritual in Art,* 36.
7. Swimme, *Universe,* 45.
8. Maturana and Poerksen, *From Being to Doing,* 197.
9. Greene, *Releasing the Imagination,* 3.
10. Levi, "Sentient Heart," 8.
11. Howell, *Jungian Symbolism,* 71.
12. Saint-Exupéry, *Little Prince.*
13. Perkins, *Shapeshifting,* 128–29.
14. Mails, *Fools Crow,* 79.
15. Levi, "Sentient Heart," 1, 5, 7, 8.
16. "Cantar en un coro hace al corazón más saludable."
17. Buhner, *Plant Intelligence,* 340.
18. Pearce, *Biology of Transcendence,* 69.
19. Wolff, *Original Wisdom,* 157–58.
20. BBC Worldwide Ltd. Programs, *Planet Earth* video series.
21. Tressider, *Dictionary of Symbols,* 92.
22. Swimme, *Universe,* 62–63.
23. Briskin et al., *Centered on the Edge,* 43.
24. Greene, *Releasing the Imagination,* 155–56.
25. Gold, *Navajo and Tibetan Wisdom,* 83.

CHAPTER 16.
REBIRTH

1. Blake, "Auguries of Innocence," in *Selected Poems,* 135.
2. Capra, *Hidden Connections,* 68.
3. Briggs and Peat, *Seven Life Lessons,* 162.
4. Boff, *Essential Care,* 37.
5. Bateson, "Form, Substance," 23.

6. Briggs and Peat, *Seven Life Lessons,* 164.

7. Sheldrake, *Rebirth,* 223.

8. Bateson, "Form, Substance," 467–68.

9. In Briskin et al., *Centered on the Edge,* 29.

10. Morin, *Seven Complex Lessons,* 62.

11. Judith, *Waking,* 221.

12. Prechtel, *Secrets,* 283.

13. Laszlo, *Quantum Shift,* 86.

14. Gillette and Gillette, *Soul Truth,* 264.

15. Macy and Brown, *Coming Back,* 44.

16. Gillette and Gillette, *Soul Truth,* 264.

17. Prechtel, *Secrets,* 283.

18. Swimme, *Universe,* 132, 146.

Bibliography

Abram, David. *Becoming Animal: An Earthly Cosmology.* New York: Vintage, 2010.

Anderson, Chris. "Responses to 'The New Humanists' Essay." In Brockman, *The New Humanists.* New York: Barnes and Noble, 2003.

Angakkorsuaq, Angaangaq. "Melting the Ice in the Heart of Man." IceWisdom (blog), Aug. 2015.

Atlee, Tom. "Collective Intelligence Is Only One-Fifth of Co-Intelligence." Co-Intelligence Institute (website).

———. "Co-Stupidity." Co-Intelligence Institute (website).

Audlin, James David. *Circle of Life: Traditional Teachings of Native American Elders.* Santa Fe, N.M.: Clear Light, 2005.

Bache, Christopher. "The Living Classroom." In Laszlo, *The Akashic Experience.* Rochester, Vt.: Inner Traditions, 2009.

Barrios, Carlos. *The Book of Destiny: Unlocking the Secrets of the Ancient Mayans and the Prophecy of 2012.* New York: Harper One, 2009.

Bateson, Gregory. "Form, Substance, and Difference." In Bateson, *Steps to an Ecology of Mind.* Chicago: University of Chicago Press, 1972.

———. *Sacred Unity: Further Steps to an Ecology of Mind.* Edited by Rodney E. Donaldson. New York: Harper Collins, 1991.

BBC Worldwide Ltd. Programs. *Planet Earth.* 2007.

Bear Heart, with Molly Larkin. *The Wind Is My Mother: The Life and Teachings of a Native American Shaman.* New York: Clarkson N. Potter, 1996.

Bennett, Hal Zina. *Spirit Animals and the Wheel of Life.* Charlottesville, Va.: Hampton Roads, 2000.

Beresford-Kroeger, Diana. *The Global Forest: Fifty Ways Trees Can Save Us.* New York: Penguin, 2011.

Blake, William. *The Selected Poems.* Edited by Bruce Woodcock. Hertfordshire, U.K.: Wordsworth Poetry Library, 1994.

Bly, Robert. *The Sibling Society.* New York: Vintage, 1996.

Bly, Robert, and Marion Woodman. *The Maiden King: The Reunion of Masculine and Feminine.* New York: Henry Holt, 1998.

Boff, Leonardo. *Ecología: Grito de la tierra, grito de los pobres.* Madrid: Editorial Trotto, 1996.

———. *Essential Care: An Ethics of Human Nature.* Waco, Tex.: Baylor University Press, 2008.

Boff, Leonardo, and Rose Marie Muraro. *Femenino y masculino.* Madrid: Editorial Trotto, 2004.

Bohm, David. *On Creativity.* Edited by Lee Nichol. New York: Routledge, 1998.

———. *On Dialogue.* London: Routledge, 1996.

———. "The Physicist and the Mystic." In Wilber (ed.), *The Holographic Paradigm and Other Paradoxes: The Enfolding-Unfolding Universe.* Boston: New Science Library, 1982.

———. *Wholeness and the Implicate Order.* London: Routledge & Kegan Paul, 1980.

Boldt, Laurence G. *The Tao of Abundance: Eight Ancient Principles for Abundant Living.* New York: Penguin/Arkana, 1999.

Briggs, John, and F. David Peat. *The Seven Life Lessons of Chaos.* New York: Harper Perennial, 1999.

Briskin, Alan, Sheryl Erickson, J. Lederman, John Ott, David Potter, and C. Strutt. *Centered on the Edge: Mapping a Field of Collective Intelligence and Spiritual Wisdom.* Kalamazoo, Mich.: John E. Fetzer Institute, 2001.

Brockman, John, ed. *The New Humanists: Science at the Edge.* New York: Barnes & Noble, 2003.

Buhner, Stephen Harrod. *Plant Intelligence and the Imaginal Realm.* Rochester, Vt.: Bear & Co., 2014.

Butler, Bill, and Simonne Butler. *Our Last Chance: Sixty-Six Days Adrift.* Miami, Fla.: Exmart Press, 1991.

Buxton, Simon. *The Shamanic Way of the Bee: Ancient Wisdom and Healing Practices of the Bee Masters.* Rochester, Vt.: Destiny, 2004.

"Cantar en un coro hace al corazón más saludable." *La Nación* (San José, Costa Rica), July 21, 2013.

Capra, Fritjof. *The Hidden Connections: A Science for Sustainable Living.* New York: Anchor, 2002.

————. *The Turning Point*. New York: Bantam, 1982.

Castaneda, Carlos. *A Separate Reality: Further Conversations with Don Juan*. New York: Pocket Books, 1975.

Cerdas, Daniela E. "El 98% de los romeros cree en milagros." *La Nación* (San José, Costa Rica), July 30, 2015.

Chevalier, Jean, and Alain Gheerbrant. *The Penguin Dictionary of Symbols*. New York: Penguin, 1996.

Chödrön, Pema. *The Places That Scare You: A Guide to Fearlessness in Difficult Times*. Boston: Shambhala, 2001.

Chopra, Deepak. *Quantum Healing*. New York: Bantam Books, 1989.

Clark, Andy. "Natural Born Cyborgs?" In Brockman, *The New Humanists*. New York: Barnes & Noble, 2003.

Cowan, Tom. *Fire in the Head: Shamanism and the Celtic Spirit*. San Francisco: Harper San Francisco, 1993.

Cunningham, Lori Bailey. *The Mandala Book: Patterns of the Universe*. New York: Sterling, 2010.

Curott, Phyllis. *Witch Crafting: A Spiritual Guide to Making Magic*. New York: Broadway, 2001.

Daly, Emma. "Couple Credit C.R. Saint for 'Miracle Rescue.'" *Tico Times* (San José, Costa Rica), Aug. 25, Sept. 1, 1989.

————. "Ticos Join Shipwrecked Pair Thanking 'Negrita.'" *Tico Times* (Costa Rica), Sept. 1, 1989.

Dossey, Larry. *Recovering the Soul: A Scientific and Spiritual Search*. New York: Bantam, 1989.

————. *Space, Time, and Medicine*. Boston: Shambhala, 1982.

Dwoskin, Elizabeth, and Tony Romm. "Facebook Says It Has Uncovered Coordinated Disinformation Operation ahead of 2018 Midterm Elections." *Washington Post* (website), July 31, 2018.

Dychtwald, Ken. "Commentaries on the Holographic Theory." In Wilber, *The Holographic Paradigm and Other Paradoxes*. Boston: Shambhala, 1982.

Einstein, Albert. "The Merging of Spirit and Science." ccreationvsevolution .blogspot.com

Eisler, Riane. *The Chalice & the Blade*. San Francisco: Harper & Row, 1987.

Eliade, Mircea. *The Sacred and the Profane: The Nature of Religion*. New York: Harcourt, Brace & World, 1956.

Eves, Howard. *Mathematical Circles Adieu*. Boston: Prindle Weber & Schmidt, 1977.

Ferguson, Marilyn. *Aquarius Now.* York Beach, Maine: Red Wheel/Weiser, 2005.

Freire, Paulo. *Pedagogy of Freedom.* Lanham, Md.: Rowman & Littlefield, 1998.

Frey, Nancy Louise. *Pilgrim Stories: On and Off the Road to Santiago.* Berkeley: University of California Press, 1998.

Fried, Robert L. *The Passionate Learner.* Boston: Beacon Press, 2001.

Frost, Robert. "Mending Wall." In Oscar Williams (ed.), *The New Pocket Anthology of American Verse.* New York: Pocket Books, 1972.

Galland, China. *Longing for Darkness: Tara and the Black Madonna.* New York: Penguin, 1990.

Gallegos Nava, Ramón. *Holistic Education: Pedagogy of Universal Love.* Brandon, Vt.: Foundation for Educational Renewal, 2001.

Georgescu-Roegen, Nicholas. "Energy and Economic Myths." *Southern Economic Journal* 41, no. 3 (Jan. 1975).

Gillette, Sheila, and Marcus Gillette. *The Soul Truth.* New York: Tarcher/ Penguin, 2008.

Gold, Peter. *Navajo and Tibetan Sacred Wisdom: The Circle of the Spirit.* Rochester, Vt.: Inner Traditions, 1994.

González Chaves, Alfredo, and Fernando González Vásquez. *La casa cósmica Talamanqueña y sus simbolismos.* San José, Costa Rica: Editorial Universidad de Costa Rica and Editorial Universidad Estatal a Distancia, 1989.

Goodman, Paul. *Compulsory Mis-education and the Community of Scholars.* New York: Vintage, 1962.

Gordon, James S. *Manifesto for a New Medicine.* Reading, Mass.: Perseus, 1996.

Gough, Andrew. "The Bee." A three-part article (June 2008–Aug. 2008) posted on Gough's website.

Gowdy, John, and Susan Mesner. "The Evolution of Georgescu-Roegen's Bioeconomics." *Review of Social Economy* 56, no. 2 (summer 1998).

Greene, Maxine. *Releasing the Imagination.* San Francisco: Jossey-Bass, 1995.

Gustafson, Fred. *The Black Madonna.* Boston: Sigo Press, 1990.

Gutiérrez, Francisco. *Doctorado de la tercera cultura: En busca del sentido.* San José, Costa Rica: Universidad de La Salle, 2006.

Halifax, Joan. *The Fruitful Darkness: Reconnecting with the Body of the Earth.* New York: Harper Collins, 1993.

Hamilton, Craig. "Come Together: The Mystery of Collective Intelligence." *What Is Enlightenment* magazine 25 (May–June 2004): 1–18.

Harner, Michael. *The Way of the Shaman.* San Francisco: Harper & Row, 1980.

Hauser, Marc D. "Animal Minds." In Brockman, *The New Humanists: Science at the Edge*. New York: Barnes & Noble, 2003.

Heaven, Ross. *Vodou Shaman: The Haitian Way of Healing and Power*. Rochester, Vt.: Destiny Books, 2003.

Heid, Markham. "You Asked: Are the Honeybees Still Disappearing?" *Time* (website), April 15, 2015.

Henderson, Hazel. *Building a Win-Win World: Life beyond Global Economic Warfare*. San Francisco: Bennett-Koehler, 1996.

Hiltner, Carol. "What Is a *Kurgan*, and Why Does It Matter?" AltaiMir (website).

Hock, Dee. *Birth of the Chaordic Age*. San Francisco: Berrett-Koehler, 1999.

Howell, Alice O. *Jungian Symbolism in Astrology: Letters from an Astrologer*. Wheaton, Ill.: Quest, 1987.

Humphrey, Chevy. "'Killer' Bees May Do More Saving than Killing!" Huffington Post (website), Aug. 19, 2014.

Ingerman, Sandra. *The Practice of Shamanism in the Twenty-first Century*. Shamanism Global Summit, the Shift Network, Aug. 2015 (audio).

Ingerman, Sandra, and Hank Wesselman. *Awakening to the Spirit World: The Shamanic Path of Direct Revelation*. Boulder, Colo.: Sounds True, 2010.

Jenkins, Elizabeth B. *The Fourth Level: Nature Wisdom Teachings of the Inka*. Naalehu, Hawaii: Pu'umaka'a Press, 2013.

———. *Initiation: A Woman's Spiritual Adventure in the Heart of the Andes*. New York: G. P. Putnam's Sons, 1997.

———. *Journey to Q'eros: Golden Cradle of the Inka*. Naalehu, Hawaii: Pu'umaka'a Press, 1998.

Johnson, Steven. *Emergence: The Connected Lives of Ants, Brains, Cities, and Software*. New York: Scribner, 2001.

Judith, Anodea. *Waking the Global Heart: Humanity's Rite of Passage from the Love of Power to the Power of Love*. Santa Rosa, Calif.: Elite Books, 2006.

Jung, Carl G. *Memories, Dreams, Reflections*. Translated by Richard and Clara Winston. Glasgow: Collins Fountain, 1962.

———. *The Red Book: Liber Novus*. Edited by Sonu Shamdasani. New York: W. W. Norton, 2009.

Kaku, Michio. *Visions*. New York: Anchor, 1997.

Kalweit, Holger. *Dreamtime and Inner Space: The World of the Shaman*. Boston: Shambhala, 1988.

Kandinsky, Wassily. *Concerning the Spiritual in Art.* Translated by M. T. H. Sadler. New York: Dover, 1977 [1914].

Kazmier, Robin. Pilgrimage to Copacabana: The Role of the Researcher in Ethnography. Weinberg College of Arts and Sciences (website), May 7, 2004.

Kenny, Robert. "Calling Out Our Potential." Collective Wisdom Initiative (website), 2007.

Kharitidi, Olga. *Entering the Circle: Ancient Secrets of Siberian Wisdom Discovered by a Russian Psychiatrist.* San Francisco: HarperSanFrancisco, 1996.

———. *Master of Lucid Dreams.* Charlottesville, Va.: Hampton Roads, 2001.

Kurzweil, Ray. "The Singularity." In Brockman, *The New Humanists: Science at the Edge.* New York: Barnes & Noble, 2003.

La Chapelle, David. "What Supports the Emergence of Collective Wisdom?" Collective Wisdom Initiative (website), 2007.

Lambert, Johanna. *Wise Women of the Dreamtime: Aboriginal Tales of the Ancestral Powers.* Rochester, Vt.: Inner Traditions, 1993.

Lame Deer, John Fire, and Richard Erdoes. *Lame Deer: Sioux Medicine Man.* London: Davis-Poynter, 1973.

Lanier, Jaron. "One Half of a Manifesto." In Brockman, *The New Humanists: Science at the Edge.* New York: Barnes & Noble, 2003.

Laszlo, Ervin. *The Akashic Experience: Science and the Cosmic Memory Field.* Rochester, Vt.: Inner Traditions, 2009.

———. *Quantum Shift in the Global Brain: How the New Scientific Reality Can Change Us and Our World.* Rochester, Vt.: Inner Traditions, 2008.

———. *Science and the Akashic Field: An Integral Theory of Everything.* Rochester, Vt.: Inner Traditions, 2004.

Levi, Renee A. "Holographic Theory and Groups." Collective Wisdom Initiative (website), 2001.

———. "The Sentient Heart: Messages for Life." Collective Wisdom Initiative (website).

Lipton, Bruce H., and Steve Bhaerman. *Spontaneous Evolution: Our Positive Future.* Carlsbad, Calif.: Hay House, 2009.

Macy, Joanna, and Molly Young Brown. *Coming Back to Life: Practices to Reconnect Our Lives, Our World.* Gabriola Island, B.C.: New Society Publishers, 1998.

Magee, Matthew. *Peruvian Shamanism: The Pachakúti Mesa.* Kearney, Neb.: Middle Road Publications, 2002.

Mails, Thomas E. *Fools Crow: Wisdom and Power.* Tulsa, Okla.: Council Oak Books, 1991.

Markale, Jean. *Cathedral of the Black Madonna: The Druids and the Mysteries of Chartres.* Rochester, Vt.: Inner Traditions, 2004.

Maturana, Humberto R., and Bernhard Poerksen. *From Being to Doing: The Origins of the Biology of Cognition.* Heidelberg, Germany: Carl-Auer Verlag, 2004.

Maturana, Humberto R., and Francisco J. Varela. *The Tree of Knowledge.* Boston: Shambhala, 1998.

McCartney, Paul. "Somedays." *Flaming Pie.* YouTube.

McNiff, Shaun. *Trust the Process: An Artist's Guide to Letting Go.* Boston: Shambala, 1998.

McTaggart, Lynne. *The Field: The Quest for the Secret Force of the Universe.* New York: Harper Collins, 2002.

Men, Hunbatz. *Secrets of Mayan Science/Religion.* Santa Fe: Bear & Co., 1990.

Miller, Peter. "Swarm Theory." *National Geographic,* July 2007, 130–47.

Miró-Quesada Solevo, Oscar. *The Path of the Universal Shaman: Transforming Our World through Sacred Living.* The Shift Network, 2016.

Moravec, Hans. "Making Minds." In Brockman, *The New Humanists: Science at the Edge.* New York: Barnes & Noble, 2003.

Morin, Edgar. *Seven Complex Lessons in Education for the Future.* UNESCO, 2001.

Morin, Edgar, and Anne Brigitte Kern. *Homeland Earth: A Manifesto for the New Millennium.* Cresskill, N.J.: Hampton Press, 1999.

Morse, Melvin, and Paul Perry. *Where God Lives: The Science of the Paranormal and How Our Brains Are Linked to the Universe.* New York: Cliff Street Books, 2000.

Moss, Nan, and David Corbin. *Weather Shamanism: Harmonizing Our Connection with the Elements.* Rochester, Vt.: Bear & Co., 2008.

Murdock, Maureen. *The Heroine's Journey.* Boston: Shambhala, 1990.

Nachmanovitch, Stephen. "Gregory Bateson: Old Men Ought to be Explorers." *Coevolution Quarterly,* 1981.

Negroponte, Nicholas. *Being Digital.* New York: Vintage, 1995.

Payán de la Roche, Julio César. *Lánzate al vacío, se extenderán tus alas.* Bogotá, Colombia: McGraw Hill Interamericana, 2000.

Pearce, Joseph Chilton. *The Biology of Transcendence: A Blueprint of the Human Spirit.* Rochester, Vt.: Park Street Press, 2002.

Peat, F. David. *Blackfoot Physics*. York Beach, Maine: Red Wheel/Weiser, 2005.

———. *Synchronicity: The Bridge between Matter and Mind*. New York: Bantam, 1988.

Peirce, Penney. *Frequency: The Power of Personal Vibration*. New York: Atria, 2009.

Pellegrino, Charles. *Unearthing Atlantis: An Archaeological Odyssey*. New York: Vintage, 1991.

Perkins, John. *Shapeshifting: Shamanic Techniques for Global and Personal Transformation*. Rochester, Vt.: Destiny, 1997.

———. *The World Is as You Dream It: Shamanic Teachings from the Amazon and Andes*. Rochester, Vt.: Destiny, 1994.

Perkins, John, and Shakaim Mariano Shakai Ijisam Chumpi. *Spirit of the Shuar: Wisdom from the Last Unconquered People of the Amazon*. Rochester, Vt.: Destiny Books, 2001.

Petersson, Peter. "Cymatics: The Science of the Future" World-Mysteries (blog), Dec. 13, 2011.

Pfeiffer, Bill. "Leon and Maria in the Altai." Petersham, Mass.: Sacred Earth Network, 2006.

———. *Wild Earth, Wild Soul: A Manual for an Ecstatic Culture*. Winchester, U.K.: Moon Books, 2013.

Popcorn, Faith. "The Humanoid Condition." *The Economist: The World in 2016*.

Powell, James N. *The Tao of Symbols: How to Transcend the Limits of Our Symbolism*. New York: Quill, 1982.

Prechtel, Martín. *Long Life, Honey in the Heart*. New York: Tarcher/Putnam, 1999.

———. *Secrets of the Talking Jaguar*. New York: Tarcher/Putnam, 1998.

Redmond, Layne. *When the Drummers Were Women*. New York: Three Rivers, 1997.

Richo, David. *When the Past Is Present: Healing the Emotional Wounds That Sabotage Our Relationships*. Boston: Shambhala, 2008.

Ronnberg, Ami, and Kathleen Martin. *The Book of Symbols: Reflections on Archetypal Images*. Cologne, Germany: Taschen, 2010.

Rudloe, Jack. *Search for the Great Turtle Mother*. Sarasota, Fla.: Pineapple Press, 1995.

Sagot, Jacques. "Desazón de una sospecha." *La Nación* (San José, Costa Rica), Feb. 9, 2015.

Saint-Exupéry, Antoine de. *The Little Prince*. New York: Harcourt Brace Jovanovitch, 1943.

Sams, Jamie, and David Carson. *Medicine Cards: The Discovery of Power through the Ways of Animals*. Santa Fe: Bear & Co., 1988.

Sarangerel. *Chosen by the Spirits*. Rochester, Vt.: Destiny, 2001.

Schneider, Michael S. *A Beginner's Guide to Constructing the Universe*. New York: Harper Collins, 1994.

Seed, John, Pat Fleming, Joanna Macy, and Arne Naess. *Thinking like a Mountain*. Gabriola Island, B.C.: New Society Publishers, 1988.

Sheldrake, Rupert. *Dogs That Know When Their Owners Are Coming Home*. New York: Three Rivers, 1999.

———. *The Rebirth of Nature: The Greening of Science and God*. Rochester, Vt.: Park Street Press, 1991.

Somé, Malidoma Patrice. *Ritual: Power, Healing, and Community*. New York: Penguin Compass, 1997.

Stevens, José Luis. *Awaken the Inner Shaman: A Guide to the Power Path of the Heart*. Boulder, Colo.: Sounds True, 2014.

Swimme, Brian. *The Universe Is a Green Dragon*. Rochester, Vt.: Bear & Co., 2001.

"Technology in Africa." *The Economist*, Nov. 11, 2017, 3–14.

Theobald, Robert. *Reworking Success: New Communities at the Millennium*. Gabriola Island, B.C.: New Society Publishers, 1997.

Tressider, Jack, ed. *Complete Dictionary of Symbols*. San Francisco: Chronicle Books, 2005.

Tucker, Linda. *Mystery of the White Lions: Children of the Sun God*. Carlsbad, Calif.: Hay House, 2001.

Turkle, Sherry. *Alone Together: Why We Expect More from Technology and Less from Each Other*. New York: Basic Books, 2011.

———. *Life on the Screen: Identity in the Age of the Internet*. New York: Simon & Schuster, 1995.

Villoldo, Alberto. *Shaman, Healer, Sage: How to Heal Yourself and Others with the Energy Medicine of the Americas*. New York: Harmony Books, 2000.

Walker, Barbara G. *The Woman's Dictionary of Symbols and Sacred Objects*. San Francisco: Harper & Row, 1988.

———. *The Woman's Encyclopedia of Myths and Secrets*. San Francisco: Harper & Row, 1983.

Wang, Amy. "Former Facebook VP Says Social Media Is Destroying Society." *Washington Post,* Dec. 12, 2017.

Wan Ho, Mae. "The Entangled Universe." *Yes! A Journal of Positive Futures,* Spring 2000. In Pearce, *Biology of Transcendence.* Rochester, Vt.: Park Street Press, 2002.

Warren, Robert Penn, and Albert Erskine, eds. *Six Centuries of Great Poetry.* New York: Dell, 1955.

Wilber, Ken, ed. *The Holographic Paradigm and Other Paradoxes.* Boston: Shambhala, 1985.

Wilcox, Joan Parisi. *Masters of the Living Energy: The Mystical World of the Q'ero of Peru.* Rochester, Vt.: Inner Traditions, 1999.

Wohlleben, Peter. *The Hidden Life of Trees: What They Feel, How They Communicate.* Vancouver, B.C.: Greystone, 2016.

Wolff, Robert. *Original Wisdom: Stories of an Ancient Way of Knowing.* Rochester, Vt.: Inner Traditions, 2001.

Wordsworth, William. "The World Is Too Much with Us." In Warren and Erskine, *Six Centuries of Great Poetry.* New York: Dell, 1955.

Zapp, Ivar, and George Erikson. *Atlantis in America: Navigators of the Ancient World.* Kempton, Ill.: Adventures Unlimited, 1998.

Index